Planting Churches
Cross-Culturally

Planting Churches Cross-Culturally

North America and Beyond

Second Edition

David J. Hesselgrave

Baker Academic

Grand Rapids, Michigan

© 2000 by David J. Hesselgrave

Published by Baker Academic
a division of Baker Publishing Group
P.O. Box 6287, Grand Rapids, MI 49516-6287
www.bakeracademic.com

Printed in the United States of America

Library of Congress Cataloging-in-Publication Data
Hesselgrave, David J.
    Planting churches cross-culturally : North America and beyond / David J. Hesselgrave.—2nd ed.
        p.   cm.
    Includes bibliographical references (p.   ) and index.
    ISBN 10: 0-8010-2222-3 (pbk.)
    ISBN 978-0-8010-2222-7 (pbk.)
    1. Church development, New—Biblical teaching. 2. Missions—Theory—Biblical teaching. 3. Missions—Biblical teaching. 4. Evangelistic work—Biblical teaching. 5. Bible. N.T.—Criticism, interpretation, etc. I. Title.
BV652.24.H4   2000
266—dc21   99-054928

Unless otherwise indicated, Scripture quotations are from the New American Standard Bible, © the Lockman Foundation 1960, 1962, 1963, 1968, 1971, 1972, 1973, 1975, 1977. The other versions quoted are the King James Version (KJV), the New International Version (NIV), and the Revised Standard Version (RSV).

To Gertrude,
loving wife and mother,
faithful companion and helpmate,
devoted Christian and layperson

Contents

Foreword to the Revised Edition

After almost twenty years, a new edition of *Planting Churches Cross-Culturally* is being released. With this edition David Hesselgrave's work takes another step toward becoming a classic. What was it about the first edition that caused its popularity? I believe the answer lies in the fact that with equal concern it looks both back to the early church and forward to contemporary culture. This dual perspective is essential. Indeed, a growing number of us who were involved in attempting to re-shape the missionary enterprise at the end of the twentieth century realize that something is drastically wrong with the contemporary Western paradigm of missions. We see entire movements of churches with an appalling lack of leaders. Almost all of these movements are on course for producing but a nominal fourth generation. Some argue that this downturn is inevitable, yet many of us believe that the biblical ideal suggests that the fourth generation of churches should be the strongest generation to date. With the coming postmodern global village, these churches must be sufficiently strong to realize the potential of fostering a worldwide expansion of the gospel such as has not been seen since the early church.

In a very real sense, this new edition continues the conversation that Roland Allen's groundbreaking work initiated concerning Western missions and New Testament patterns. At the turn to the twentieth century, Allen began calling the church back to what he termed "the way of Christ and the apostles." He set forth a contrast between New Testament missionary methods and the modern missionary movement. In the first edition of *Planting Churches Cross-Culturally* Hesselgrave continued the call to return to the missionary methods of Paul, a message that has received a wide audience over the last two decades. The heart of this call to return to the New Testament Hesselgrave calls the Pauline Cycle. His entire book is organized around this cycle.

In going back to the New Testament model for missions, Hesselgrave is in essence calling us to return to the biblical paradigm, which unfolds in the Book of Acts. Luke understood that his two-volume history—Luke and Acts—was catechetical in nature (Luke 1:1–4; Acts 1:1). Acts was in essence a catechism for carrying out the Great Commission, that is, for multiplying churches worldwide. The essence of this catechism is the model of missions structured by Luke around the missionary journeys of Paul: he evangelized strategic cities, established churches, and trained leaders to continue the process. Yet Hesselgrave's book is not only a return to the Pauline paradigm, but also an anticipation of building a culturally relevant paradigm based upon the principles of the Pauline Cycle. Though the strength of the book is in identifying the core biblical elements of the "way of Christ and the apostles," Hesselgrave also introduces modern missiological research. He raises an awareness of the need to exegete culture as well as the biblical text as we go about building contemporary strategies for missions.

How one might best approach Hesselgrave's church-planting manual deserves a brief comment at this point. Obviously it would be ideal to begin at the beginning and read the book carefully from cover to cover. However, many of us are inclined to begin from our own point of need; and if a portion of a book captures us, we are then pulled into the whole. A reader so inclined might begin with chapter 3, "Church-Planting Strategy," where Hesselgrave describes the essence of the Pauline Cycle. Then, after grasping the ten parts of the cycle, the reader might turn to the chapter devoted to that part of the cycle that most applies to one's ministry at the time. This should confirm the need to give the book a thorough reading at a future date. I have read through this book several times. It has become the core text of our flagship course at BILD International—a course that is being used in over thirty countries.

The new edition maintains the same structure as the first edition, but includes new and updated information strewn throughout every section. To guide future generations, the essence of the original edition remains intact. But the extent of the update demands that those of us who have used the first edition in our ministries replace it. This work is an excellent advancement of the conversation on mission begun by Allen and others a century ago. Now, at the turn to the twenty-first century, *Planting Churches Cross-Culturally* serves a strategic purpose in helping us strategize for the new millennium. It is destined to take on classical status as we move through the century before us. If it is widely read and followed, it will move us a long way toward accomplishing the critical task of establishing movements of churches worldwide. We applaud the decision to release this new edition and anticipate that the work will continue to be a leading voice calling for the return to New Testament foundations as we attempt to build relevant cultural models for the twenty-first century.

Jeff Reed
Director, BILD International
and The Center for Church-Based Theological Education
December 1999

Foreword to the First Edition

Here is a great book on Christian mission—lucid, wide-ranging, and biblical. David Hesselgrave of Trinity Evangelical Divinity School knows mission theory, theology, methodology, and history—and describes them well.

Hesselgrave puts the missions of many churches in many lands in his debt as he expounds what mission is and how it should be carried out in the enormously different settings found in the multitudinous societies which constitute our world. Missiologists will rejoice in this book. Teachers of missions will make it required reading for their classes.

The structure of the book arises systematically from the key idea that the essential task in a world where three-fourths of all men and women have yet to believe in Jesus Christ as God and only Savior is that of planting new churches. The process of mission commanded by Christ and demonstrated by Paul is set forth as consisting of ten steps. Hesselgrave is far too competent a missiologist to allow readers to think that these steps are all there is to mission. But it is remarkable how much of mission in all six continents can be properly catalogued and understood under the following headings: Missionaries Commissioned, Audience Contacted, Gospel Communicated, Hearers Converted, Believers Congregated, Faith Confirmed, Leaders Consecrated, Believers Commended, Relationships Continued, Sending Churches Convened, and, finally, More Missionaries Commissioned.

Discrimination, good judgment, and unswerving dedication to the heart of mission mark this book. One example will illustrate this excellence. In chapter 16 Hesselgrave speaks of continuing relationships between churches and missions. After quoting Harvie Conn to the effect that ultimately church and mission are to be integrated, Hesselgrave agrees and then quickly goes on to say, "However, we must not forget two factors. First, most missions exist under the aegis of sending churches [and hence are already church]. Second, as long as governments allow missions the freedom to evangelize . . . , the responsibility and opportunity to do so should not be forfeited in order to integrate with churches which do not have a vision for that God-given task."

A special merit of this book is its systematic development of each major topic. The framework, varying only slightly from chapter to chapter, keeps thought focused on the basic objectives. Career missionaries and candidates in training will profit from this masterly presentation.

Church leaders busily engaged in redefining mission to mean "everything God wants Christians to do" (our plain Christian duty) will not like this book, but churchmen and missiologists who define mission as cross-cultural propagation of the gospel will be pleased with it. The seventy-five thousand missionaries at work on all six continents will acclaim its clarity, breadth, and depth. As congregations, denominations, and missionary societies multiply churches and carry out the Savior's will in the most responsive world ever to exist, they will do their task better for having read *Planting Churches Cross-Culturally.*

Donald A. McGavran, Founding Dean
School of World Mission
Fuller Theological Seminary
Pasadena, California

Preface

Christ loved the church and gave himself for her. Though in seemingly inconsequential ways by comparison, I too have loved the church and given myself to her. For over fifty years it has been my high privilege to serve Christ in the fellowship of the Evangelical Free Church, in local churches in North America, in church-planting ministries in Japan, and in a teaching ministry at Trinity Evangelical Divinity School.

This book, therefore, grows out of fifty years of pioneering and pastoring, reading and researching, and learning and lecturing in company with literally thousands of people who have been my instructors and inspiration in service for Christ and his church. The following are but representative of the larger number.

I thank congregations in Radisson (Wisconsin), Minneapolis-St. Paul, Rockford (Illinois), and Chicago, and in Urawa, Warabi, and Kyoto (all in Japan), for their patient support and prayers. Heartfelt gratitude is expressed to my colleagues on the faculty at Trinity who have provided stimulation and inspiration. The personnel at Free Church headquarters have been supportive. Trinity students have been most helpful. Over the years I enjoyed a number of contacts with Donald McGavran, and on each occasion I was the beneficiary. His foreword to the first edition of this book is most appreciated, as is Jeff Reed's foreword to the second. And, as has been the case in every endeavor, my wife Gertrude and my children David Dennis, Ronald Paul, and Sheryl Ann have directly and indirectly made irreplaceable contributions.

I want to acknowledge here the special contribution of Earl Blomberg to my thinking and to this volume. A former professor at our Free Church seminary in Venezuela and a theologian in his own right, Blomberg was a student in one of my classes on church planting at Trinity Evangelical Divinity School about the time that the original manuscript was being prepared. As the class proceeded through the ten steps of the Pauline Cycle, he shared such significant insights on the theology involved that I asked and received permission to include many of them in the text. Many of those insights remain in this updated edition, and both my readers and I are the richer for them. For this I express profound gratitude.

Numerous books on church growth and church planting have been published in recent years. The church of Christ has been strengthened by these literary contributions. The present volume is somewhat unique in its attempt to combine a biblical and step-by-step approach to church planting with cultural and experiential data designed to facilitate the founding of new congregations in unreached areas of the world. As such, it can be successful only to the extent that the servants of Christ transmute its concepts into churches. I commend it, therefore, to the Lord and to his servants, in the hope that any strengths it may possess will aid them in their labors, and with the prayer that its weaknesses will not detract from their success.

        David J. Hesselgrave
        Rockford, Illinois

Part One

The Christian and the Christian Mission

The Heart of the Christian Mission 1

The church is a storm center of contemporary society. Communists have viewed it as a chain anchoring the proletariat to the past. Secularists think of it as a vestigial organ without which society and individuals could function just as effectively, or more so. Liberals often see the church as fulfilling its purpose when it permeates society and loses its separate identity. Most conservative Christians, on the other hand, are convinced that the church is at the heart of the divine purpose for the present age and view growth as one of its major responsibilities.

Adding to the confusion occasioned by these diverse views, theologians distinguish the visible church and the invisible church, the church militant and the church triumphant, and the universal church and local churches. Missiologists write about the indigenous church, the responsible church, older and younger churches, sending and receiving churches, and national and nativistic churches. Church analysts talk about formal and informal churches, traditional and innovative churches, and structured and unstructured churches.

We should make it clear at the outset that when we use the word "church," we may be referring to that universal body which is built upon the foundation of the apostles and prophets, which is composed of all true Christian believers, and of which Christ is the head. Or we may be referring to any duly constituted local body of Christian believers who corporately engage in worship and witness, and who serve each other and the world in accordance with the Word of God. From a biblical point of view, these are the only entities that can rightly be called "church."

The thesis of this chapter is simple: The primary mission of the church and, therefore, of the churches is to proclaim the gospel of Christ and gather believers into local churches where they can be built up in the faith and made effective in service; thus new congregations are to be planted throughout the world. Of course there are many other important tasks to be carried out by Christian believers both individually and corporately. But few of these objectives will be realized unless new believers are constantly being added to local churches, unless new local churches are being added to the universal church, and unless existing churches are growing up into the fullness of him who is their head.

The Divine Plan for the Church

Countless pages have been written on the place of the church and its mission in the plan of God.[1] It can be demonstrated from the biblical record that God was not taken by surprise when Adam sinned. God had a prior plan that provided a way whereby humans could be reconciled and restored to fellowship with him. As an integral part of that plan God chose Abraham and his descendants as a people through whom the world would be blessed (Gen. 12:1–3). In one sense they failed, but the plan did not fail. Neither the continued provincialism of the Jewish people nor their ultimate rejection of the Messiah could obstruct the divine purpose. Rather, "by their transgression salvation has come to the Gentiles" (Rom. 11:11b). Believing Gentiles have been made "fellow heirs and fellow members of the body, and fellow partakers of the promise in Christ Jesus through the gospel" (Eph. 3:6). And "this was in accordance with the eternal purpose [lit., purpose of the ages] which [God] carried out in Christ Jesus our Lord" (Eph. 3:11).

As Paul makes abundantly clear, the present arrangement whereby Jew and Gentile alike become members of a spiritual body by faith in Christ does not mean that the promises to Israel as a nation have been nullified. Certainly not. The blindness of their eyes and the hardness of their hearts are partial and temporary until the "fulness of the Gentiles has come in." Then "all Israel will be saved" (Rom. 11:25–26). Israel will still have her day!

In the meantime the present age constitutes a unique period of history. It can correctly be called the church age. When our Lord was ministering on earth, he prophesied that he would build his church and that the gates of Hades would not overpower it (Matt. 16:16–18). When he died on the cross, he provided for the church, giving himself in death that the church might be born and grow (Eph. 5:25). Now that he is in heaven, he is sanctifying or calling out the church and preparing it for its final presentation (Eph. 5:26–27). When he comes again, he will gather the church to glorify it in the presence of the Father (1 Thess. 4:13–18; Rev. 4–6).

Various metaphors describe the church in its relation to Christ. It is his building—"built upon the foundation of the apostles and prophets, Christ Jesus Himself being the corner stone" (Eph. 2:19–21). It is his

---

1. See, e.g., Johannes Blauw, *The Missionary Nature of the Church* (New York: McGraw-Hill, 1962); and Gary F. Vicedom, *The Mission of God* (St. Louis: Concordia, 1965).

spiritual body—"the fulness of Him who fills all in all" (Eph. 1:23; see also 1 Cor. 12:12–13). It is, as it were, his bride—the object of his love and provision (Eph. 5:25–33).

The church, then, is not an afterthought in the mind of God. He planned for it in eternity past and provided for it in the death and resurrection of his Son (Eph. 1:19–23). And the Son prepared for its formation and development by instructing his followers as to their mission and empowering them by his Spirit (Acts 1:4–8). The church and the churches have no friend like their Lord! If Christians are to love what their Lord loves, they must love the church—and the churches! In the final analysis, Christology is closely allied with ecclesiology. When we inquire into a person's faith, we do well to ask what that individual thinks of Christ and his church!

The Great Commission

If there is any lingering doubt as to the central task to which Christ calls his people, it should be dispelled by an inquiry into the nature of the final command of Christ and the result of obedience to that command on the part of the early believers. Not that the Great Commission is overlooked! Perhaps no single passage of Scripture is more widely used to challenge Christians to faithfulness to their primary task than is Matthew 28:16–20:

> But the eleven disciples proceeded to Galilee, to the mountain which Jesus had designated. And when they saw Him, they worshiped Him; but some were doubtful. And Jesus came up and spoke to them, saying, "All authority has been given to Me in heaven and on earth. Go therefore and make disciples of all the nations, baptizing them in the name of the Father and the Son and the Holy Spirit, teaching them to observe all that I commanded you; and lo, I am with you always, even to the end of the age."

Despite its widespread use as a challenge, however, exhorters seldom take the time to exegete the passage carefully and compare it with parallel passages. As a result, the essence and method of mission are often lost in exhortations to undertake it!

It is important to recognize that the one who issued the Great Commission is the risen Christ to whom all authority *(exousia)* has been given. (The Holy Spirit will provide the power or might *[dynamis]* to fulfil the command [Acts 1:7–8].) The commission itself is clearly related to Christ's authority by the word "therefore." Two meanings are possible: (1) all authority is behind the command; and (2) those commanded to go can do so in the assurance that all authority belongs to Christ.

Figure 1
Complementary Statements of the Great Commission

The Statements	The Authority	The Enablement	The Sphere	The Message	The Activities
1. Matt. 28:18–20	The authority given to Christ ("all authority . . . in heaven and on earth")	Christ is with us to the very end of the age	The nations (Gentiles)	All things Christ has commanded	Disciple by going, baptizing, and teaching
2. Mark 16:15			All the world ("all creation")	The gospel	Go and preach (proclaim)
3. Luke 24:46–49	"In His (Christ's) name"	Promise of the Father . . . power	All nations beginning from Jerusalem	Repentance and the forgiveness of sins	Preach (proclaim) and witness
4. John 20:21	Sent by Christ as he was sent by the Father				
5. Acts 1:8		Power of the Holy Spirit	Jerusalem, all Judea, Samaria, and even to the remotest part of the earth	Christ	Witness

From David J. Hesselgrave, Communicating Christ Cross-Culturally (Grand Rapids: Zondervan, 1978), 54.

Both are true. Though the former meaning is usually assumed in this case, the latter should not be overlooked.

The word which is translated "go" is a participle in the original and not an imperative. A literal translation would be "going" or "as you go." But that should not be allowed to blunt the force of the word. The same construction is found in Acts 16:9: "Come over [lit., coming over] to Macedonia and help us." Obviously, if Paul does not "come," he cannot "help"! And if we do not "go," we cannot accomplish our mission. On the other hand, the emphasis is not on the going but on the reason for going.

"Make disciples" is the sole imperative and the central activity enjoined in the Great Commission. To make converts and believers is certainly involved. But faith and discipleship can never be divorced. Obedience is required, not just on the part of the one who brings the gospel message, but also on the part of the one who receives it. Converts and believers as popularly conceived might do their own thing, so to speak. But disciples obviously must do the will of their Master.

"Of all the nations" has reference to the Gentiles, who, as we have seen, are now to be brought into the church on the same basis as are the Jews. Previously our Lord had sent his disciples to "the lost sheep of the house of Israel" (Matt. 10:6). Gentiles had not been included. Why? Because God was still dealing with Israel as a people. Christ had not been rejected and crucified. All was not ready. But following the crucifixion and the resurrection, the gospel could go to the Gentiles also.

"Baptizing them in [or, into] the name . . ." has reference to the means or method by which disciples are made. In the original, "baptizing" is a participle which derives imperatival force from the main verb. Converts are to be baptized into [eis] the name of the Father, and the Son, and the Holy Spirit. This implies that they come into the ownership of the Triune God.

"Teaching them to observe all that I commanded" is parallel to the former participial construction. Disciples are made by a process of baptizing and teaching. And what is to be taught? All that Christ commanded. For we live by "every word that proceeds out of the mouth of God" (Matt. 4:4).

"Lo, I am with you always . . . ." No one who is sent, and goes, goes alone. Christ himself will accompany his servants to the ends of the earth and until the consummation of the age.

Though the most complete and oft-quoted statement of the Great Commission is found in Matthew 28, parallel passages should not be overlooked. They serve to underscore its central motifs (see figure 1). A comparison of these varied statements of the Great Commission clearly shows that they are neither redundant nor contradictory. They are complementary.

In an effort to make a case for a social understanding of the Christian mission, some interpreters have concluded that the Johannine statement (John 20:21) takes precedence over the Synoptic statements. These interpreters say that our Lord's use of the phrase "as the Father has sent Me" indicates that our commission is to continue the ministry that he began in the world. Of course, there is a sense in which we are to continue his ministry. But these interpreters quickly move on to the passage in Luke 7:19–23 where John the Baptist sent his disciples to ask Jesus if he indeed was the one who was to come (i.e., the Messiah). Jesus' answer was concise and clear: "Go . . . tell John . . . how that the blind see, the lame walk, the lepers are cleansed, the deaf hear, the dead are raised, to the poor the gospel is preached" (KJV). This, these interpreters say, is the work that we are to carry on. And so, putting the other statements of the Great Commission aside, they place the ministries of healing and social betterment, and the struggle for justice, at the very heart of our mission.

Now there can be no question but that believers are created in Christ for good works (Eph. 2:10) and that they are to "do good unto all men, especially unto them who are of the household of faith" (Gal. 6:10 KJV). And if one is disposed to say that all things that believers are commanded of God to do constitute their mission in the world, there is a sense in which we can agree. But to say that good works constitute the Great Commission, or the heart of our mission, or that the Johannine statement supersedes the Synoptic statements, is to fly in the face of sound exegesis and clear thinking. Neither the grammar nor the context of John 20:21 will support it. Furthermore, in Luke 7 Jesus was clearly substantiating his messiahship by reference to that miraculous ministry which John, familiar as he was with Old Testament prophecy, had been openly anticipating. The passage as such does not constitute a divine mandate for the continuing exercise of miracles, for the attempt to reproduce them as nearly as possible by the application of medicine, or for social and political redress.

In sum, the Johannine statement of the Great Commission does not change the direction of the statements in the Synoptic Gospels. Rather, it underscores the necessity of going into the world to disciple the nations by preaching, baptizing, and teaching. To allow any understanding of mission to obscure the proclamatory, sacramental, and didactic responsibility of the church is to put the knife to the heart of the Christian mission. To substitute other activities for those distinctly specified by our Lord is to attempt a heart transplant—one that sooner or later will certainly be rejected.[2]

2. Andreas J. Köstenberger, *The Missions of Jesus and the Disciples according to the Fourth Gospel* (Grand Rapids: Eerdmans, 1997), 197–213.

Pentecost

The event that initially expanded Christianity was Pentecost. The fact is that the early Christians did not inspire themselves to carry out the Great Commission by reminding each other of its provisions and cruciality. Rather, the Holy Spirit came upon those early believers and transformed them into witnesses even as the Lord had promised. According to Acts 1:8, he had told them that when the Holy Spirit came upon them, they would (1) receive needed power or strength, (2) testify regarding the Christ whom they had seen and heard and in whom they believed, and (3) go to Jerusalem, Judea, Samaria, and the ends of the earth. After the Holy Spirit came, they discovered experientially that the Holy Spirit is also the missionary Spirit. He carried out the commission in and through them.[3]

And what was the result? Luke informs us that following Pentecost "the Lord was adding to their number day by day those who were being saved" (Acts 2:47). Later, when the Jerusalem disciples were scattered by persecution, they "went about preaching the word" (Acts 8:4). After this persecution the churches in Judea, Galilee, and Samaria "enjoyed peace, being built up; and, going on in the fear of the Lord and in the comfort of the Holy Spirit, [they] continued to increase" (Acts 9:31). In Antioch "a large number who believed turned to the Lord" (Acts 11:21).

Pointing to the use of the word "church" in connection with the gathering of believers at Antioch (Acts 13:1), Francis Schaeffer comments: "Here was a functioning local congregation called 'the church.' From here on the New Testament clearly indicates that churches were formed wherever some became Christians."[4] Luke reports, for example, that when Paul and Silas traveled through Syria and Cilicia on the second missionary journey, they confirmed the churches that had been established previously. These churches were "strengthened in the faith, and were increasing in number daily" (Acts 16:5).

Paul and the Mission of the Church

The apostle Paul was the person especially charged with the responsibility of taking the gospel to the Gentiles. His missionary ministry, therefore, is of special importance to an understanding of our mission:

> In a little more than ten years St. Paul established the Church in four provinces of the Empire: Galatia, Macedonia, Achaia, and Asia. Before

---

3. Harry R. Boer, *Pentecost and Missions* (Grand Rapids: Eerdmans, 1961).
4. Francis Schaeffer, *The Church at the End of the Twentieth Century* (Downers Grove, Ill.: InterVarsity, 1970), 60.

A.D. 57 St. Paul could speak as if his work there was done, and could plan extensive tours into the far West without anxiety lest the churches which he had founded might perish in his absence for want of his guidance and support.

The work of the Apostle during these ten years can therefore be treated as a unity. Whatever assistance he may have received from the preaching of others, it is unquestioned that the establishment of the churches in these provinces was really his work. In the pages of the New Testament he, and he alone, stands forth as their founder. And the work which he did was really a completed work. So far as the foundation of the churches is concerned, it is perfectly clear that the writer of the Acts intends to represent St. Paul's work as complete. The churches were really established. Whatever disasters fell upon them in later years, whatever failure there was, whatever ruin, that failure was not due to any insufficiency or lack of care and completeness in the Apostle's teaching or organization. When he left them, he left them because his work was fully accomplished.[5]

And why was Paul so successful? There were many reasons, of course. But one important reason was that Paul considered the preaching of the gospel and the establishment of churches as his primary task. The biblical record leaves no room for thinking that either Paul or the members of his team were basically engaged in raising living standards, ameliorating social conditions, imparting secular knowledge, ministering to medical needs, or dispensing aid from previously established churches. There can be little doubt that allegiance to Christ on the part of converts in the churches entailed these effects as by-products of faith even to the sending of needed aid back to the Jerusalem church (a kind of reverse flow). That the missionaries were concerned about social relationships, and about minds and bodies as well as souls, is patently true. But Paul's primary mission was accomplished when the gospel was preached, people were converted, and churches were established. Obedience to the Great Commandment to love one's neighbor was part of the commission to teach all things Christ commanded. But good works were the fruit—not the root—of Paul's mission:

> It would be well at this point to remember Paul's practice. Were there no poor in Corinth? Were there no race problems in Ephesus? Did all the children in Asia Minor have enough to wear? Paul's letters to the congregations in various cities demonstrate his deep concern for the poor and socially disenfranchised (Gal. 2:10). He exhorts the Christians in Corinth to follow the example of other congregations in taking up a generous offering for the poverty-stricken saints of Jerusalem (2 Cor. 8–9). Yet his

5. Roland Allen, *Missionary Methods: St. Paul's or Ours?* (Grand Rapids: Eerdmans, 1962), 3.

uniform practice in spreading the gospel of love and brotherly concern was to establish congregations. To ignore the apostolic practice, then, is to overlook the very heart of the methodology whereby the gospel spread around the Mediterranean in the first century. Furthermore, it overlooks a vital way by which the spiritual and physical needs of people may be met.[6]

No wonder Paul was so effective in multiplying believers and churches. Not only was he a gifted, Spirit-controlled man, he had a singleness and clarity of objective that have escaped many of his successors. He gave all of his boundless energy and unusual abilities to the building of the church of Jesus Christ!

The Church and Its Mission in the Modern Era

If there is confusion as concerns the heart of our mission today, it does not stem from the Scriptures but from the blinders devised by history, and other blinders of our own making.

An Understanding of Mission That Is Too Broad

The Reformers of the sixteenth and seventeenth centuries recovered the message of the church, but (for the most part) were too preoccupied with the problems of Europe to give much impetus to mission in other parts of the world. It remained for the Pietists, Moravians, and a Baptist by the name of William Carey to recover the sense of urgency to take the gospel to the whole world.

In the great missionary advance of the nineteenth century, however, missionaries were not always clear as to their objectives. Mission took the forms of establishing schools and hospitals, opposing inhumane practices such as suttee and footbinding, and launching campaigns for sanitation. Christians can be justly proud of the great achievements of loyal sons and daughters who accomplished these tasks at the cost of great personal sacrifice. They deserve to be applauded by all people and emulated by contemporary Christians. But in and of themselves these worthy activities did not make disciples nor did they establish churches. Thus when history bequeaths to us the misunderstanding that the mission of the church consists in any worthy enterprises Christians may undertake, enterprises that may deter us from our primary task, history does us a disservice.

For our own part, we moderns have tended to perpetuate confusion at this point. We have multiplied parachurch missions as arms

6. Paul Benjamin, *The Growing Congregation* (Cincinnati: Standard, 1972), 54.

of the church in order to undertake every conceivable type of good work from feeding the hungry to immunizing populations against disease to introducing new strains of corn and cattle. These are worthy endeavors and according to Galatians 6:10 qualify as Christian undertakings. But organizations formed to accomplish them do not really qualify as missions unless upon entering needy areas they keep the church's primary mission primary. Wherever it is possible to proclaim the gospel and form churches, only those organizations that support evangelism and church planting in a significant way should be thought of as missions. If they do not engage in or support evangelism and church planting, they are not only parachurch, they are paramission.

An Understanding of Evangelism That Is Too Narrow

If history sometimes affords us an understanding of mission that is too broad, it also provides us with an understanding of evangelism that is too narrow. In the last decades of the nineteenth century and in the twentieth century, evangelism became identified too closely with great campaigns or crusades designed to win individuals to a commitment to Jesus Christ. This on the one hand. And on the other hand there developed a number of carefully thought out methods of personal evangelism with the same end in view. Both campaign evangelism and personal evangelism are to be encouraged. But as often practiced they do not place new believers in vital contact with local churches. Proportionately, too much emphasis has been placed upon multiplying converts—and not nearly enough emphasis has been placed on multiplying congregations.

It is true that to evangelize means to "gospelize"—to spread the Good News of Christ. But in the New Testament, evangelism does not stand alone. To extend the statement of Francis Schaeffer quoted earlier:

> Thus, here [at Antioch] was a functioning local congregation called "the church." From here on the New Testament clearly indicates that churches were formed wherever some became Christians.
>
> In a sense we have a complete picture of what the church ought to be: Individuals were becoming Christians, but not individualistic ones; the congregation covered the full spectrum of society; the members were all tellers not only at home but abroad. And when the Holy Spirit said that Barnabas and Saul should be sent on the first missionary journey, the members did not function only as individual Christians, but as a unit, as a church.[7]

7. Schaeffer, *Church at the End of the Twentieth Century,* 60.

Schaeffer puts his finger on a crucial issue. If people had become individualistic Christians without a commitment to, and participation in, local churches, how would the church have moved forward in her mission to disciple the nations? Indeed, one basic reason why the church of the early centuries triumphed in the Roman Empire was that

> the little "cells" or "societies of the Way of Jesus" enjoyed a community life never before achieved. Here was a new society with a new power to practice a new way of life, because it was living in fellowship with the perfect Man who is one with God.
>
> This Christian church became the best-organized community in all the empire. Its local churches were living cells in a far-flung body covering every part of the empire. They were linked together by the travels of the bishops. They found fellowship in smaller and greater councils, through common ways of worship, through reading the same Scriptures, and, above all, through burning loyalty to and communion with one everliving Christ.[8]

So intimate is the relationship between gospel proclamation and church planting that they cannot be divorced without doing violence to the mission of the church. Note how the Church Growth specialist Donald McGavran defines evangelism: "Increasingly the primary assignment of missions is evangelism: the proclamation of the Good News and assisting in the emergence of churches which, rooted in the soil and with their own leaders, will be witnesses to the Good News."[9]

Putting Mission and Evangelism Together Again

We should be grateful for men like Bartholomew Ziegenbalg, Gustav Warneck, Henry Venn, Rufus Anderson, John Nevius, Roland Allen, and Donald McGavran. Spanning more than two centuries, they have reminded us that whatever else of good may issue from our obedience to the Great Commission, it must also result in the establishment of churches among the peoples of the world. We should also thank God for Kenneth Strachan, Francis Schaeffer, Michael Green, and others who have reminded us that New Testament evangelism results in new converts coming into the Christian fellowship of congregations new and old, and in new congregations being established in communities around the world.

It is noteworthy in this regard that Ralph Winter, who had earlier written about what he called M-1, M-2, and M-3 mission, could so easily

8. Basil Mathews, *Forward through the Ages* (New York: Friendship, 1960), 17–18.
9. Donald A. McGavran, *The Bridges of God* (New York: Friendship, 1955), xiii.

change the nomenclature to E-1, E-2, and E-3 evangelism at the International Congress on World Evangelization at Lausanne and mean essentially the same thing.[10] Did he not know that missionaries often engage in educational, medical, linguistic, and other ministries in which evangelists as we know them seldom become involved? Of course he did. But his primary concern was with mission narrowly defined as winning people to Christ and establishing churches. And with evangelism broadly defined in the same way. Accordingly, he might well have used the designations ME-1, ME-2, and ME-3.

In this book we will often use the hyphenated terms "mission-evangelism" and "missionary-evangelist," and the designation ME, in order to communicate the idea that mission and evangelism go together. When we are talking about the heart of the Christian mission and the larger implications of evangelism, the two are really inseparable. Although on occasion, in order to avoid redundancy, we may use these words separately, they are to be understood as having essentially the same meaning.

Winter also made a helpful contribution by his use of numbers to indicate the cultural distance involved in carrying out our task. Geography as such does not affect the goal of the church in mission. The words of our Lord in Acts 1:8 are important here. Grammarians are quick to point out that the Greek construction in Acts 1:8 binds Jerusalem, Judea, Samaria, and the uttermost parts together in one inseparable entity. (Southern Baptists, therefore, are scriptural when they refer to a new church as a mission whether it is located in Asia or North America!) What changes as we go from place to place (and sometimes as we stay in one place) is the cultural adaptation that must be made in order to communicate the message meaningfully and "grow a church." With this in mind, Winter uses the numbers 1, 2, and 3 to indicate the degree of cultural distance involved when a missionary-evangelist moves out to obey the Great Commission. Of course, this degree depends upon the cultural orientation of both the missionary-evangelist and the audience. For example, when a Swedish-American in Los Angeles wins other Swedish-Americans to Christ and establishes them in churches, he has not surmounted any significant cultural barrier whatsoever. That is ME-1 mission-evangelism. If he were to win Los Angeles Latinos, the cultural distance traversed would likely be much greater. That would be ME-2 mission-evangelism. But if the Swedish-American were to go to Venezuela and learn an entirely new language and culture in order to communicate Christ and plant

---

10. Ralph Winter, "The Highest Priority: Cross-Cultural Evangelism," in *Let the Earth Hear His Voice*, ed. J. D. Douglas (Minneapolis: World Wide, 1975), 213–25.

churches, the cultural distance would be greater still. That would be ME-3 mission-evangelism. Note again that geographical distance per se has little to do with the difference. If the Swedish-American Christian were to learn Spanish and adapt to the culture of new Venezuelan immigrants in the Los Angeles area, that might still be ME-3 mission-evangelism.

There are a number of reasons why we will use these designations in this book. In the first place, they constitute a neat sort of shorthand. Second, they are widely used by all who are familiar with Church Growth materials. Third, they bring mission and evangelism together in one formula. Finally, they call attention to the fact that while mission and message do not change, our methods will change as we encounter cultural differences. (It should be borne in mind that when assigning the numbers 1, 2, and 3, we are taking a North American perspective.)

Today's Priority: Cross-Cultural Church-Planting

Ralph Winter's indefatigable mind did not stop with the distinction between ME-1, ME-2, and ME-3 mission-evangelism. At Lausanne and subsequently he emphasized that the church's highest priority today must be to cross cultural boundaries in order to win people to Christ and establish communities of Christians. If we are to fulfil the Great Commission, we must recapture the pioneer spirit and move out to unreached people everywhere. To make clear what is involved, Winter divided the world into four major groupings: Bible-believing Christians, other Christians, culturally near non-Christians, and culturally distant non-Christians. These groupings became the basis for the global analysis which appeared in the Manila Manifesto of the second Lausanne Congress on World Evangelization (1989). They are also the basis of a more recent analysis that will serve our present purpose.[11]

First, there are 570 million (10 percent of the world's population) Bible-believing Christians. They represent both a tremendous potential and an ever present danger. The potential is that they can win others to the faith. The danger is that they may become ingrown and simply occupy themselves with nurturing their own faith rather than winning others.

Second, there are 1,300 million (20 percent of the world's population) other Christians. They stand within the Christian tradition but are not committed Christians. They need renewal or what we might call ME-0 mission-evangelism since no significant cultural barrier has to be

---

11. "John R. Stott Sums Up the World," with illustrations and explanations by Ralph D. Winter, *Mission Frontiers Bulletin*, May-June 1995, p. 11.

crossed in reaching them. They represent a great potential for the church because they are relatively easy to reach. But they also represent a danger in that Bible-believing Christians tend to expend most of their resources of time and money in reaching them.

Third, there are 1,660 million (30 percent of the world's population) culturally near non-Christians. They live in cultures that have already been penetrated by the Christian faith. They may be geographically distant from active Christian churches, but any cultural barriers that exist are minimal and may be largely of the Christians' own making. Sensitive ME-1 mission-evangelism is needed here.

Fourth, there are 2,170 million (40 percent of the world's population) culturally distant non-Christians. These people may or may not be far removed from active Christians geographically. But they are far removed linguistically, socially, economically, and culturally. In no way can they be expected to come into existing congregations. New churches must be planted among them. But the cultural distance involved makes many of them all but invisible. They are the hidden peoples! We must first discover them. Then, depending upon the situation, ME-2 or ME-3 mission-evangelism will be required to reach them.

One may be tempted to question some of these statistics. Nevertheless, the analysis is most perceptive. It graphically communicates the immensity of the task. It also indicates a strategy. Namely, identify cultural groupings, especially among the hidden unreached peoples of the world, and devise a method for planting believing congregations among them. Priorities must be rearranged if the church is to reach the whole world for Christ. It is all too easy to concentrate on those who are near us and most like us, while neglecting those who are far away. "Out of sight, out of mind," tends to be the case.

But our task is both/and, not either/or. Many—perhaps most—of the 1,300 million other Christians are Christians only in name. Rather than being Christians who need renewal, they are unbelievers who need regeneration. Sometimes the cultural barriers between evangelical (Bible-believing) Christians and nominal (other) Christians loom as large as do the barriers between evangelicals and culturally near non-Christians. Furthermore, though many cultural barriers between evangelicals and both of these groups are of our own making as evangelicals, we must also recognize that Western culture as a whole is becoming post-Christian. This means that barriers erected out of the worldviews of naturalism and humanism are very real. Unless we take these barriers into account, our evangelistic communication will be understood by an ever decreasing number of people in the West. Thus we must keep our near neighbors in mind while we focus on culturally distant peoples around the world among whom no Christian church yet exists. All need the gospel and Bible-teaching churches.[12]

Let every denomination, every mission, every congregation, and every Christian take a fresh look at all four of Winter's categories and ask themselves what they are doing among these respective peoples. Where people have geographical and cultural access to existing churches, let us call them into fellowship with Christ and his church. Where they do not, let us cross geographical and cultural barriers in order to preach Christ and plant the church! This book is designed to aid true Christians in this latter task. In it we do not distinguish between ME-0 and ME-1 church-planting evangelism. The vast majority of church-planting situations today entail some measure of cultural adaptation.

Allow me to quote a graduate of Trinity Evangelical Divinity School (identified only as B.A.) who wrote in the school paper a number of years ago:

> There's a new wind blowing, and it's wafting our way, soon to turn into a gale. Its theme is reflected in this simple little epigram:
>
>> If you want to grow something to last a season—
>>   plant flowers.
>> If you want to grow something to last a lifetime—
>>   plant trees.
>> If you want to grow something to last through eternity—
>>   plant churches.[13]

Call it what you will. Call it church planting, church development, church growth, or church-extension evangelism. Or call it mission-evangelism. The task is the same anywhere in the world. Any community of people without an accessible church—whether they reside in North America or South Africa—is a mission field. And it is the responsibility of believers in existing churches to fill those spiritual voids with believing congregations. As has often been remarked, neither a mission-less church nor a churchless mission is in accordance with the plan of God. The same must be said regarding an unevangelistic church and a churchless evangelism. As Donald McGavran writes, mission is "an enterprise devoted to proclaiming the good news of Christ and persuading men to become disciples and dependable members of his church."[14]

12. Carl F. H. Henry, "Evangelicals: Out of the Closet but Going Nowhere?" *Christianity Today* 24.1 (4 Jan. 1980): 16–22.

13. "The Free Church—Going to Seed: A Prophecy," *The Scribe* 1 (Spring 1976): 7 (Trinity Evangelical Divinity School).

14. Donald A. McGavran, *Understanding Church Growth* (Grand Rapids: Eerdmans, 1970), 34.

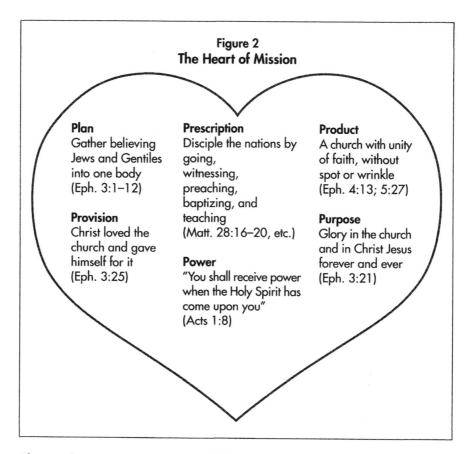

Figure 2
The Heart of Mission

Plan
Gather believing Jews and Gentiles into one body (Eph. 3:1–12)

Provision
Christ loved the church and gave himself for it (Eph. 3:25)

Prescription
Disciple the nations by going, witnessing, preaching, baptizing, and teaching (Matt. 28:16–20, etc.)

Power
"You shall receive power when the Holy Spirit has come upon you" (Acts 1:8)

Product
A church with unity of faith, without spot or wrinkle (Eph. 4:13; 5:27)

Purpose
Glory in the church and in Christ Jesus forever and ever (Eph. 3:21)

Those who are sent to accomplish this basic task are missionaries and evangelists in the best sense of these words. To be sure, to win people of other worldviews, languages, and customs to Christ and to establish them in congregations of believers require special training and tools. And while it will be helpful to use designations such as ME-1, ME-2, and ME-3 to denote the degree of cultural adaptation that will be necessary, we must keep in mind that, at its heart, our mission is the same irrespective of where it is performed or who constitutes our audience. This is what the universal church—and churches and missions—should be doing, and doing as effectively as they can, and doing now (see figure 2)!

Planning for Church Planting   2

Planning for the Task

The churches are task forces. They have a job to do. But too often the job is undertaken haphazardly and without thinking it through. A missionary once (probably facetiously) objected to planning on the grounds that Abraham "went out not knowing where he was going." The analogy breaks down, however. Abraham didn't know where he was going, but he knew what he was going to do when he got there. The missionary knew where he was going, but evidently did not know what to do when he got there!

The Bible has abundant evidence of God's plan. God is the greatest planner of all! Before creation he devised a plan for humanity and history that took every contingency into account. When Christ was ministering on earth, he had a plan for deploying his disciples and getting the kingdom message to the "lost sheep of the house of Israel" (Matt. 10). After his death and resurrection he revealed the basics of his plan for the discipling of the Gentile nations (Matt. 28:18–20; Acts 1:8). During the period covered by the Book of Acts the Holy Spirit had a plan to fulfil the Great Commission even when the apostles didn't, and increasingly that plan became a matter of discussion and deliberation on the part of his people. Finally, Paul set about the work of establishing the church as a body in which Jew and Gentile participate on an equal basis; this work was not an afterthought or even a back-up plan, but part of the eternal plan of God, though only now fully revealed (Eph. 3:1–12).

Is it not peculiar that God had a plan for history; that ordered households plan budgets, weekly schedules, and the education of the children; but that churches and missions often have no well-thought-out and prayed-about plan for the most important task of all? Is it not sad that, since God cannot count on obedience and wise stewardship in this matter, he often has to use church splits and ad hoc means to get new congregations of believers started? How much better it would be if we had a plan—his plan!

33

Figure 3
Steps in Accomplishing a Task

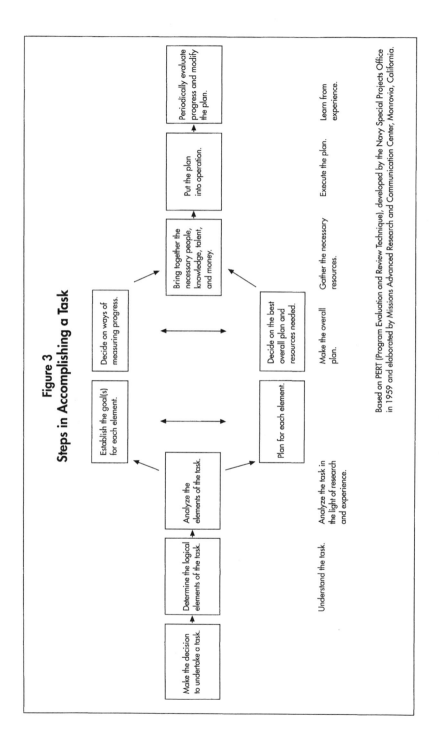

| Make the decision to undertake a task. | Determine the logical elements of the task. | Analyze the elements of the task. | Establish the goal(s) for each element. | Decide on ways of measuring progress. |
| | | | Plan for each element. | Decide on the best overall plan and resources needed. | Bring together the necessary people, knowledge, talent, and money. | Put the plan into operation. | Periodically evaluate progress and modify the plan. |

| Understand the task. | Analyze the task in the light of research and experience. | Make the overall plan. | Gather the necessary resources. | Execute the plan. | Learn from experience. |

Based on PERT (Program Evaluation and Review Technique), developed by the Navy Special Projects Office in 1959 and elaborated by Missions Advanced Research and Communication Center, Monrovia, California.

How does one develop a plan for winning others to Christ and planting viable churches? Experts tell us that there are six steps involved in accomplishing a task:

1. Understand the task.
2. Analyze the task in the light of research and experience (identify helpful and useless approaches).
3. Make an overall plan to accomplish the task.
4. Gather the necessary resources.
5. Execute the plan.
6. Learn from experience (and use what is learned to modify the plan).[1]

These steps can be better understood if we plot them on a simplified chart (see figure 3). The chart helps us understand what is involved in the various steps. It is basically self-explanatory and needs no elaboration at this point. It should be noted that in this book we are primarily concerned with the first three steps. It should be borne in mind, however, that as important as planning is, the exercise will mean little until we go on to gather our resources, execute the plan, and modify the plan as new understandings and circumstances may require.

The first of the six steps mentioned above—understanding the task—was dealt with in chapter 1. There we identified church-planting evangelism, especially among unreached populations, as being central to the fulfilment of the Great Commission. However, only when church planters focus on a particular culture, location, and people does the task become concrete and occasion the kind of planning advocated here.

The second and third of the six steps—analyzing the task in the light of research and experience, and then making an overall plan—constitute the central focus of the remainder of this book. Of course, as Christians doing Christ's work, we will not restrict ourselves to the kind of knowledge gained from research and experience. The Word of God that prescribes our task also provides principles and precedents designed to guide us in its accomplishment. For church-planting planners, then, there are three major sources of relevant information:

1. Revelation (the Bible)
2. Research (especially in the social sciences)
3. Reflection (especially on church-planting experience) (see figure 4)

1. *Planning and PERT* (Program Evaluation and Review Technique) (Monrovia, Calif.: Missions Advanced Research and Communication Center, 1966).

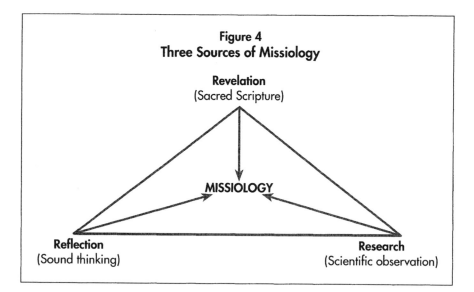

Figure 4
Three Sources of Missiology

Revelation
(Sacred Scripture)

MISSIOLOGY

Reflection
(Sound thinking)

Research
(Scientific observation)

The Three Sources of Missiology

Revelation in Scripture

The Scriptures are first in order of importance. They are the only completely authoritative rule of both faith and practice. Apart from them not only would our understanding of God be limited, but our understanding of the way in which he wants us to build his church and call out a people for his name would be limited as well. If we are to do his work, we must give attention to his Word. No true Christian would dispute this, but that is not the end of the matter. Growing out of biblical authority are at least two implications that are of paramount importance in planting and growing new congregations, particularly in those cultures and among those peoples where the Christian faith is generally unknown or largely forgotten.

First, the Bible itself—all of it and as it is—constitutes the true message. This seems self-evident. Down through history, however, a nagging question has doggedly pursued missionary pioneers. It has to do with the starting point for Christian preaching and teaching. Is it better to begin by presenting Christ and his work, or by introducing the true God, his character and attributes? The controversy is more complex than it appears to be, and through the centuries has taken many twists and turns. What, after all, is our message? What aspects of it take priority? What cultural adaptations are legitimate? What approach would be most effective?

In more recent times such questions have elicited responses at two levels among conservative evangelicals. At an activist level the gospel has been introduced by widespread showings of the *Jesus* film, by the presentation of schematics designed to arouse interest (e.g., "Four Spiritual Laws" and "Six Things God Wants You to Know"), by the use of questions (e.g., "If God asks why he should let you into his heaven, what would you say?") to encourage dialogue, and by analogies reminiscent of the redemptive work of Christ (e.g., the Peace Child rituals of West Irian). At a more reasoned level, discussions have focused on contextualization or ways of making the Christian message understandable to and effective for people in their specific religious, cultural, and linguistic settings. Contextualizers realize that the Christian message is not communicated best by using the same form or formula in all cultures. In fact, that approach may ensure that in some cultures the Christian message will be misconstrued and not really communicated at all! Only by tailoring the message form (and, for that matter, the method as well) to the target culture will the biblical gospel be truly heard!

It is not difficult to trace the hand of God in the progress of world evangelization. No knowledgeable practitioners would argue that their particular formula is the formula of heaven. And no serious theorist would claim to have all the answers. God has used and continues to use a variety of approaches in the communication of the gospel because the worldviews, thought patterns, and motivations of the world's peoples vary significantly.

All of that having been said, the author is in a growing company of theologians and missiologists who are persuaded that the Bible itself—not just a statement of basic doctrines, or a list of biblical ideas, or a succession of fragmented Bible stories—constitutes the contextualization that God himself has provided, prescribed, and promised to prosper (see Matt. 28:20; 2 Tim. 3:16–17). Various approaches might be used to make contacts, awaken interest, and gain a hearing. But in the making of disciples—students and followers of Christ—the larger story and full compass of Scripture must be taught, understood, and embraced. That is the way old idolatrous worldviews are exchanged for the divinely inspired worldview of the Bible, an exchange that is basic to biblical conversion and spiritual maturation.[2]

Second, turning from message to strategy and method, we can make a case that Scripture provides not only the message, but also practical guidance on how to go about the twin tasks of communicating the gospel and building the church. There is, however, an important differ-

---

2. See David J. Hesselgrave, *Scripture and Strategy: The Use of the Bible in Postmodern Church and Mission* (Pasadena: William Carey Library, 1994), esp. chs. 3, 6, and 7.

ence here. While in the final analysis the biblical statement of the gospel message is normative and foundational to churches of all times and places, the biblical account of the strategies and methods employed by Christ and the apostles is largely descriptive. This is so in the case of our Lord, who trained the Twelve but planted no particular church. It is also true in the case of the apostle Paul, who led various missionary teams in the planting of numerous churches. Paul makes it clear that he received his message directly from the Lord; accordingly, it is not to be altered (Gal. 1:11–12). But he makes no such claim with regard to his strategy as a "master builder" of the church of Christ (1 Cor. 3:10). So his strategy is prescriptive only to the degree that it mirrors biblical principles and teachings. Otherwise it is descriptive—a strategy to be pondered and studied, but not necessarily to be followed in every case.

With this caveat in mind, there can be little doubt that insofar as a pattern for church planting is discoverable in the New Testament, it is to be discovered in those passages that describe the ministry of the apostle Paul. The lion's share of the Acts record, for example, is devoted to the ministry of Paul and his coworkers. Moreover, much of the remainder of the New Testament is made up of Paul's correspondence to those coworkers and the churches he had founded.

It is possible, therefore, to extrapolate from the biblical record specific aspects of Paul's overall strategy and special methods that can be applied to contemporary situations. For example, Paul's strategy was to concentrate on cities located on major routes of communication and commerce. He utilized his tentmaking ability to provide for both his own needs and the needs of some of his coworkers. He did not subsidize newly planted churches with monies from the outside. The works of Roland Allen highlight these aspects of Paul's method and apply them to church-planting efforts today.[3] Donald McGavran takes a somewhat similar approach, but he concentrates more on the sociological aspects of Paul's ministry. As he proceeded from city to city, Paul sought out relatives, friends, and business associates of people he had known in Antioch and other places. These contacts became bridges to bring the gospel into new places and among new peoples.[4] Of course, Allen and McGavran have by no means exhausted the basic features of Paul's strategy. A number of other theorists have made similar studies and point to Paul's reliance on a missionary team, for example, and the usefulness of multinational teams in our contemporary world.

---

3. See, e.g., Roland Allen, *Missionary Methods: St. Paul's or Ours?* (Grand Rapids: Eerdmans, 1962).
4. Donald A. McGavran, *The Bridges of God* (New York: Friendship, 1955).

Though we will not hesitate to draw attention to various details of Paul's strategy and methodology, we will concentrate instead on his overall approach. That is, we will concentrate on those essential elements in Paul's approach to church planting that are not only clear from the biblical text, but also so obviously necessary that they require the formation of intermediate plans within the overall plan. Since the same sequence of essential elements occurs over and over in different locations and among different target peoples, we will refer to it as the Pauline Cycle. Because an understanding of this cycle is so germane to what follows in this book, we will devote an entire chapter (ch. 3) to it.

Research in the Sciences

That most planning programs (including the six-step program we highlighted earlier) fail to take biblical revelation into account is not at all surprising. Secularists are limited to information stemming from research and experience. In planning for church planting and growth, on the other hand, we have recourse to God's Word. What value, then, should we place on research and experience?

After his conversion Augustine faced much the same question when he inquired into the usefulness of that knowledge he had acquired at university. Could "Egyptian knowledge" be put to kingdom service? Summed up in his classic statement that "gold from Egypt is still gold," Augustine's conclusion serves us quite well as a guiding principle today. Truth obtained from any source is still truth, and not only can but should be used in kingdom service. However, Augustine added two caveats that are of almost equal importance: (1) all such knowledge should be thoroughly tested in the light of Scripture to make sure that it is real gold (i.e., true) and not fool's gold; and (2) scriptural knowledge is qualitatively (and even quantitatively) more important than secular knowledge.[5]

It should be noted that the word "research" in the present context should not be thought of in the narrow sense of controlled experimentation, but primarily as understandings growing out of the social sciences (we are not necessarily excluding experimentation and technology of various sorts). Since the late nineteenth century, but especially since World War II, Western missions have become increasingly dependent upon the methods and findings of such disciplines as anthropology, linguistics, communications, psychology, and marketing.

In this regard, it will be helpful to consider briefly the general orientation of one of the most influential mission movements of the last half

---

5. Augustine, *On Christian Doctrine*, trans. D. W. Robertson Jr. (New York: Liberal Arts, 1958), book 2.

of the twentieth century—the Church Growth movement. There was in much of the work of Donald McGavran, Alan Tippett, and their associates a certain tension between theology and the sciences. Sometimes the latter seemed to drive the former. It is well to be aware of this. Nevertheless, their general approach had a number of advantages. First, they put the growth of the church front and center in evangelism and mission theory and practice. Second, at a very practical level they demonstrated that, rightly understood and employed, social science findings can be expected to make a signal contribution to our knowledge of the ways in which the church grows. Third, they made it clear that this kind of knowledge is important when making and implementing bold plans for growing the church. Fourth, they also made it clear that knowledge of such topics as the variegated mosaics of societies, receptivity and resistance, and the dynamics of group decision-making needs to be augmented by an understanding of the ways in which churches have grown or stagnated in the past, that is, by reflection on experience.

Reflection on Past Experience

Experience is a great teacher, but effective only to the degree that it attracts willing students. McGavran and his colleagues were not troubled by the myopia that plagues many church-growth studies today. They carried out thoroughgoing studies both of the larger history of church and mission and of particular churches. Membership statistics for particular churches were gathered and plotted on a graph. The graph was carefully studied. The various elements involved in growth (conversion from the world, birth of children, transfer from other churches), the number of (and reasons for) withdrawals from membership, and likely causes of growth, plateauing, and downswings were analyzed. On the basis of this and similarly relevant information, McGavran and his colleagues then plotted other graphs indicating the potential for future growth and developed plans for achieving that potential.

Certain weaknesses in this approach are apparent. In addition to the weakness of its theological underpinnings, critics pointed to the overemphasis on quantitative growth, a rather naive understanding of causation, and the focus on existing churches to the neglect of planting new congregations. In addition to making church growth a central concern, however, and to his everlasting credit, McGavran pointed to far more egregious weaknesses in the approaches of many of his predecessors and contemporaries. Many were unconcerned about the two billion souls who (in his time) had not heard the gospel of Christ. Some had established mission stations that effectively sealed missionaries off from the very peoples they needed to evangelize. Some had allowed the missionary enterprise to metamorphose into a vast program of social concern well calculated to ameliorate human ills, but not to effect the spiritual redemption without which men and women will be poorer in this life and in the life to come. Some, on the other hand, had gained a few converts and then, spending all their efforts in perfecting them, failed to reach out to new populations.

It is highly instructive that in his later years the indomitable and insightful Father of Church Growth lent his wholehearted support to the establishment of a society (the Evangelical Missiological Society) dedicated to Great Commission mission and based on a commitment to the cardinal doctrines of the Christian faith. Were he alive today, we can be sure that he would still devote himself to reaching the unreached with the gospel of Christ, to dissipating the universal fog that obscures church growth, and to decrying the overemphasis in some circles on marketing the church, a practice that risks raising up churches that please humans but provoke God!

Church-Planting Strategy— The Pauline Cycle

3

There can be little question that if there is a biblical model of the best way to go about the task of evangelizing populations and planting Christian congregations all around the world, it is to be found in the ministry of the apostle Paul. Yet we are also mindful that our Lord in response to the apostle Peter's affirmation of faith prophesied, "You are Peter, and upon this rock I will build My church; and the gates of Hades shall not overpower it" (Matt. 16:18). As all know, this statement has been the subject of considerable controversy. Often overlooked in that controversy is that the Book of Acts records that the apostle Peter was not only empowered by the Holy Spirit to speak the Word at Pentecost, but was also directed by that same Spirit to open the door of salvation to the Gentile Cornelius and his household (Acts 11:13–14), and to defend at the Jerusalem Council the ministry of Paul to the Gentiles (see Acts 15:7–14).

Nevertheless, once the apostle Paul had been converted and commissioned, and his message and ministry had been vindicated, the Acts record focuses almost exclusively upon Paul's mission among peoples in a broad area extending from Jerusalem throughout the Mediterranean world to the door of Western Europe. Moreover, under the direction of the Holy Spirit at least thirteen of the twenty-one letters that constitute a major portion of the New Testament were authored by this same Paul. In addition, the Holy Spirit inspired Paul to identify himself as a "wise master builder" of church foundations (1 Cor. 3:10). Surely, then, if we are warranted in examining and following the example of anyone at all in this important business of planting churches in new places and among new peoples, that person must be the apostle Paul, who, we have assumed up to this point, had a definite strategy in view.

Did Paul Have a Strategy?

We have used the words "strategy" and "method" without stopping to define them. "Strategy," of course, is a military term now more widely used to refer to large-scale planning and directing of operations toward a certain goal. "Method," on the other hand, is usually taken to refer to a scaled-down way of going about a task. These words are often used without being defined, so we will depend upon the reader to determine what they mean in context. We will, however, generally use them in the way just indicated. At the same time, they are often so closely intertwined that the answer to a question such as "Did Paul have a strategy?" will be understood as relating to Paul's methods as well as to his strategy per se.

Our answer to the question "Did Paul have a strategy?" will determine how we proceed from this point. If, as Michael Green seems to believe, Paul had little or no strategy, and "the Gospel spread out in an apparently haphazard way as men obeyed the leading of the Spirit, and went through doors he opened,"[1] then all we can learn from Paul is to depend upon that same Spirit. If, on the other hand, Donald McGavran is right when he says that while Paul was in Antioch he devised a strategy for reaching a great part of the Mediterranean world with the gospel,[2] then we can learn from Paul's strategy as well as from his dependence upon the Holy Spirit.

A mediating position seems to square with the data. Green is quite right when he insists that we "must not organize [Christ] out of the picture," and when he warns against the idea that "efficiency on the evangelistic production line will inevitably produce results."[3] But he seems to overstate his case. If Paul had no plan, the Holy Spirit could not have changed it (see Acts 16:6–10)! On the other hand, McGavran's discussion of Paul's strategy for reaching "people on the bridge" (people related to believers) is fascinating and instructive. But at times McGavran too seems to overstate his case. J. Herbert Kane's words are worth pondering:

> We might begin by asking: Did Paul have a missionary strategy? Some say yes; others say no. Much depends on the definition of strategy. If by strategy is meant a deliberate, well-formulated, duly executed plan of action based on human observation and experience, then Paul had little or no strategy; but if we take the word to mean a flexible *modus operandi* developed under the guidance of the Holy Spirit and subject to His direction and control, then Paul did have a strategy.
>
> Our problem today is that we live in an anthropocentric age. We imagine that nothing of consequence can be accomplished in the Lord's work

1. Michael Green, "Evangelism in the Early Church," in *Let the Earth Hear His Voice*, ed. J. D. Douglas (Minneapolis: World Wide, 1975), 174.
2. Donald A. McGavran, *The Bridges of God* (New York: Friendship, 1955), 25–35.
3. Green, "Evangelism in the Early Church," 174.

without a good deal of ecclesiastical machinery—committees, conferences, workshops, seminars; whereas the early Christians depended less on human wisdom and expertise, more on divine initiative and guidance. It is obvious that they didn't do too badly. What the modern missionary movement needs above everything else is to get back to the missionary methods of the early church.[4]

We tend to agree with Kane's basic position, but we would modify his statement somewhat. Paul, of course, had comparatively little opportunity to base his strategy on observation and experience. But with two thousand years of missions history behind us we should have a "deliberate, well-formulated, duly executed plan of action based on human observation and experience." However, to be Christian, that plan should not be based primarily on human observation. It must be "developed under the guidance of the Holy Spirit and subject to His direction and control." As for flexibility, any strategy that is not flexible is simply bad strategy.

Let's agree, then, that "what the modern missionary movement needs above everything else is to get back to the missionary methods of the early church." That is the starting point. It would be as foolhardy for us to disregard the Holy Spirit–inspired record of the way in which the early Christians, and especially Paul and his cohorts, actually built up the churches of their day as it would have been for Paul to disregard the Holy Spirit's guidance received in Arabia and Antioch. At the same time, it would be as unthinkable for us to discount the understanding that has come to us through two thousand years of experience and study as it would have been for Paul to discount the processes of the Hellenization of culture and the religious penetration of Judaism in his own day. Nevertheless, Kane's warning is not to be ignored. If our dependence is on the overall strategy and the method of its implementation rather than on the wisdom and power of the Holy Spirit, we cannot claim to be true to the New Testament, nor will our witness be as effective as was that of the first-century believers.

Is Pauline Strategy Applicable Today?

To say that Paul's missionary labors resulted from thinking as well as praying and working does not end the matter. We must ask whether or not Pauline strategy is applicable in our day. To that question we answer yes.

4. J. Herbert Kane, *Christian Missions in Biblical Perspective* (Grand Rapids: Baker, 1976), 73.

In the first place, the first-century world of Paul bears some remarkable similarities to our world of today. Of course, we must admit that the twenty-first century is not a carbon copy of the first century, and that, when compared to the situation in which modern foreign missionaries usually find themselves, Paul's situation was quite different. Paul was a citizen of his missionary world. He did not have to learn a strange tongue in order to communicate. Moreover, from the very beginning of his ministry he was familiar with the thought patterns of his audience. At the same time, as E. M. Blaiklock, professor of classics at Auckland University in New Zealand, is reported to have said, "Of all the intervening centuries, [ours] is most like the first."[5] There was considerable intercultural flow of peoples of different races and backgrounds. There was a widespread bankruptcy of ideas and ideals. And there was a group of people scattered throughout the Roman Empire who, by virtue of their contact with or commitment to Jewish monotheistic and ethical ideas, constituted a prepared audience for the gospel.

In the second place, Paul claimed to be a master builder of the church (1 Cor. 3:10). While not inferring from that fact that we are to slavishly follow every approach employed by the great apostle to the Gentiles, we can at least profit from a careful study of his strategy and even his methodology. After all, modern architects study the works of master architects of the past even though they may not design and build identical buildings. Just so, we can learn from Paul. As Richard Longenecker has written:

> It has often been devotionally said: "The world has yet to see what God can do with a man wholly committed to Him." Paul was such a man, and the world has witnessed the effect. He possessed a firmness of commitment to his Lord, a fervency of spirit, a compassion of heart, a breadth of outlook, a keenness of perception, and a constant openness to the Spirit. Such an example of a Christian life and ministry stands as both a paradigm and an inspiration to us today.[6]

To What Extent Is Paul's Methodology Normative?

It is clear from the New Testament Scriptures that Paul's message is normative. To the Galatians—troubled as they were by the Judaizers—he could say, "But even though we, or an angel from heaven, should preach to you a gospel contrary to that which we have preached to you, let him be accursed" (Gal. 1:8). To the Corinthians—plagued as they

5. Quoted in Ray Stedman, *Body Life* (Glendale, Calif.: Regal, 1972), 129.
6. Richard Longenecker, *The Ministry and Message of Paul* (Grand Rapids: Zondervan, 1971), 112.

were with church difficulties—he could write, "For I received from the Lord that which I also delivered to you" (1 Cor. 11:23a).

It is also clear from the New Testament that, in a secondary sense, Paul the man was a normative example of what a Christian should be and do. To the Corinthians, who desperately needed an example of what a Christian should be, he could make that remarkable statement, "Be imitators of me" (1 Cor. 11:1a). But Paul was not perfect. He knew it. And therefore he added those all-important words, "just as I also am of Christ" (1 Cor. 11:1b). So Paul's example of Christian living is normative to the degree that it reflected the perfect pattern—that of Jesus Christ himself.

Then what about Paul's missionary method? There seems to be little to indicate that the Holy Spirit expects us to slavishly follow every Pauline procedure in our evangelistic outreach. On the other hand, there is explicit teaching in the Epistles which directs us to carry on the same activities in a similar way—namely, to go where people are, preach the gospel, gain converts, gather them into churches, instruct them in the faith, choose leaders, and commend believers to the grace of God. And where could we find a pattern for these activities that is less likely to lead us into blind alleys than is the apostle Paul's missionary work? As A. R. Hay writes, "Paul's ministry and that of his companions is recorded in detail because he and they provide a typical example for the exceedingly important permanent ministry of church planting."[7]

We conclude, then, that Paul's message is absolutely normative, and that his manner of life and missionary methodology are less normative. It is a matter of degree. There is room for adaptation in each case, but less in the case of his message and more in the cases of his lifestyle and methodology. Those of us who are two thousand years removed from the physical presence of the Master and his apostles would do well to learn from Paul's preaching, person, and program in dependence on the Word and the Holy Spirit.

To put it in words that will be used throughout this book, church planners and planters should always be faithful to biblical principles, and they should always be attentive to biblical precedents. In every phase of both planning and planting they should both give themselves to prayer and exhort coworkers and converts alike to do the same. Little or nothing will be accomplished without prayer! Little or nothing will be accomplished without thinking and working. Ask the apostle Paul! Consult the biblical record!

---

7. A. R. Hay, *New Testament Order for Church and Missionary* (Audubon, N.J.: New Testament Missionary Union, 1947), 220.

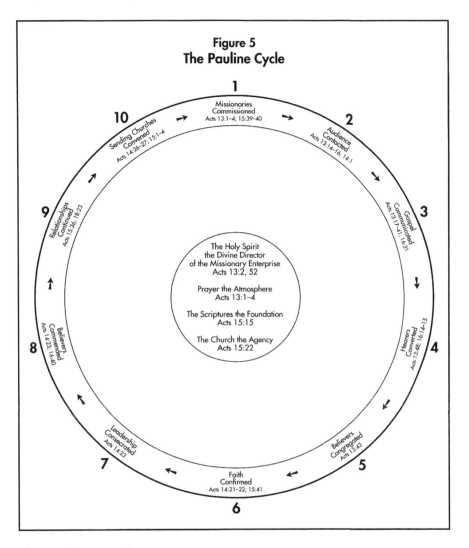

Figure 5
The Pauline Cycle

1 Missionaries Commissioned — Acts 13:1–4; 15:39–40

2 Audience Contacted — Acts 13:14–16; 14:1

3 Gospel Communicated — Acts 13:17–41; 16:31

4 Hearers Converted — Acts 13:48; 16:14–15

5 Believers Congregated — Acts 13:43

6 Faith Confirmed — Acts 14:21–22; 15:41

7 Leadership Consecrated — Acts 14:23

8 Believers Commended — Acts 14:23; 16:40

9 Relationships Continued — Acts 15:36; 18:23

10 Sending Churches Convened — Acts 14:26–27; 15:1–4

The Holy Spirit the Divine Director of the Missionary Enterprise — Acts 13:2, 52

Prayer the Atmosphere — Acts 13:1–4

The Scriptures the Foundation — Acts 15:15

The Church the Agency — Acts 15:22

The Pauline Cycle

The Logical Elements in Paul's Master Plan of Evangelism

What were the logical elements (steps) in Paul's master plan of evangelism and church development? These elements will be analyzed later. At this point we will simply list them and display them in diagrammatic form (see figure 5):

1. Missionaries Commissioned—Acts 13:1–4; 15:39–40
2. Audience Contacted—Acts 13:14–16; 14:1; 16:13–15

3. Gospel Communicated—Acts 13:17–41; 16:31
4. Hearers Converted—Acts 13:48; 16:14–15
5. Believers Congregated—Acts 13:43
6. Faith Confirmed—Acts 14:21–22; 15:41
7. Leadership Consecrated—Acts 14:23
8. Believers Commended—Acts 14:23; 16:40
9. Relationships Continued—Acts 15:36; 18:23
10. Sending Churches Convened—Acts 14:26–27; 15:1–4

Possible Objections to the Pauline Cycle

To some the steps in the Pauline Cycle may seem to be almost too obvious to be really important. Our response is that for people who are thoroughly acquainted with a given task, the logical elements which go to make it up should be obvious. Chemists would be hampered in working with hydrochloric acid if its molecular structure were not common knowledge in their laboratories. Once the basic elements of anything are discovered, they are more or less obvious. At that point the only real expertise that is required is in working with them.

To others the Pauline Cycle may seem somewhat contrived. Ten steps, alliterative phrases—the whole thing seems too tidy to be true, too programmatic to be practical. Our response is that there is nothing sacrosanct about this particular way of breaking the task down into manageable elements. In this sense the mission of the church is not analogous with a molecule of hydrochloric acid. Variation is possible. Nevertheless, we believe that careful analysis of the missionary task will reveal something very similar to the steps in the Pauline Cycle. It makes little difference to us how those steps are identified.

To still others it may seem that the cycle is not really Pauline. They may grant that Paul engaged in these various activities, but not necessarily in every locality. If that is the case, is not the cycle a sort of hybrid or composite inferred from a total ministry rather than the basis for a plan in any given local situation? Our answer is fourfold.

1. Paul did not establish a church in every locality he visited. He did not plan to do so. As far as Paul was concerned (and as far as we know), in Athens, for example, the cycle went through the contact and communication steps and stopped with the conversion of Dionysius, Damaris, and certain others (Acts 17:34). We know that later on there was a church in Athens. But as far as the biblical record and Paul's ministry are concerned, we have no further information about it. Athens was a layover for Paul. It was not his kind of city.

2. By using the phrase "Pauline Cycle" we do not mean to imply that Paul himself carried out every step in every place he went. Paul led a

team of men. The record is clear that he delegated responsibilities to other members of the team. For example, Paul wrote to Titus, "The reason I left you in Crete was that you might straighten out what was left unfinished and appoint elders in every town, as I directed you" (Titus 1:5 NIV).

3. The more complete the biblical record in the case of any given local situation, the more explicit the steps in the cycle become. Take, for example, the case of the church at Ephesus. There the basic steps are made explicit in the biblical record:

Audience Contacted—Acts 18:19; 19:1, 8–9
Gospel Communicated—Acts 19:4, 9–10
Hearers Converted—Acts 19:5, 18
Believers Congregated—Acts 19:9–10
Faith Confirmed—Acts 20:20, 27
Leadership Consecrated—Acts 20:17, 28; 1 Tim. 1:3–4; 2:2
Believers Commended—Acts 20:1, 25, 32
Relationships Continued—Acts 20:17; Eph. 1:1–3, 15–16

4. While the cycle grows out of Pauline methodology instead of being imposed upon it, nevertheless it also grows out of logicality and the larger experience of missions. Given the nature of the task to which we have been commissioned, the steps in the cycle are practical and reasonable. Look at them again. If any of us as the modern counterparts of Paul, Peter, Thomas, or Timothy were to go to a designated city to evangelize and establish a church, would we not carry out these very same steps? And would we not carry them out in this order, more or less?

Four Important Aspects of the Pauline Cycle

Before we close our preliminary discussion of the Pauline Cycle, four aspects of it should be especially noted.

1. The cycle has a beginning and an ending. This avoids a shortcoming of a large number of recent books in the area of church growth and development, some of which do afford stimulating reading for those concerned about the mission of the church. Practitioners who are trained in the church-growth principles advocated by these books contemplate church-extension evangelism in a new area only to find that they don't know how to string these pearls of wisdom on one strand! They don't know where to begin! And they have not even thought about how to end. By thinking in terms of a cycle with a beginning and an end and logical steps in between, it may be possible to overcome this weakness. One of the many strengths of Tom A. Steffen's fine work on church

planting is that he underscores the critical importance of "passing the baton" from church planter to succeeding pastor. The successor must take up responsibility for every stage in the church-planting plan and process.[8]

2. Though we speak of a beginning and an ending to the cycle, there is a sense in which it does not admit of either. When Paul was recommissioned in Antioch before his second missionary journey (Acts 15:39–40), he reestablished contact with, and continued his ministry to, fledgling groups of believers, confirming them in the faith (Acts 15:41). At the same time he was pressing the frontiers of the gospel a little farther from the home bases in Jerusalem and Antioch. To legitimately think of a beginning and an ending, then, one must be thinking of the church-planting task in relation to only one church or one limited area.

3. The cycle must be viewed synchronically as well as diachronically. That is, while we can think of progressing from the contact stage to communication, to conversion, to congregating believers, and so on, we must also remember that as we proceed through time to the more advanced stages of development, we must still carry on the activities of the initial stages (or see to it that they are carried on). For example, we must always be making new contacts and working for new conversions from the world even as we are confirming previous believers in the faith. Not to do so is to displease the head of the church. Therefore, bold lines should not be drawn between the major elements of the cycle. In one sense they are distinct and sequential. In another sense they impinge upon, and flow into, one another.

4. It is of vital importance that the Pauline Cycle strategy be applied to existing churches as well as to pioneer situations. By evaluating an existing church step by step from "audience contacted" right on through "relationships continued," the pastor and responsible believers can analyze where their church is successful and where it is falling down on the job! Then they can make necessary changes in their overall plan, decide on standards, gather resources, and put promising innovations into operation. In addition, they will constantly gain new insights into the mission of the church at home and abroad.

Effective missionizing and evangelizing requires careful, prayerful planning and strategizing. When God was preparing to lead his people out of Egypt and into the Promised Land, he called Moses and communicated a plan: "Go and gather the elders of Israel together, and say to them . . . and you with the elders of Israel will come to the king of Egypt,

8. Tom A. Steffen, *Passing the Baton: Church Planting That Empowers*, 2d ed. (La Habra, Calif.: Center for Organizational and Ministry Development, 1997).

and you will say to him . . . But I know that the king of Egypt will not permit you to go. . . . So I will stretch out My hand, and strike Egypt with all My miracles" (Exod. 3:16–20). When God was ready to bring believing Jews and Gentiles into a new community of faith, he arrested Saul and said, "But arise, and stand on your feet; for this purpose I have appeared to you, to appoint you a minister and a witness" (Acts 26:16). And when Saul—now Paul—had ministered, witnessed, and established groups of believers from Syria in the East to Macedonia and Achaia in the West, he wrote to one church, "I planted, Apollos watered, but God was causing the growth. . . . We are God's fellow workers; you are God's field, God's building. According to the grace of God which was given to me, as a wise master builder I laid a foundation, and another is building upon it. But let each man be careful how he builds upon it" (1 Cor. 3:6, 9–10). Above all, the accomplishment of God's plans and purpose requires divine wisdom, intervention, and grace. But it also requires that a Moses and his elders, or a Paul and his companions, dedicate themselves—body, heart, and mind—to the task.

Part Two

The Christian Leader and the Christian Mission

Leading the Mission 4

The Leaderless Army

Imagine an army without generals or a resident commander in chief. It has tens of thousands of troops. It has corporals, sergeants, lieutenants, and captains. It has airplanes, trucks, tanks, and the latest weaponry. It has administrative buildings, schools, and barracks. It has mess sergeants, kitchens, dining halls, and an almost limitless supply of food. It has specialists in military strategy, logistics, communications, and physical fitness. And it has bands complete with drum and bugle corps. But it has no generals and no resident commander in chief.

Everyone in our imaginary army is busy. Wherever one goes throughout the length and breadth of the encampment one is amazed at the activity. Classes are in session. Units are marching. Bands are playing. Traffic is moving. In fact, special units quite regularly take it upon themselves to go out and harass the enemy in territory they invaded and occupied long ago. Periodically there are special maneuvers in which some entrepreneuring individuals rally everyone together just long enough to put on a full display of men and machines—and within sight of the enemy! Remember, however, our imaginary army has no generals and no resident commander in chief.

"Stop right there," some loyal member of the Christian army protests. "I see what you are saying. But our Christian army does have a commander in chief, and generals too. We are pressing the battle on many fronts. And we are taking captives and winning back some ground too!"

Granted. The analogy may be overdrawn. But if one were to travel the length and breadth of our land and spend months and even years inspecting the battlefields in every part of the world, one would probably agree that the analogy has some validity.

Oh, there are many Christians in our army. And there is no small amount of expertise. We have some sophisticated equipment too. And activity on every side. But all too often the units of the Christian army are out of touch with one another. Generals there are, but not a few of them give the appearance of being self-appointed. Those who do not, often seem to be so preoccupied with logistics that they have precious little time or inclination to map out an overall strategy or direct an assault on the enemy. Finally, there is the disconcerting fact that many members of the army claim to be getting directives that are contradictory and self-defeating. One wonders: Are they setting themselves to obedience, or to do their own thing in the hope that somehow the larger cause will be aided?

How unlike the campaign of Paul and his apostolic band—the campaign that won a foothold in city after city and province after province right up to and including the palace of the pagan emperor! One can understand why. Under God, Paul was at the forefront of that campaign. If there were defections and disagreement, there was also direction. Read the record: "Now those who conducted Paul brought him as far as Athens; and receiving a command for Silas and Timothy to come to him as soon as possible, they departed" (Acts 17:15); "For this reason I left you [Titus] in Crete, that you might set in order what remains, and appoint elders in every city as I directed you" (Titus 1:5). It seems obvious that the early missionary enterprise was characterized by discipline and direction. No wonder the leader of that apostolic band could humbly write in terms of accomplished tasks and occupied territory: "For I will not presume to speak of anything except what Christ has accomplished through me . . . that from Jerusalem and round about as far as Illyricum I have fully preached the gospel of Christ" (Rom. 15:18–19); "I have fought the good fight, I have finished the course, I have kept the faith" (2 Tim. 4:7).

We of the twenty-first century will never return to apostolic authority (in the personal sense) and first-century simplicity. But there must be much more strategic thinking and serious direction on the part of those who have been duly appointed as leaders of the church and its missions—and much more disciplined involvement on the part of the soldiers of the cross—if we are ever to accomplish what should be accomplished in the time that remains to us to obey our commission and complete our mission.

Leadership and Strategy for Home Missions

Our understanding of the task can never be complete until it is defined in terms of specific target areas. But who decides what areas should be entered with a view to establishing new churches? Who determines the master plan for actually doing so? And who gathers the resources that make it possible? The answer should be obvious. Church and mission leaders.

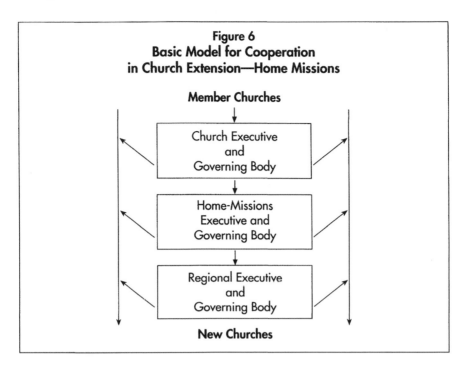

Figure 6
Basic Model for Cooperation
in Church Extension—Home Missions

Home-mission leaders must resist the temptation to become only, or primarily, caretakers of the churches already established. Some of their most important functions should be to encourage an overall plan for church extension, to suggest ways and means of carrying out the plan, and to provide leadership in implementation. Obviously there are alternative ways of going about the task. But acceptable ways should be agreed upon and elaborated into master plans, and those plans should be studied in the churches and missions. Laypersons and pastors often stand ready to devote themselves to the task. What are often lacking are the leadership and organization required for their recruitment and deployment.

Given an understanding of our missionary task and the elements that go into it, the next requirement is a basic organization that will provide for direction and cooperation in carrying out a plan to retake ground occupied by the enemy and extend the frontiers of the church of Christ. In the suggested model (see figure 6) this requirement is met by organizing leaders in such a way that they can take responsibility for planning strategy and for gathering and deploying human and financial resources for the task. Of course, organizational and procedural details must be worked out in accordance with the governing rules of the denomination or mission involved.

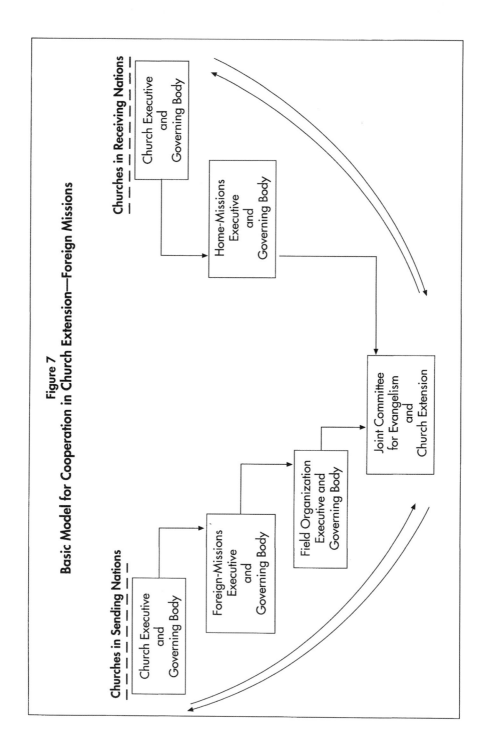

Figure 7
Basic Model for Cooperation in Church Extension—Foreign Missions

Churches in Receiving Nations

Church Executive
and
Governing Body

Home-Missions
Executive
and
Governing Body

Joint Committee
for Evangelism
and
Church Extension

Field Organization
Executive and
Governing Body

Foreign-Missions
Executive
and
Governing Body

Church Executive
and
Governing Body

Churches in Sending Nations

Leadership and Strategy for Overseas Missions

Missions overseas are the arms of the churches. Their executives must see to it that missionaries and evangelists are not simply deployed and busy—but are deployed in a way advantageous to the communication of the gospel and the building of churches. In fact, of the many services that missionary executives perform for the field missionary, perhaps the most important is that they ensure that the men and women on the field are so informed and situated that they can work in harmony with their colleagues in accordance with a meaningful strategy and clearly defined goals.

This is no small order, as those experienced in overseas missions will recognize. Field organizations tend to be characterized by egalitarianism and rotating leadership. Endless hours can be spent in keeping the field organization functioning, in the decision-making process, and in secondary activities. Moreover, the national churches have prerogatives which are divinely ordained but which greatly complicate the field situation and may frustrate the missionaries. Proper organization and planning at home and abroad, however, will assure missionaries with great church-planting potential that they will not be lost in the crowd at home or frustrated in the ministry overseas.

In those cases where administrative arrangements with national churches might jeopardize the outreach of expatriate missionaries, the nature and implications of these arrangements should be carefully spelled out to missionary candidates before they commit themselves to a particular field. Sending churches and receiving churches alike should also be very cautious lest they discourage or wrongly deploy those who are called to, and gifted for, extension work. The Scriptures are clear enough as to what the primary task is. Convenience is a poor substitute for obedience on the part of any church or mission. (A viable framework for cross-cultural mission may well be some variation of figure 7.)

Liaison between Home and Overseas Mission Societies

Finally, meaningful liaison and cooperation between home and overseas mission societies and departments should be established in this new day that has dawned for the church. It is of course true that the administration of an enterprise involving the regulations of foreign governments and cooperation with Third World churches entails unique problems that require special expertise. And obstacles will almost always increase as we move out from ME-1 to ME-2 and ME-3 mission-evangelism. Nevertheless, we should be carrying on the same basic ministry at home and abroad. It follows that there should be a high de-

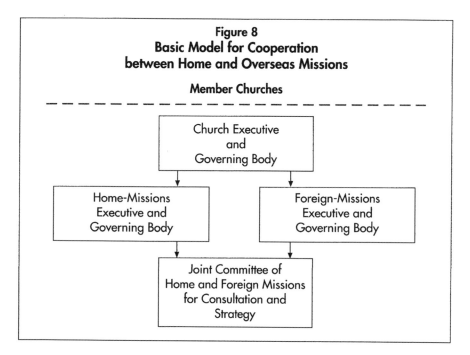

Figure 8
Basic Model for Cooperation
between Home and Overseas Missions

Member Churches

Church Executive
and
Governing Body

Home-Missions
Executive and
Governing Body

Foreign-Missions
Executive and
Governing Body

Joint Committee of
Home and Foreign Missions
for Consultation and
Strategy

gree of correlation between strategies employed by home and overseas missions. No longer can we afford the luxury of missions going their separate ways. They must instead join together in prayer and consultation to form master plans. The elaboration and execution of those plans for specific intra- and cross-cultural areas are quite enough to occupy the attention of the separate departments. (Figure 8 suggests an organizational model for mutually beneficial consultation and planning on the part of home and overseas missions.)

Before concluding this introductory consideration of mission leadership, we do well to flash certain caution lights:

1. One of the perennial problems of church-planting efforts has to do with the style of leadership at various levels of operation and stages of development. In his excellent book on the subject John Westermann elaborates on six styles of leadership.[1] They range from authoritarian, where the leader alone decides and directs, to the hands-off approach, where the leader neither communicates nor gets involved with those actually doing the work. In between these two unacceptable extremes Westermann discusses four more-appropriate styles: consultative, participatory, visionary, and supportive.

1. John J. Westermann, *The Leadership Continuum: A Biblical Model for Effective Leading* (Deer Lodge, Tenn.: Lighthouse, 1997), 13–26.

Westermann is well worth reading at this point. In church-planting situations any problems associated with leadership style will often be aggravated by problems stemming from geographical distance and the number of organizational levels at which the leaders are involved. Another problem is the frustration that arises when church planters have little regard for individual gifts and local conditions. Further, when there are no overall strategy and modus operandi in evidence and church planters are left to their own devices, factionalism may well be the result. It is imperative that more-desirable approaches be considered, clarified, and decided upon.

2. Representatives from the congregations participating in any church-extension effort should be involved in planning as well as in carrying out the plans. This is especially true in democratic societies, but it has universal application.

A seminar on church planting was held in the Far East some years ago. After several hours were spent discussing the raw materials of a master plan, one participant volunteered, "But we already have a master plan upon which all have agreed." He was correct. The plan was available. It was relatively sound. And all had agreed to it—formally. But when inquiry was made as to why the plan had not actually been put in operation, a problem became apparent. The leader had drawn up the plan and presented it to the various congregations that were going to be involved. For reasons that were largely cultural they had voted to accept it. But their attitude was, "That is not our plan. It is yours. You carry it out."

3. Though there is great wisdom in including representatives of cooperating churches in the planning stages of church extension, there is always the danger of exhausting cooperative input in decision making and planning. The lion's share of energy should be conserved for the far tougher tasks connected with actually getting the job done. Planning for witness in a new area is important. But actually contacting the people and bringing them under the message of the gospel is imperative.

Selecting Target Areas　　　　5

Often we are too vague when it comes to the mission of the church. When we see our primary task as winning people to Christ and establishing them in the faith and in local churches, we will have come a long way in our understanding. But even that is just a beginning. Before we can get on with the task, we must decide on definite areas and peoples that will become the foci of our immediate attention and labors. One of the fundamental problems with many studies on church growth is that principles are discussed but not incorporated into a plan for reaching a specific target area. In a very real sense the task does not become clear until we answer the questions of who and where. In overseas missions especially, the process of selecting target areas and peoples has precipitated some rather heated debates that are relevant to missions both at home and abroad.

Deciding on Priorities

Priority to Home Missions?

Shall we do all that we can at home before devoting our efforts to needy areas abroad? Many earnest Christians insist upon this and for seemingly good reasons. They cite Acts 1:8 as evidence that we are to witness first in our Jerusalems, then in our Samarias, and, finally, to the ends of the earth. They also insist that unless we have a strong home base we cannot hope to evangelize the rest of the world.

These arguments are not without some validity, but more must be said. First, the grammatical construction in Acts 1:8 ties the target areas together: "You shall be My witnesses both in Jerusalem, and in all Judea and Samaria, and even to the remotest part of the earth." The field is the world, and its parts are here tied together in a way that will not allow us to think of one part to the exclusion of another. Second, the growing, dynamic religious movements of our day have a vision for the whole world even when, for logistic or economic reasons, they are confined to one part of it. It seems that, in most cases, a world vision is required to win our Jerusalems!

Certainly we need a strong work at the home base. A strong overseas-mission program cannot long survive a weak home-missions program. As we said previously, it is both/and, not either/or!

Priority to Responsive Peoples?

Shall we grant priority in our planning to tribes, classes, cities, and nations that prove particularly receptive? Or should priority be given to maintaining a witness among all groups irrespective of their receptivity or resistance to the gospel?

A major contention of the Church Growth movement has been that great growth can occur only when we concentrate our efforts on those areas and peoples where responsiveness assures us that large numbers will embrace Christ and join the churches. Resistant areas should have a missionary witness, but it should be more of a holding action until the people become more responsive to the gospel.

Understandably, those who work among difficult populations in North Africa, Europe, and Asia, and in the inner cities of North America, are disturbed about this ordering of priorities. They do not dispute the need to reach responsive peoples. But they are greatly concerned that concentration upon receptive areas will diminish interest in resistant areas, where, they feel, we have little more than a holding action at present.

Balance is needed. Our Lord did tell his disciples to shake the dust of unresponsive houses and cities off their feet and go on to others (Matt. 10:11–15). And when Paul's message was rejected by the Jews he said, "This salvation of God has been sent to the Gentiles; they will also listen" (Acts 28:28). But we should not lose sight of the fact that in these cases the preparation afforded by previous revelation should have assured a response. These cases are hardly parallel to some resistant areas today. Years of patient preevangelistic endeavor may be the price of responsiveness. In faithfulness to Christ, most missions should give consideration to maintaining a witness in some difficult area(s) even as they send reapers into the whitened harvest fields of receptive populations.

Priority to the Unreached?

Still another controversy has to do with whether we should give priority to those who are unreached—those who have never had a chance to hear and believe the gospel. Subsidiary questions here have to do with the advisability of devoting vast resources to reaching tribal groups whose population is actually decreasing, and what it means to "hear" the gospel.

A great deal of mental effort has been devoted to these questions. The number of peoples without any portion of the Word of God in their language has been the subject of continued inquiry. Ways of reaching the unreached have been explored in conferences and seminars. Prodigious efforts to communicate the gospel by means of radio, television, and literature to people who are sealed off from a missionary presence have been undertaken. Strategies for reaching populations behind closed doors that are now opening up are being researched. The true Christian can only rejoice at these efforts, for the Word of God does single out for special attention those who have never heard about Christ. Missionaries are to be sent so that such people might hear and be saved (Rom. 10:11–15).

Once again, however, balance is needed. The question of priorities should never be settled on the basis of simple slogans like "Why should anyone hear the gospel twice before everyone has heard it once?" How many Christians would there be in the world if the number were reduced to those who believed after only one hearing? And how will the gospel continue to go to remote tribes and hidden peoples unless we plant growing churches elsewhere—churches that provide the resources for those operations?

Priority to Urban or Rural Areas?

Still another debate has to do with the relative importance of urban as opposed to rural areas. At an earlier period in missions history, it was quite usual for missionaries to head for the hills, where people were perishing not only without Christ but also without culture. More recently, increased attention has been given to the large cities, which are centers not only of population, but also of ideas and economic potential.

Though the need of peoples in rural areas is not to be overlooked, it does seem that the increased attention being given to urban centers—and especially to large cities—is warranted if for no other reason than their sociological significance. To the unreflective observer the city is different from the countryside simply because it has crowds of people, tall buildings, lots of excitement, and economic opportunity. But there are differences much deeper and more important that entail entirely different sets of problems and potentialities for the missionary.

Cities are focal points of change. Anthropologist George Foster writes that most changes first occur in the city among the upper classes and spread downward to the lower classes and then outward to the countryside.[1] He is referring specifically to social and economic changes, but a visit to Bombay, Bangkok, Tokyo, Manila, Nairobi, Kinshasa, or Ibadan will convince one that there is also a tremendous po-

1. George M. Foster, *Traditional Cultures and the Impact of Technological Change* (New York: Harper and Row, 1962), 29.

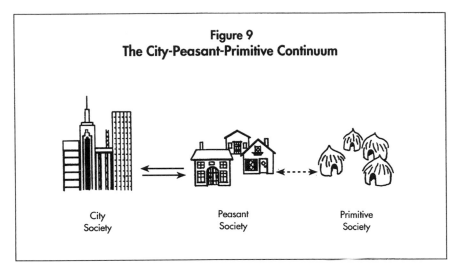

**Figure 9
The City-Peasant-Primitive Continuum**

City
Society

Peasant
Society

Primitive
Society

tential for Christian evangelism and growth in the cities, and from the cities to the surrounding countryside. Of course, not all cities are centers of change to the same degree. Whether a city has educational institutions and is located on main commercial lines will determine its degree of openness and innovativeness.

It is important in this regard to note an important difference between Western and non-Western urban areas. Especially in the inner core of most Western cities, Christianity with its stately but often cavernous cathedrals and churches may be identified with the past. Therefore, the closer one comes to that inner core, the more difficult it may be to win a hearing for the gospel and establish, or renew, churches. In the non-Western world this usually is not true. Christianity is new and represents a viable option to many.

It is also important to distinguish two fundamentally different types of rural societies. One type is tied to the city in the sense that the city is the source of much of its resources, whether of finance, material goods, or new ideas and values. The other type is isolated and self-contained. It views the city from afar, if at all. The first type of rural society is variously designated as a folk, village, traditional, or peasant society. The words "primitive" and "tribal" are often applied to the second type. Social scientists view these two types of rural society very differently and for good and obvious reasons (see figure 9).

Paul's Selection Strategy

From a reading of the New Testament it would appear that there were at least five aspects of what we might call Paul's selection strategy.

1. Though Paul was desirous of bearing testimony among his own people and in Jerusalem itself, he was especially prepared and commissioned to go to Gentile peoples (Acts 26:15–18). The New Testament makes it abundantly clear that, though both our Jerusalems and the uttermost parts are included in the Great Commission, the call to some to bear the gospel to and build the church on the spiritual frontiers is a major part of the divine plan. Paul's strategy and ministry cannot be understood at all apart from recognition of this larger plan of God for his fallen world.

2. Though Paul had a concern for all, he gave a certain priority to Jews and Gentiles who might be expected to respond to the gospel. At least in the earlier stages of his ministry he went to the synagogues, where he found both Jews and God-fearing Gentiles. When many Jews proved to be resistant to the gospel, he turned increasingly to Gentiles. But even then he gave a certain priority to Gentile God-fearers whose hearts God had already prepared through their association with the Jews and their worship of the God of Abraham, Isaac, and Jacob.

New Testament examples are numerous but in no place clearer than in Paul's ministry in Corinth. There from the first he lived and labored with Aquila and Priscilla, a Jewish couple recently come from Italy. Then he ministered in the synagogue and within the Jewish community. When they proved highly resistant, he turned to the Gentile community (though Luke is careful to point out that Paul went to the house of the God-fearer Titius Justus, who lived hard by the synagogue). Ultimately many Corinthians believed and were baptized (see Acts 18:1–8). There can be little doubt that Paul's strategy entailed priorities, and that receptivity was among them.

3. Paul had a special concern for peoples who had not heard the gospel and places where the church had not been planted. This aspect of his strategy is apparent in all of those cases where, after gaining and gathering converts, he refused to settle down for a long stay but pressed on instead to new frontiers. It is especially apparent when, while still in Corinth, he writes to the Roman Christians. In that letter he makes it clear that he aspires to preach Christ where he is not yet named and build the church where foundations have not yet been laid (Rom. 15:20–21). Then, not once but twice, he adds that he hopes to visit Rome en route to Spain (Rom. 15:24–28).

4. Paul gave priority to establishing churches in strategically located cities. In the Book of Acts, when Paul's extensive missionary endeavors are related to a specific area, the reference is usually to a city. He considered an area evangelized when a church was planted in its major city.

In church-extension evangelism there is much to be said for giving a certain priority to cities. But that does not end the matter. Roland Allen notes that "all the cities, or towns, in which he [Paul] planted churches were centres of Roman administration, of Greek civilization, of Jewish influence, or of some commercial importance."[2] Walter Liefeld adds that they were located on major trade routes oriented towards Rome.[3] Each of these characteristics should be pondered, for each has its significance. When Paul chose a target city for missionary endeavor, he looked beyond the city to the surrounding region. That is why these characteristics were important. In this regard Liefeld's further words are instructive: "Paul's abortive attempt to evangelize northern Asia Minor should probably not be seen as a strategy, i.e., to visit sparsely settled areas, but rather as a determination to preach in several cities which lay on the northern trade route."[4]

Allen's conclusion to the matter merits careful consideration on the part of the proponents of urban strategies. He insists that more than the natural advantages for outreach that characterized certain cities of Paul's day should be considered when one analyzes Paul's strategy: "To seize a strategic centre we need not only a man capable of recognizing it, but a man capable of seizing it."[5] In other words, one significant reason that cities became important in Paul's ministry was that he was the kind of man who was capable of seizing them for Christ.

Contemporary research helps us understand the urban strategy of Paul and his choice of certain types of cities for initial contact in an area. They were such that, once he evangelized them, he could speak of the surrounding area as being evangelized. All cities are by no means the same, but in general they do present the greatest potential and possibilities for planting churches. This is due to (1) openness to change, (2) the concentration of resources, and (3) the potential for significant contact with surrounding communities.

5. Though we may question whether we are justified in using the word "strategy" in this connection, it is important to note that when it came to selecting target places and peoples, Paul always remained open to the leading of the Holy Spirit. A key and well-known passage that illustrates this openness is to be found in Acts 16:6–10. The Holy Spirit prevented Paul and his companions from stopping and speaking the word in the region of Phrygia and Galatia when they passed that way.

2. Roland Allen, *Missionary Methods: St. Paul's or Ours?* (Grand Rapids: Eerdmans, 1962), 13.

3. Walter L. Liefeld, "The Wandering Preacher as a Social Figure in the Roman Empire" (Ph.D. diss., Columbia University, 1967), 150—quoted in idem, "Theology of Church Growth," in *Theology and Mission*, ed. David J. Hesselgrave (Grand Rapids: Baker, 1978), 179.

4. Liefeld, "Theology of Church Growth," 179.

5. Allen, *Missionary Methods*, 16.

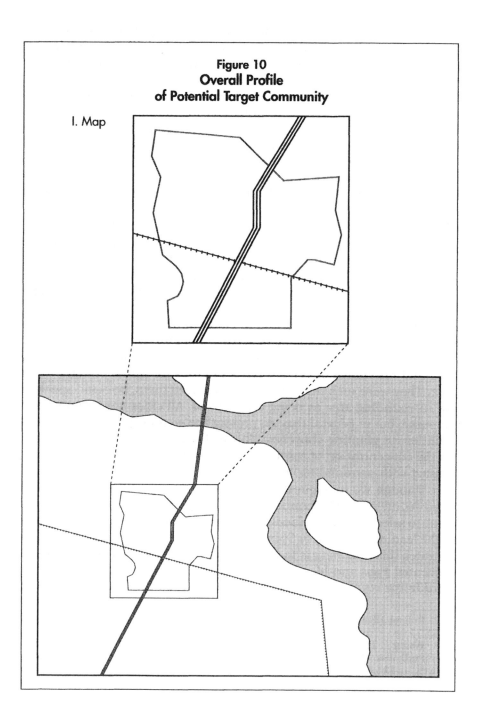

**Figure 10
Overall Profile
of Potential Target Community**

I. Map

II. Geographical Profile
Section A—Description of the Land
1. Rolling hills _____%
2. Plains _____%
3. Rivers & streams _____%
4. Mountains _____%
5. Forests _____%

Section B—Land Use
1. Farming _____%
2. Ranching _____%
3. Lumber _____%
4. Commercial _____%
5. Unused _____%
6. Other _____%

Section C—Transportation
1. Railroads
2. Roads
3. Airport
4. Rivers

Analysis:_____
_____

III. Population Profile
Section A—Population
1. Population in 1900 _____, 1990 _____, 2000 _____
2. Present Population _____
3. Density (number of persons per square mile) _____

Section B—Population Growth or Decline
1. Population growth or decline (1980–2000)
   a. Growth _____ (_____%)
   b. Decline _____ (_____%)
2. Population projections for 2005 _____, 2010 _____, 2020 _____

Analysis:_____
_____

IV. Economic Profile
Section A—Occupation
1. Farming or ranching _____%
2. Business or clerical _____%
3. Education _____%
4. Government or military _____%
5. Other _____ _____%

Section B—Income
1. Less than X _____%

2. Between X and Y   _____%
3. More than Y   _____%
Analysis:_____

V. Sociological Profile
Section A—Ethnic Groupings
   1. _____   _____%
   2. _____   _____%
   3. _____   _____%
Etc.
Section B—Classes, Castes, Clans
   1. _____   _____%
   2. _____   _____%
   3. _____   _____%
Etc.
Section C—Age
   1. Under 18   _____%
   2. Between 18 and 35   _____%
   3. Between 36 and 50   _____%
   4. Over 50   _____%
Analysis:_____

VI. Religious Profile
Section A—Christian Population
   1. Roman Catholic   _____%
   2. Eastern Orthodox   _____%
   3. Liberal Protestant   _____%
   4. Conservative Protestant   _____%
   5. Other   _____%
Section B—Non-Christian
   1. Muslim   _____%
   2. Hindu   _____%
   3. Buddhist   _____%
   4. Jewish   _____%
   5. Unaffiliated   _____%
   6. Other   _____%
Analysis:_____

VII. Overall Evaluation

When they wanted to go into Bithynia, the Holy Spirit did not allow them to go there either. It was then that Paul had a Holy Spirit–inspired vision of a Macedonian man calling for help. The record says, "Immediately we sought to go into Macedonia, concluding that God had called us to preach the gospel to them" (Acts 16:10). At that point Paul began his remarkable ministry to the Western world. Subsequent history has revealed something of the debt we all owe to Paul's willingness to follow the guidance of the Holy Spirit!

Analysis of Target Areas and Peoples

After the leaders of home and overseas missions have prayerfully thought through the issues and settled upon a definite target area as a part of an overall plan, the target area itself must be analyzed. We cannot completely understand our task until we are able to define it in relation to the particular area to be entered. That will require continued study. But analysis should begin before workers actually enter the area. No area should be entered with a church-planting effort simply because some believer, however saintly, has a desire or vision for a work, however noble and lofty. We need corporate study of whatever demographic data are readily available. Many city, county, town, and village planning commissions can provide maps with data on residences, businesses, parks, roads, zoning, and future plans. In some instances detailed studies of businesses and utility companies will be available. This is invaluable information. If an area is zoned for industrial use, for example, there obviously will be no population representing church-growth potential. Further, industrialization will determine the kind of people who eventually will live in the adjacent communities.

The choice of specific target areas, then, should be preceded by the gathering of data essential to the carrying out of the church-development task:

1. The need for an evangelical church and the potential for its growth and for the planting of still other churches.
2. A map of the area showing zoning as well as the location of buildings and other places where people often congregate.
3. A demographic projection to ascertain the ethnic, socio-economic, educational, and religious background of the target-area population, the districts where various homogeneous groupings are located, areas of future growth, and the types of people who will be located in those areas.[6] (See figure 10.)

6. Among the various publications designed to assist in making such a survey is Paul Benjamin, *Analyzing the Community* (Cincinnati: Standard, 1973).

Figure 11
Rating Sheet for Church-Planting Priorities

Communities Profiles	Community A	Community B	Community C	Community D	Etc.
Geographical profile					
Population profile					
Economic profile					
Sociological profile					
Religious profile					
Total score					
Priority					

1. Rate the respective profiles of each potential target community on a scale from 1 to 10 (1 = lowest rating; 10 = highest rating).
2. Set priorities: the community with the highest total score is #1, the next highest #2, etc.

Once such an analysis of potential target communities has been carried out, priorities for church-planting efforts should be set. A prayerful evaluation can be made on the basis of a rating system such as is found in figure 11.

It is imperative that church leaders give prayerful consideration to the selection of areas for evangelism and church planting. Selecting an area where there is no real potential and the Holy Spirit has not prepared a people can mean years of unrewarding and frustrating service. Thus the matter of selecting fields of labor cannot be left to individual or ad hoc decisions.

Deploying the Resources 6

The Holy Spirit has his ways of deploying all of the human, material, and spiritual resources that God has made available to the church. There is little to indicate that apostolic Christianity would have spread very far or fast from its Jerusalem and Judean home apart from the intervention of the Holy Spirit. To assure that the churches would grow and multiply, the Holy Spirit gave visions that communicated the divine provision for people of other nationalities and areas (e.g., Acts 10 and 16:6–10); and he even allowed persecution to scatter the believers as seed for a greater harvest (e.g., Acts 8:1). Assuredly, the Holy Spirit is the missionary Spirit who prods the church to move onward. But his primary method is to work in the hearts of God's people so that in loving obedience they will—without waiting for painful prods—purposively move out to claim new peoples and places for the kingdom.

It is good stewardship as well as good planning to determine what a task will cost in terms of people, time, talent, and money, and then to assess our resources. Our Lord had rather critical words about the man who began to build a tower but did not have resources to finish it (Luke 14:28–30). As we proceed with the building of a church in any location, our prayer will be that new resources become available as people turn to Christ. But as we begin (or begin anew with a plan), we do so primarily with that which we have and are by his grace—not so much with what we hope to have and be. Faith we must have. Presumption we can do without. When looking ahead to a new work, therefore, let the planners make a realistic appraisal of the resources available from (1) their headquarters (the offices of the denomination or mission), (2) churches surrounding the target area, and (3) the target area itself.

Missionaries and Evangelists

The New Testament makes it clear that the ascended Christ granted person gifts to the church in order that it might grow (Eph. 4:1–13). Usually four person gifts are enumerated (or five, if pastors and teachers constitute separate categories): apostles, prophets, evangelists, pastors, and teachers (or pastor-teachers). Of special concern here are the apostles and evangelists.

In the present context it is especially significant to notice that the first of the person gifts mentioned in both 1 Corinthians 12 and Ephesians 4 is the apostle. In fact, in the former passage Paul writes, "And God has appointed in the church, first apostles . . ." (v. 28). The apostle is the missionary. (We will take a closer look at this gift in ch. 8.)

The word "evangelist" is not found in many passages in the New Testament. Philip is called an evangelist (Acts 21:8). Second Timothy 4:5 indicates that Timothy was to "do the work of an evangelist." But the New Testament does make much of the work of evangelizing or heralding the Good News of Christ. Some fifty-five passages bear upon this ministry. In fact, Paul writes, "Woe is me if I do not preach the gospel [evangelize]" (1 Cor. 9:16).

The Role of Laypersons

The fact that in the case of Timothy, for example, the roles of missionary-evangelist and pastor-teacher were combined indicates that we should not press these distinctions too far. One person can—and often does—carry on the various ministries simultaneously or successively as the case may be. Neither should we press too far the distinction between these special person-gifts and the saints who make up the great part of the spiritual body of Christ. All are given the privilege and responsibility of building up one another and the body (Eph. 4:16). The apostles or missionaries, prophets, evangelists, and pastor-teachers are to take the lead and perfect the saints so that the saints can minister also. Thus we are justified in concluding that in a very real sense every member of the church is a person gift to all the others.

Without question, the fact that New Testament churches were established and grew as rapidly as they did was due in significant measure to the contribution of dedicated laypersons. Though the origin of the church at Rome, for example, is obscure, it seems likely that it was founded by Jews and proselytes who had been present at Pentecost (Acts 2:10), and also that some of the people mentioned in Romans 16 had been converted in the Eastern churches and taken the message of Christ to Rome. Suetonius mentions that the emperor Claudius "expelled the Jews from Rome because they kept rioting at the instigation of Christus." This may indicate that when the message was preached, unbelieving Jews in Rome rebelled, as was the case with their counterparts in Thessalonica, Berea, and other places.[1]

---

1. *Harper's Bible Dictionary*, ed. Madeleine Miller and J. Lane Miller, 7th ed. (New York: Harper and Row, 1962), 622.

At any rate, as victims of Claudius's edict, Aquila and Priscilla moved to Corinth where they continued their occupation as tentmakers (Acts 18:2–3). From a human perspective the founding and growth of the Corinthian church (to say nothing of the success of Apollos—Acts 18:24–28) were due in large part to the ministry of these well-informed and dedicated laypeople.

These humble believers—and a host of others like them, both named and unnamed in the record—had a vital part in the planting of churches in the Apostolic Era. And this was as it was supposed to be. It was entirely in keeping with the teaching of Peter himself, who wrote that believing people constitute a "chosen race" and a "royal priesthood" (1 Peter 2:9).

History reveals that one of the most successful missionary movements of the modern era was that of the Moravians. Within twenty years (1732–52) they started more missions than did all Protestants put together in the two preceding centuries. Why? Because the Moravians saw evangelization as essential and made it a common concern of their community. How? By sending small groups of ordinary believers to establish themselves in new areas and testify for Christ. In the case of the Moravians, they sent nuclei of believers to even the remote areas of the world! The proportion of Moravian missionaries to communicant members over a two-hundred-year period was one in twelve![2]

The Use of Teams in Church Planting

Teams in missions and evangelism are popularly associated with the gospel teams used in campaign and crusade efforts. Christians who are acquainted with the world missionary enterprise will be aware of the use of international teams that are sent out in the hope that they will be able to identify with audiences of various ethnic and social backgrounds. At times this hope has been realized. At other times it has not. American-born blacks and American-born Orientals may actually be at a disadvantage in the lands of their roots because they do not know the language or culture even though their physical features suggest that they should.

A more successful team-strategy—one that seems to be reflected in the Scriptures—is the deployment of teams whose members complement one another in their gifts and ministries. Paul made strategic use of such a team. Included at various times were Luke, Silas (the Silvanus of the Epistles), Timothy, Sopater, Aristarchus, Secundus, Gaius, Ty-

2. J. Herbert Kane, *A Global View of Christian Missions* (Grand Rapids: Baker, 1971), 79–80.

chicus, Trophimus, and others (Acts 20:4). These team members were of various ages and backgrounds and possessed complementary gifts. Paul often left team members behind, or sent them to places visited previously in order to complete the cycle and help develop mature, responsible local churches.

Talents and Spiritual Gifts

In taking stock of available resources the world speaks of talent, abilities, know-how, competency. Talents and abilities are often referred to as natural talents or native abilities. The Christian, of course, recognizes that they are really God-given and that they must be developed and used for God's purposes and glory. Such diverse abilities as those of the surgeon, mechanic, pilot, musician, radio technician, writer, artist, and linguist can be and should be utilized in evangelism and church extension.

Those responsible for directing the mission of the church must exercise caution in this regard, however. In the first place, talent, ability, and expertise are not to be confused with the spiritual gifts enumerated in Romans 12 and 1 Corinthians 12. In the second place, there is the very real danger of recruiting missionary-evangelists primarily on the basis of their abilities and expertise. "Whatever your special interest is, we can use it in our mission" is an all-too-common approach to recruitment. As a result, many workers become frustrated when their special ability is not fully utilized; they react by simply doing their own thing and contributing only indirectly to the task of planting churches. Consequently, the so-called secondary or supporting ministries have a way of becoming primary and actually eclipsing the central task!

Finances and Material Resources

Roland Allen makes a case that three rules guided the practice of the apostle Paul in regard to finances: (1) he did not seek financial help for himself; (2) he took no financial help to those to whom he preached; and (3) he did not administer local church funds.[3] Yet Allen was not hard-pressed to find certain exceptions to these rules. In any case, perhaps his sagest advice in this regard is, "What is of supreme importance is how these arrangements, whatever they may be, affect the minds of the people, and so promote, or hinder, the spread of the gospel."[4] On the one hand, it is imperative that we do not enter a new area with so much

3. Roland Allen, *Missionary Methods: St. Paul's or Ours?* (Grand Rapids: Eerdmans, 1962), 49–61.
    4. Ibid., 49.

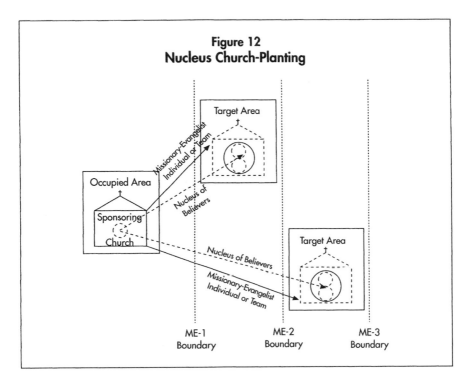

Figure 12
Nucleus Church-Planting

manpower, talent, and money as to create the impression that local initiative is not needed. On the other hand, those undertaking the task of developing churches must not discourage local participation by saddling local people with responsibilities that neither we nor our predecessors could have borne!

Nucleus and Pioneer Church-Planting

The geographical and cultural boundaries to be crossed in establishing new churches will require a variety of personnel and approaches. Basically, the existing church (and its leadership) has two possible courses of action. First, guided by the Holy Spirit, it can plan to start another church on its own. Second, it can cooperate with other like-minded churches (which belong, for example, to the same denomination or mission association) in such an enterprise. The first option is often feasible in our Jerusalems and Judeas where considerable Christian work has been carried on, but where many churchless communities are still to be found. The second option is more viable in the Samarias and uttermost parts where great populations of relatively unreached and unchurched people are located.

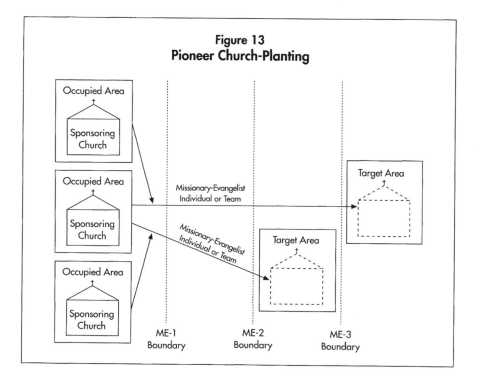

Figure 13
Pioneer Church-Planting

The former option usually involves ME-1 or ME-2 programs. It can be called nucleus church-planting because, in most cases, a nucleus of believers (from the sponsoring church or already residing in the target area or both) will be on hand to aid the missionary-evangelists (see figure 12). The latter option usually involves ME-2 or ME-3 programs. It can be called pioneer church-planting because, in most cases, there will be only a small (or no) nucleus of believers with which to start (see figure 13).

Of course, there are many variations of the nucleus and pioneer models. Isaac Saoshiro recalls that Roger Greenway once outlined some fifteen different models for a class in missions, and that Peter Wagner presents twelve models in his book *Church Planting for a Greater Harvest*. Saoshiro himself settles on six different models—pioneer, propagation, sodality, branch, seeding, and helping first.[5]

A great variety of factors must be considered when we are determining the exact relationship between existing denominations, parishes,

5. Isaac T. Saoshiro, "Dynamics of Church Expansion in Urban Kenya: A Multiple Case Study in Nakuru" (Doctor of ministry/missiology major project, Trinity Evangelical Divinity School, Dec. 1997), 150–58.

congregations, and believers on the one hand, and target places and peoples on the other. But the counsel of those who are experienced and knowledgeable along with the guidance of the Holy Spirit in response to corporate prayer will be both necessary and sufficient in any given case. We can be sure that God has provided the church of Christ with all that is needed for its mission in the world. The challenge to the church is to dedicate itself to Christ and deploy its resources in accordance with his will.

Measuring Growth 7

An old adage says, "Aim at nothing and you will probably hit it." Goals are essential, especially in a task as important as that of planting churches cross-culturally. Most will agree with that. But in spite of that agreement we often lack well-understood goals. Why? For four main reasons. First, because measurable goals sometimes seem incompatible with spirituality. Second, because we lack discipline. Third, because we are confused as to what the goals should be. Fourth, because even when we establish goals, they are often too general and imprecise.

None of the four reasons offers a sufficient excuse for the lack of well-understood goals. Goals are necessary if we want to be effective, faithful stewards of the resources God has given to us. Measurement is essential in order to analyze progress and make in-course corrections. This chapter will consider some of the primary questions related to growth, the establishment of goals, and ways of measuring progress.

Basic Questions relating to Church Growth

Quantitative or Qualitative Growth?

Growth can be quantitative or qualitative (Acts 9:31; 16:5). The former has to do primarily with the number of believers being added to the churches and the number of new congregations being established. The latter has to do with the level of understanding, Christian life, and dedication demonstrated by church members.

A rather pedantic and somewhat pointless argument has occurred between proponents of these two types of growth as to their priority and relationship. Advocates of the Church Growth school of thought have put so much emphasis on the number of members and percentages of membership growth that they have been the targets of a great deal of criticism. Church Growth proponents have responded to this criticism by noting that (1) it is evident in Scripture that God is interested in numerical (quantitative) growth, and (2) one of the best measures of qualitative growth is numerical increase.

The first response has validity. The second leaves something to be desired. There is a relationship between the two kinds of growth, to be sure. But some churches made up of quality Christians in such widely separated areas as Morocco, Mindanao, and Montana are experiencing very limited numerical growth. Moreover, numerical growth in receptive areas can actually be deceptive as a measurement of qualitative growth. After all, numerical growth occurs in non-Christian movements as well as Christian ones. Sometimes it occurs in Christian churches that employ Madison Avenue techniques at the expense of scriptural standards of Christian ethics and spirituality.

There is certainly nothing unspiritual about numerical growth (unless one considers the post-Pentecost church at Jerusalem unspiritual). But numerical growth must be accompanied by spiritual growth. Goals for numerical growth should be set, but one can feel an empathy with the North American pastor who said, "My people are so fed up with numbers that the mere mention of a membership goal turns them off completely. What do I do?" (Probable solution: Set goals but do not overemphasize them.)

Can Qualitative Growth Be Measured?

In most situations numerical growth is an indicator of spiritual growth. But it is not the only indicator. It is important to realize that qualitative growth is measurable in ways other than taking a head count (or preparing a financial report)! The Jehovah's Witnesses (who are vitally concerned about numerical growth) regularly test members on their ability to present their teachings to others. Soka Gakkai Buddhism has a system of voluntary examinations which all believers who want increased responsibilities are expected to pass. And, to turn to instances of Christian outreach, one historic mission in Korea required candidates for baptism to first win another to Christ. The church among an illiterate Indian tribe in Mexico required believers to produce witnesses that they were living out the Bible truths under study before they could go on to study new truths! Where there is discipline there is a way!

How Do Churches Grow Numerically?

Church Growth specialists distinguish between three kinds of growth: biological growth (children of Christian parents come to know the Lord), conversion growth (people convert from the world and are brought into the fellowship of the church), and transfer growth (new members transfer from other churches).

Depending upon birth and death rates in the target area, biological growth is more or less predictable. Specialists calculate that the average church in North America can anticipate a biological growth rate of about 25 percent per decade. Of course, the vitality of the local church and its Christian homes is an important factor here. We cannot simply assume that children of Christian parents will become believing members of the church.

Conversion growth from the swelling ranks of those multitudes of unbelievers who are unrelated to the church is essential if the church is to grow significantly. In the first place, and again depending on the target area involved, the birth rate among Christians may be lower than among non-Christians. In the second place, the addition to the church of people converted from the world has a salutary effect on the spiritual temperature of the local church. The freshness and devotion of those who have been rescued from spiritual rebellion and despair lend encouragement to the church and strengthen its outreach.

Transfer growth is not to be frowned upon unless it represents sheep stealing from other churches that are faithful to the testimony of Jesus Christ. Of course, it is imperative that believers who move into the areas of our churches be brought into fellowship (and membership) as soon as possible. At the same time, transfer growth must be seen for what it is: the removal of believers from one church and their addition to another. The gain of one congregation represents the loss of another congregation! Transfer growth can never be a substitute for biological and conversion growth!

How Big Is Too Big?

Recently—particularly in America—a good deal has been said and written about the size of Sunday schools and churches. Bigness is certainly one measure of success—and perhaps the most obvious one. Some of what is said pro and con on the issue tends to be self-serving. But there is a serious argument for large churches that merits consideration in great urban centers around the world. Robert Schuller, pastor of the flourishing Garden Grove Church in California, maintains that large churches with multiple staffs can best meet the expectations and needs of mushrooming areas and mobile populations. Furthermore, they can have an influence and ministry that reach far beyond the immediate environs.[1]

There is something to be said for Schuller's argument. Perhaps the cause of Christ is best served by having some superchurches when God gives the appropriate form of leadership and circumstances are right. But several additional factors must be considered. (1) A large church that does not provide for identification with small groups included within the whole cannot possibly meet the spiritual and psychological

1. Robert H. Schuller, *Your Church Has Real Possibilities* (Glendale, Calif.: Regal, 1974), 7–18.

needs of its members. (2) Large churches generally are not as effective as smaller churches in terms of the utilization of believer potential.[2] (3) A large church may be so self-contained that the members do not move outside it to serve the community. (4) Some societies are better suited to the multiplication of small churches than they are to the formation of large churches. (5) Today's dream of a large, impressive edifice, once realized, can become tomorrow's nightmare of large maintenance costs and unimpressive echoes! Meaningful answers to these disadvantages of large churches can come only in relation to specific target areas and leadership.

In conclusion, let it be said that God desires both quantitative and qualitative growth for his churches, but neither at the expense of the other. Certainly our Lord desires fruitfulness—and fruitfulness is measurable in a number of ways (John 15:16). But he also requires faithfulness. Measured by human yardsticks, the two will in many situations seem unfriendly to each other. But in the divine economy they usually are closely related.

Measuring and Analyzing Growth in the Church

Unquestionably, God is desirous of spiritual growth in his people. But spiritual life precedes spiritual growth. Unbelievers must first be converted and become members of the family of God. Leaving the consideration of spiritual growth for later chapters, let us think now in terms of measuring and analyzing numerical growth in a local church. This is a matter that should be carefully studied by church leadership in anticipation of entering a target area to plant a new church. Otherwise goals will be nebulous, proper records will not be kept, and meaningful analysis of progress will be difficult. Three tasks are imperative in this connection: (1) the establishment of measurable goals; (2) the keeping of accurate records; and (3) analysis of past progress.

The Establishment of Measurable Goals

When a target area has been adequately surveyed and studied, it should be possible to make some meaningful projections as to growth in the new work. Even when based upon sound data, any such projections will be expressions of faith for only God can "grow a church." But just that kind of faith is needed. If our survey of the target area reveals, for example, that it contains two comparatively static congregations, that the population of six thousand is increasing at an average of five

2. Charles L. Chaney, "A New Day for Churches," *Church Growth Bulletin* 12.4 (March 1976): 512–16.

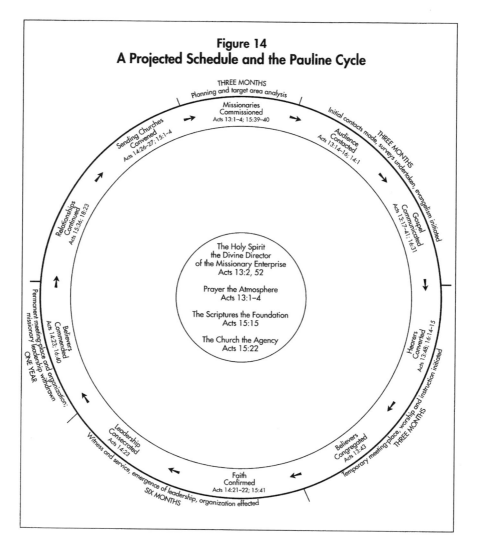

Figure 14
A Projected Schedule and the Pauline Cycle

THREE MONTHS
Planning and target area analysis

Missionaries
Commissioned
Acts 13:1–4; 15:39–40

Sending Churches
Convened
Acts 14:26–27; 15:1–4

Initial contacts made, surveys undertaken, evangelism initiated
THREE MONTHS

Audience
Contacted
Acts 13:14–16; 14:1

Gospel
Communicated
Acts 13:17–41; 16:31

Relationships
Continued
Acts 15:36; 18:23

The Holy Spirit
the Divine Director
of the Missionary Enterprise
Acts 13:2, 52

Prayer the Atmosphere
Acts 13:1–4

The Scriptures the Foundation
Acts 15:15

The Church the Agency
Acts 15:22

Permanent meeting place and organization;
missionary leadership withdrawn
ONE YEAR

Believers
Commended
Acts 14:23; 16:40

Hearers
Converted
Acts 13:48; 16:14–15

Leadership
Consecrated
Acts 14:23

Witness and service, emergence of leadership, organization effected
SIX MONTHS

Faith
Confirmed
Acts 14:21–22; 15:41

Believers
Congregated
Acts 13:43

Temporary meeting-place, worship and instruction initiated
THREE MONTHS

hundred annually, that the residents tend to be of similar class and ethnic background, that a majority of the present residents are not committed to another faith, and that newcomers tend to be responsive (with a significant number of committed Christians among them), then we have good grounds for projecting a certain growth rate.

Such projections will have two primary aspects: the number of people we anticipate will be brought into the local body of believers, and the time required to reach successive stages of growth. By superimposing this information upon the Pauline Cycle in the manner of figure 14, the workers will see the task in a new light. They can plan and pray according to projections based on faith and knowledge. If the work does not progress on schedule, they will ask what they might be doing wrong, and will change their approach or revise their expectations in accordance with experience. If progress exceeds expectations, they can revise their projections upward!

The Keeping of Accurate Records

One of the most serious problems encountered by specialists who are asked to analyze the growth patterns of local churches and denominations is the lack of adequate records. All too often church records are ambiguous, incomplete, or altogether lacking. When there is a record of the number of church members in a given year with no corresponding records of average attendance, the manner of entrance into the church (transfer or confession of faith, for example), and the number of members removed from the church rolls (whether by discipline, death, or transfer), the membership statistic means little. In fact, unless such records are available over a period of years, it becomes all but impossible to diagnose the health of a church.

Denominational and mission leaders should see to it that accurate and uniform records are kept in new churches from the very first. The resultant statistics will enable the church planter to ascertain whether the projected goals are being reached through the first months and years of the church-planting effort. Later on, those statistics will be invaluable in ascertaining the growth patterns of the church on a long-term basis. At the very least, membership records should include:

1. The results of initial surveys
2. Information concerning successful contacts (i.e., contacts who have responded by confessing faith and/or coming to church meetings), including how they were first approached
3. Attendance figures for the various meetings of the developing congregation
4. Membership statistics (from the time the new church is organized), including data as to how new members are gained (whether by transfer from other churches or by confession of faith [when children make confession of faith, it should be noted whether their parents are believers or unbelievers]), and why former members are lost to the membership

Analysis of Past Progress

A prominent preacher once announced to a Midwestern congregation that the sermon they were about to hear was being preached for the

1,030th time and that it had always brought results! Before criticizing the preacher, we should take stock. A sermon that has been in for 1,030 tune-ups can be expected to be a fairly good sermon! Besides, if it always gets results, it certainly bears repeating! One would wish that our plans for extending the church of Christ were as carefully devised, thoroughly mastered, regularly reviewed, and universally effective as that sermon!

An overall or master plan requires periodic evaluation and modification. We should change our plan, not by scrapping the whole and initiating a new one each time we encounter a problem or some new idea is promulgated, but by modifying the part that is ineffective or rendered obsolete. This we can do by changing conditions or by adding new insights.

We are reminded again of the seminar in which, after much discussion, one of the participants remembered that a five-year plan for evangelism and church planting had been developed several years before. A thorough search extricated a copy of this master plan from the secretary's file cabinet! It had been carefully devised, prayerfully considered, unanimously passed, and promptly forgotten! Periodic evaluation and modification are essential. In fact, they are part of the plan!

One of the most widely used small books on church growth (it has been translated into about fifty languages) focuses on analyzing membership statistics. The author, Vergil Gerber, explains in simple steps how growth patterns over a period of time can help diagnose the strengths and weaknesses of a church.[3] Using a ten-year span for the sake of convenience, we can outline the basic steps Gerber recommends:

Step One: Compile membership statistics for the ten-year period.

Step Two: Plot these statistics on a graph.

Step Three: Calculate the growth rate of the church for the decade. In the case of Church A in figure 15:

Current membership	180
Membership ten years ago	-100
Ten-year increase	80
The growth rate is	80 percent

This gives the overall picture. Of course if one also calculates the annual growth rates and compares them, it is possible to ascertain whether the rate of growth is increasing or declining. In the case of Church A, after a

3. Vergil Gerber, *A Manual for Evangelism/Church Growth* (South Pasadena, Calif.: William Carey Library, 1973), 43–62. See also Bob Waymire and C. Peter Wagner, *The Church Growth Survey Handbook* (Santa Clara, Calif.: O.C. Ministries, 1980).

period of stagnancy there was a steady growth of ten members for each of the last three years; but since the total membership increased each year, the rate of growth actually declined somewhat.

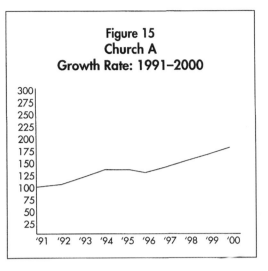

Figure 15
Church A
Growth Rate: 1991–2000

Step Four: Compare the actual growth with the biological growth. As a rule of thumb, biological growth is about 25 percent per decade. This means that the average church over the span of a decade will have a growth rate of about 25 percent apart from conversions from the world and transfers from other churches. On the basis of biological growth Church A added 25 percent to its original 100 members over the ten-year period:

Ten-year increase	80
Typical biological increase	-25
Increase from conversion and transfers	55

Obviously, further analysis is needed to see how healthy and strong Church A really is.

Step Five: Refine the data. Some members are lost to the church. They fall into three categories: reversion (or excommunication), transfer, or death. Very few churches keep statistics that are this accurate and detailed, even though such statistics would be highly revealing. Consider, for example, the bar graph in figure 16, which gives this very kind of information for Church B over a five-year period. Even a cursory analysis is revealing. Notice that the number of conversions is consistently higher than the number of reversions. That is as it should be. In the last year, however, the ratio of reversions to conversions has been higher. That certainly needs prayerful consideration. Notice also that, with the exception of one year, considerably more members have been transferring out of Church B than have been transferring in. Perhaps this indicates that something is wrong in the church. Or perhaps people are just leaving the area. In either case, something must be done or Church B will not continue to exist!

Step Six: Analyze the church's growth patterns. When the kind of study suggested has been done, one can look back and analyze the re-

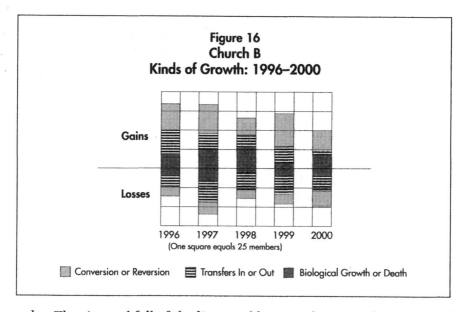

Figure 16
Church B
Kinds of Growth: 1996–2000

Gains

Losses

1996   1997   1998   1999   2000
(One square equals 25 members)

▨ Conversion or Reversion   ▤ Transfers In or Out   ▦ Biological Growth or Death

sults. The rise and fall of the lines and bars on these simple graphs tell the story of successes and failures, of strengths and weaknesses.

Step Seven: Set goals for the future. For the starting of new churches as well as the strengthening of existing ones, this is a most important step. In the pioneer situation about the only way to set goals for the future is to look at the record of surrounding churches or churches in similar situations. An existing church can project goals on the basis of its past record, expected biological growth (25 percent per decade), and faith in what the Lord will do in response to praying, planning, and working. In the case of Church A, the goal might well be something like 225 members at the end of five years (see figure 17).

Current literature on church growth is chock-full of ideas designed to increase the number of church attenders and members. Some of those ideas come from Scripture, but the bulk of them emanate from the experience of the authors or from such fields as management, marketing, and social theory. To choose but one example out of literally scores, the Southern Baptist growth specialist Andy Anderson makes use of the so-called Flake Formula, which maintains that there are five steps essential to the growth of any organization: (1) locating new prospects; (2) providing space for them; (3) enlisting and training workers; (4) enlarging the organization by creating new units within it; and (5) contacting and recruiting prospective members.[4] Anderson explains

4. Andy Anderson, *The Growth Spiral: The Proven Step-by-Step Method for Calculating and Predicting Growth Potential in Your Church* (Nashville: Broadman and Holman, 1993).

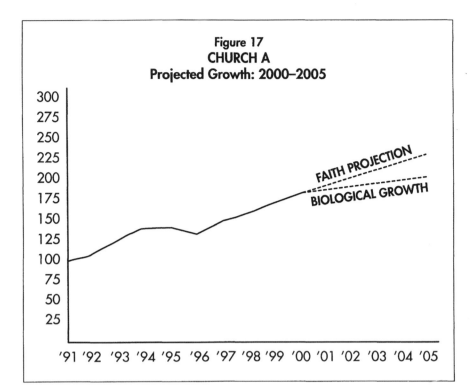

Figure 17
CHURCH A
Projected Growth: 2000–2005

how he first came to use this formula and then goes on to describe how following its steps can help achieve balanced and continuous growth.

We conclude that in many ways planting and growing Christian churches are much like initiating and enlarging various other types of organizations. The process involves strategic planning, gathering and deploying resources, setting goals, and plain hard work. However, planting churches is the King's business and as such is also different from any other business. Our supreme objective in planting and growing churches is to obey and glorify God. Accordingly, our plans must first of all reflect his principles and purposes.

Part Three

The Sending Church and the Christian Mission

The Missionaries Commissioned 8

Someone has said that everyone's task is no one's task. There is some truth to that statement. Some people must take the lead if anything is to be accomplished. If local churches are to be truly missionary churches, denominational leaders and local pastors and officers must furnish the required information, inspiration, and example. If the work of planting churches at home and abroad is to be advanced, specialists in pioneering (i.e., evangelists and missionaries) must be called out, trained, and sent. Of course, lay participation in the missionary task is absolutely essential, especially in accessible target areas. But someone must take the lead and, moving out into new areas, give direction to the church-planting enterprise. It is the responsibility of existing churches to respond to the Holy Spirit and see that such workers are forthcoming.

Objectives

In this chapter we are concerned with our Jerusalems and Antiochs—churches that have already been established by the grace of God and the faithfulness of our predecessors, and form the bases for further outreach. There are three basic objectives for these churches:

1. To foster the kind of missionary spirit that encourages pastors, officers, and lay believers to participate in the God-given task of planting churches in adjacent and more-distant unreached communities
2. To mobilize believers in a program of missionary outreach
3. To recognize, prepare, send, support, and cooperate with those whom Christ has specially appointed to take the leadership in this work

The Selection and Sending of Church-Planting Individuals and Teams

Biblical Principles and Precedents

1. The risen Christ bestows spiritual gifts on the church and its members. These gifts are identified in certain key passages—Romans

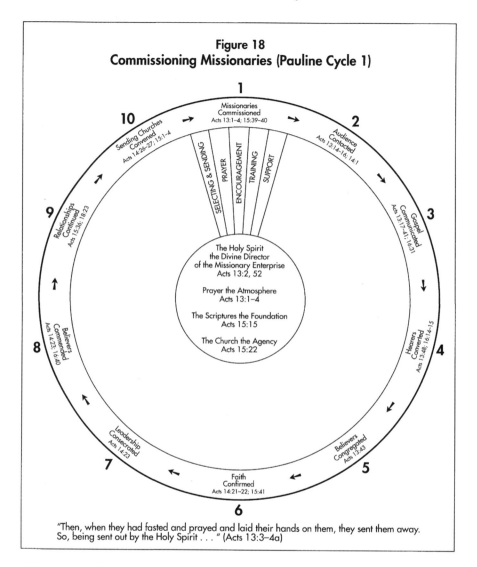

Figure 18
Commissioning Missionaries (Pauline Cycle 1)

1
Missionaries
Commissioned
Acts 13:1–4; 15:39–40

10
Sending Churches
Convened
Acts 14:26–27; 15:1–4

2
Audience
Contacted
Acts 13:14–16; 14:1

SELECTING & SENDING
PRAYER
ENCOURAGEMENT
TRAINING
SUPPORT

9
Relationships
Continued
Acts 15:36; 18:23

3
Gospel
Communicated
Acts 13:17–41; 16:31

The Holy Spirit
the Divine Director
of the Missionary Enterprise
Acts 13:2, 52

Prayer the Atmosphere
Acts 13:1–4

The Scriptures the Foundation
Acts 15:15

The Church the Agency
Acts 15:22

8
Believers
Commended
Acts 14:23; 16:40

4
Hearers
Converted
Acts 13:48; 16:14–15

7
Leadership
Consecrated
Acts 14:23

5
Believers
Congregated
Acts 13:43

6
Faith
Confirmed
Acts 14:21–22; 15:41

"Then, when they had fasted and prayed and laid their hands on them, they sent them away.
So, being sent out by the Holy Spirit . . . " (Acts 13:3–4a)

12, 1 Corinthians 12, and Ephesians 4. Though designed to enable the church to function faithfully and fruitfully, these gifts have often raised questions and even controversy. How are they to be identified? Which ones are most important? When are they to be exercised? Are all of them available to the church today? And so forth. Though such questions are indeed important, an examination of them would take us beyond the limits of the present work. Besides that, most readers will have reached their own conclusions on these matters, so they need not detain us here.

The biblical text seems to make a distinction that is often overlooked yet most germane to church-planting endeavors. Namely, the distinction between two types of gifts: gifts to persons and person gifts. To various members of the church are given such gifts as teaching, giving, exhortation, leading, and mercy (Rom. 12:7–8) as well as administration, helps, healing, and tongues (1 Cor. 12:28). But Ephesians 4 indicates that Christ also gave certain persons to the church—persons who would take the lead in various ministries and enable churches to expand and mature in faith and service. Though the person gift will be a new idea to some, it can be found in such passages as Psalm 68:18 and Mark 3:16–19.

Before we proceed to elaborate on the idea of person gifts, it is important to note that gifts to persons should also be carefully considered as we select and send out church-planting individuals and teams. Recent years have witnessed significant interest in identifying and exercising what have been lumped under the inclusive term "spiritual gifts." In fact, taking an inventory of one's spiritual gifts became at one time almost a fad in some church circles. More recently this interest has waned somewhat. For one thing, some believers saw themselves as having gifts they obviously did not have. Others identified gifts that got lost in the shuffle and were not encouraged or used. In any case, in and out of the church, fads tend to fade!

All this having been said, it is important that those whose obligation it is to help select and send church-planting individuals and teams take special note of their specific gifts or mix of gifts. Those many authors who draw our attention to the fact that certain gifts are all but indispensable to this kind of ministry do us a signal service.[1]

2. The apostles (missionaries) and evangelists were at the forefront of the early effort in church-extension evangelism. There were many ordinary saints, of whom only a few are named, who "went everywhere preaching the word" and participating in the task of planting churches. But there were also specially gifted apostles and evangelists who led the troops, so to speak.

In the New Testament there are two kinds of apostles. First, there is the relatively small group of those who were personally chosen and instructed by the Lord. These men held the office of apostle, to which there is no succession. Second, there are those men who had the gift of apostleship and were called "messengers [apostoloi] of the churches" (2 Cor. 8:23). In this group were included such men as Barnabas, Silas, Timothy, Epaphroditus, Andronicus, and Junias.

---

1. See, for example, Aubrey Malphurs, *Planting Growing Churches for the Twenty-first Century: A Comprehensive Guide for New Churches and Those Desiring Renewal* (Grand Rapids: Baker, 1992), ch. 6.

The term "missionary," of course, is not a New Testament word. Etymologically, however, it is closely related to "apostle." Both words carry the idea of one who is sent forth to do a task. The emphasis in the New Testament is more on the task to be performed than on the place to which the individual is to be sent. The task was to proclaim the gospel and plant churches, or aid those who were doing so.

The role of the evangelist was similar to that of the "messengers of the churches." The evangelist was particularly gifted by the Holy Spirit to proclaim the gospel in such a manner that those who heard were persuaded to accept the Savior. There is little evidence that the evangelists actually organized churches. That seemed to be the particular job of the apostles. Take the church on the island of Crete by way of example. Although there were undoubtedly believers who had been present in Jerusalem on the Day of Pentecost (Acts 2:11) and then returned to the island, they did not even appoint elders. It was not until Paul visited the island in the early sixties that the process of appointing elders was begun (Titus 1:5). It is apparent that some form of evangelistic work had laid the foundation for the church before Paul came, but no formal organization had been developed.

3. God calls and sends missionary-evangelists in and through the churches:

> Not even one missionary call recorded by the Holy Spirit in the Acts of the Apostles was subjective or the result of individual initiative alone. In most cases, the subjective sense of call is not the aspect of the call which is brought to our attention by the Holy Spirit. In every case either the church or another missionary had a considerable part to play in the call. God's call is based primarily on objective external events rather than on subjective, internal experience.
>
> Barnabas went to Antioch because his church sent him there (Acts 11:22). Saul went to Antioch because Barnabas brought him there (Acts 11:26). Both men went out from Antioch as a result of a decision made jointly with the other Antioch church leaders at a time of prayer and fasting (Acts 13:2). Silas joined Paul at his invitation (Acts 15:40) and so did young Timothy (Acts 16:3).
>
> How do we apply this?
>
> (1) What we find is not wild individualism or sensational guidance, but God's people working, praying, and planning together responsibly for the evangelization of the world. We see not just a selfish concern for an individual calling, but a dovetailing of God's plan for many lives.
>
> (2) A general call for missionary volunteers is not stressed in the New Testament. Missionaries went because their churches sent them, or because older missionaries brought them.
>
> (3) Our willingness to go anywhere is an intensely personal matter between us and our Master. But in order for "anywhere" to become a def-

inite "somewhere," both our home churches and the older missionaries must have a say.[2]

Turn to the record of the sending forth of Paul and Barnabas from the church in Antioch (Acts 13:1–4). Here is a delicate balance of the working of God in the church, in its leaders, and in the missionary-evangelist candidates. The direction of God is seen in the roles played by those early believers corporately and individually.

First, God spoke to the men who were to be sent. Both Paul and Barnabas had been called by God prior to this event. Paul's call is recorded in Scripture and was dramatic. Barnabas's call is not recorded and may have been less dramatic. In Paul's case, close to nine years had elapsed since his personal call. Nevertheless, he waited until God spoke to the church.

Second, God spoke to the church and its leaders. There is no evidence as to how the Holy Spirit communicated God's will. It may have been as spectacular as Paul's call or the events of the Day of Pentecost. But this is not indicated. There may have been a crisis in the church, for the group was fasting. Perhaps God placed a special burden for the lost upon the church. It seems probable that the extension of the gospel to other areas was discussed frequently. Undoubtedly the leaders had conferred with one another and with other church members as to how the gospel might be given to other peoples. In any case, the Holy Spirit spoke. He communicated to the church which men he wanted to go to new areas.

So, in God's time, the missionary-evangelists were selected by the Spirit, separated for the work, released by their followers, and sent forth by the Spirit with the laying on of hands. This official commissioning entailed both a blessing and a recognition. It entailed a blessing in that the senders acknowledged that those who were being sent had been called to and equipped for the task; they were going forth with the approval of the church. But the ceremony signified more. Just as in the Old Testament the priest laid his hands on the sacrificial victim, thus signifying that the victim was taking the place of the offerer, so in the commissioning of the missionary-evangelists the church recognized that those who were being sent were going in the place of the church.[3]

It is important to note that Paul and Barnabas were men who had demonstrated their abilities before the Spirit spoke to the church.

2. Michael C. Griffiths, *You and God's Work Overseas* (Chicago: InterVarsity, 1967), 20–21.

3. In interpreting the laying on of hands, care must be taken not to regard the church as a mediating agency. The church did not mediate Paul's call. His call was direct from God (Gal. 1:1). Therefore, we have used the words "recognition" and "blessing" in connection with the ceremony. See also Galatians 2:7–9.

There were five men in the group of prophets and teachers from which Paul and Barnabas were selected. Each one had some special qualification for the missionary task. Simeon was black. Lucius was from Cyrene and thus could have been sent there. Manaen had been brought up with Herod and could have had influence with government officials. Evidently none of these qualifications was crucial or sufficient. Barnabas was a proven quantity. He was the first teacher of note in the church. Paul was the second teacher. Under these two men the church had grown. It could be said that the church sent the best of its leadership group. At any rate, men of proven maturity and effectiveness were selected to lead the extension ministry of the Antioch church.

Relevant Research

Successful mass movements generally exhibit a succession of leadership that falls within a rather distinct pattern. Eric Hoffer notes three kinds of leaders of such movements and the order in which they appear: people of words, fanatics, and practical people of action.[4] The people of words articulate the teaching. The fanatics marshal the believers, take the message to the masses, and gain converts. The practical people of action consolidate the movement. According to Hoffer, an individual may possess the varied abilities necessary to see a movement through the various stages, but more often than not, a succession of leadership is involved. Hoffer's work qualifies as research only in the broadest sense of that word, but certain subsequent studies do indicate that his analysis has a good deal of validity.[5]

Our concerns are radically different from Hoffer's, to be sure, but there may be some value in differentiating between the theorists, the missionary-evangelists, and the consolidators in our programs of church extension. Not everyone who can begin a work can sustain it. And on the other hand, not everyone who can shepherd a congregation is effective in finding lost sheep and bringing them into the fold. The biblical distinction between various types of person gifts merits attention here.

Practical Reflection

1. We in the church have tended to let practice determine the definition of some terms that closely relate to church extension. On the one hand, we have tended to define the mission of the church very loosely.

4. Eric Hoffer, *The True Believer: Thoughts on the Nature of Mass Movements* (New York: New American Library of World Literature, 1958), 120.
5. *Dynamic Religious Movements*, ed. David J. Hesselgrave (Grand Rapids: Baker, 1978), 309.

As a consequence, foreign missionaries are those who do missionary work abroad, and missionary work is the good things foreign missionaries do for the needy people among whom they work. It follows that home missionaries are those who do good things for needy people at home. All of this may be true, but it is also vague and misleading. Actually, the central missionary undertaking is to win souls to Christ and establish churches in new areas.

On the other hand, we have tended to define evangelism very narrowly. The evangelist, then, is one who preaches (usually) the Good News and wins souls to Christ. Actually, the proclamation of the gospel is basic to the evangelist's task, but we cannot afford, and the Scriptures overall do not support, evangelism that is divorced from, or but tenuously related to, the churches.

It is incumbent upon pastor-teachers especially to carefully delineate the terms and tasks related to the growth of the church. All Christians are witnesses, but not all of them are missionary-evangelists any more than all are pastor-teachers. We need specialists who fulfil the biblical definitions and guidelines.

2. We have built the greater part of our contemporary evangelistic and missionary enterprise upon a vast program of volunteerism. New Testament missions were voluntaristic—that is, those who participated did so of their own free will. But New Testament missions were not based on volunteerism—that is, a general call for, and the sending of, anyone who would offer to go.

In overseas missions the result of our approach has been the sending of many relatively untrained missionaries to accomplish a task which is ill defined and in which they have not had experience. In home missions the result has been that those who are most successful in the ministry of local churches move on to larger churches and higher salaries rather than moving on to challenging unchurched areas where their experience and abilities could be used in starting new congregations. And because home missions is not defined primarily in terms of entering new territories for Christ, because funds are limited, and because partial self-support is not usually considered, even younger persons ready to launch out into the Christian ministry seldom begin new congregations.

Prayerful Concern for Church-Planting Missions

Biblical Principles and Precedents

The New Testament is replete with exhortations to prayer. It carefully teaches the Christian how to pray. The subject of prayer receives extensive doctrinal development in the New Testament. It is not strange, then, that much is said about prayer and missions.

Prayer and the Selection of Missionary-Evangelists

The church is commanded to pray that missionaries will be sent. When Jesus looked upon the great harvest field, he told his disciples to pray that the Lord would send forth laborers into his field (Matt. 9:38; Luke 10:2). When the church at Antioch was ministering and fasting, the Lord indicated which leaders he wanted to go to the harvest field (Acts 13:2). Clearly, the selection of missionary-evangelist candidates should be bathed in prayer.

Prayer and the Sending of Missionary-Evangelists

Just as the selection of the candidate is to be the concern of much prayer, so the commissioning of the candidate is to be accompanied by prayer (Acts 13:3). The commissioning of church planters is no different from the installation of the elder or deacon in this regard. The first deacons were commissioned only after prayer (Acts 6:6), and the elders were commended to the Lord after prayer (Acts 14:23). The normal biblical procedure is to saturate commissioning services with prayer.

Prayer and the Support of Missionary-Evangelists

Prayer for the church planter, whether at home or abroad, is part of the support which the church is to give. Paul requested prayer for himself with respect to his many needs. He asked the church at Rome to pray for his protection from enemies and the acceptance of his ministry by the saints (Rom. 15:31). He asked believers at Ephesus to pray that he might be bold in the proclamation of the message (Eph. 6:19). The Colossian Christians were asked to pray for an open door so that he could clearly present the gospel (Col. 4:2–3). The Thessalonians were requested to pray for the rapid spread of the gospel and protection from perverse men (2 Thess. 3:1–2). If to these specific requests for prayer we add the items mentioned in the general commands relating to prayer for all church leaders, it is all the more obvious that the entire church-planting operation is to be continually bathed in believing prayer.

Relevant Research

Church history reveals that there is an intimate relationship between sincere prayer and successful outreach. After several abortive attempts on the continent of Europe, a great deal of missionary activity grew out of the Pietist movement and the dedication of men like Philipp Spener (1635–1705) and August Francke (1663–1727). They supplemented their Sunday sermons with cottage meetings for prayer and Bible study. Two centuries after the Protestant Reformation the movement they fathered bore fruit in the form of successful missionary efforts.[6]

In 1723 Robert Millar wrote *A History of the Propagation of Christianity and the Overthrow of Paganism*. He pleaded for intercession for the conversion of unbelievers all around the world. Within a few years prayer groups were found throughout the British Isles. In 1746 American Christians were invited to participate in a seven-year "concert of prayer" for missions. Jonathan Edwards echoed this call in a pamphlet. Forty years later—back in England—John Sutcliff encouraged all Baptist churches in Northamptonshire to set aside the first Monday of each month to pray for the non-Christian world. Soon William Carey (1761–1834) sailed for India, and a new day dawned for Christian missions.[7]

In America, missions and evangelism were likewise the result of prevailing prayer. A burden for world mission arose in the first decade of the nineteenth century when Samuel J. Mills instituted meetings for prayer and discussion at Williams College.[8] History speaks unequivocally: the harvest is seen through opened eyes after those eyes have been closed in prayer.

Practical Reflection

Collectively and individually Christians everywhere should pray: "Lord of the church, be at work among us, and from among your sons and daughters in our fellowship call out those who will proclaim the good tidings of Christ and plant his church in needy areas of the world. For the glory of God and the good of humankind, hear our prayer offered in Jesus' name. Amen." Prayer is the starting point. God delights to answer this kind of prayer. It is always in his will to do so.

But prayer is more than the starting point. It is the continuing force behind the entire program of outreach. Over and over the apostle Paul exhorted believers in the churches to pray not just for their personal needs, but for him and for the work of Christ among the lost. And pray they did. And pray we should. After all, they and we are servants who minister to the Lord of the church. We are children who should be communicating with our Father about the family business. We are soldiers—in an army that goes forward only on its knees!

Whatever reasons we may adduce for our all too feeble and poorly attended congregational prayer meetings today, we can be assured

6. J. Herbert Kane, *A Global View of Christian Missions* (Grand Rapids: Baker, 1971), 77.
   7. Ibid., 83–85.
   8. Ibid., 86–87.

that the members of the churches of the New Testament Era would not be impressed! The fact of the matter is that contemporary prayer meetings often do not attract even some of the most likely candidates for leadership in church outreach. And why? Because the average prayer meeting in the average church does not seem to be a vital part of that outreach! This does not excuse the absentees. But it should give pause to pastors, staff members, elders, and deacons in the churches.

It is at the prayer meeting that we transact the business of the King! Whoever began the tradition of separating church business meetings from church prayer meetings and running the former according to *Robert's Rules of Order* and the latter according to the orders of the day did the churches a great disservice. Let us plan to bring business and prayer together again—with some degree of regularity. And let us bring the Word of God to bear upon the work committed to us. Let leaders in planning and outreach discuss the local work of Christ in which all should be involved in one way or another, and the more distant work of Christ in which our representatives participate. This work should be discussed not just in a general way, but in terms of a definite plan, stated programs, and real people. Let us share our thoughts on these matters—and then let us pray that God will burden and bless us, and choose and use us according to his will. And let our goal be that prayer-meeting attendance at least approximate the number of members who reside within a reasonable distance. And let another goal be that periodically the Lord will place a divine claim on some in the congregation and make of them special person-gifts to the building of his church and the blessing of all.

The Encouragement of Church-Planting Missionaries

Biblical Principles and Precedents

The Need for Encouragement

When Paul arrived in Corinth, he was a very discouraged man. Having sent Timothy to Thessalonica to ascertain the state of the believers there, he had been left alone at Athens (1 Thess. 3:1–2). He was so worried about the Thessalonians that he wished to visit them but was hindered from doing so by Satan (1 Thess. 2:18). He had failed to win many converts in Athens after successful ministries in Philippi, Thessalonica, and Berea. Perhaps this prompted him to examine his ministry. He determined to preach only the message of the crucified Christ (1 Cor. 2:2–5). Whatever the reasons, Paul seems to have been a discouraged missionary. If a man as great as Paul could become discouraged, all missionaries can become discouraged. The need for encouragement is apparent.

The Provision for Encouragement

God has provided encouragement. The Holy Spirit is the official "encourager" (*paraklētos;* John 14:16). The gift of encouragement has been given to specific individuals in the church (Rom. 12:8a NIV). An example par excellence is Barnabas (Acts 4:36). It is noteworthy that Barnabas, the "son of encouragement," is the first missionary named in Acts. It was he who introduced Saul to the skeptical apostles (Acts 9:26–27). It was he who was sent by the church at Jerusalem to Antioch (Acts 11:22). It was he who enlisted Saul to work in the Antioch church (Acts 11:25–26). Later it was he who gave John Mark a second chance and had much to do with Mark's restoration to usefulness (Acts 15:36–39; 2 Tim. 4:11). It is likely that Barnabas's encouragement is the reason Scripture records no periods of depression in the life of Paul while Barnabas accompanied him.

But Barnabas was not alone in the ministry of encouragement:

> There are a number of indications of workers whom Paul encouraged or who encouraged him in his labors. In 1 Cor. 16:10 he asks the Corinthians (believers) to "put him [Timothy] at ease among you." Paul's two letters to Timothy were in the nature of encouragements. Paul admits his loneliness in 1 Cor. 16:17–18 and tells how the coming of three friends cheered him up. He refers to the encouragement which was brought to him by the coming of Epaphroditus and gifts he brought (Phil. 4:18). More important than having his needs supplied was the thought that he was remembered and that this effort on the part of the Macedonian Christians was a sure sign of spiritual growth on their part. In Paul's letter to Philemon, Paul speaks of Philemon as giving him "much joy and comfort" (Philem. 7).[9]

In Romans 1 Paul gives an insight as to how the encourager might stimulate a depressed servant of God: "For I long to see you in order that I may impart some spiritual gift to you, that you may be established; that is, that I may be encouraged together with you while among you, each of us by the other's faith, both yours and mine" (vv. 11–12). The idea is clear. As the missionary-evangelist uses his gift, faith is stimulated in the congregation. This in turn encourages the missionary-evangelist. In other words, the depressed servant in this case is stimulated to use his spiritual gift; this creates faith on the part of the

---

9. Dale W. Bjork, "A Search for New Models" (paper submitted for a class in church-extension evangelism, Trinity Evangelical Divinity School, 19 Jan. 1978).

hearers, and the result is that the depressed missionary-evangelist is himself encouraged.

Relevant Research

Gary Collins begins his book *How to Be a People Helper* with a chapter entitled "People Helping and the Great Commission." In that chapter he shows that the discipling activity enjoined by the Great Commission requires that the Christian community be a helping and encouraging community. Though Collins's book is basically a popular treatment, he does refer to studies which reinforce his main contention. For example:

> Psychologists discovered the effectiveness of group helping many years ago. Mental patients who had been chained in unsanitary asylums were found to improve dramatically when they were treated with compassion and kindness. As part of something called "moral treatment," the hospital administrators and staff lived with the patients, ate with them, and showed that the hospital could be a therapeutic community instead of a prison-like dungeon. This idea was extended further after World War Two, when a British psychiatrist named Maxwell Jones published an account of a therapeutic community in which all of the patient's daily activities were directed toward his or her recovery. "Milieu therapy" was a term which applied to this kind of treatment. One-to-one counseling was part of the treatment but equally important was the daily support, help, and encouragement given by the staff and the patients to each other.[10]

In the present context, of course, we are not dealing specifically with therapy as such. But Collins's thesis, and numerous other studies, indicate the value of helping relationships.[11]

Practical Reflection

Encouragement is a part of the spiritual ministry of all believers. Barnabas-like spirits should take special note of young people in the church who demonstrate dedication to Christ, a cooperative spirit, the ability to communicate, dependability in inconspicuous tasks, and other gifts and qualities vital to the mission of the church. Such individuals should be singled out for counseling. They should have opportunities for discussion with visiting evangelists, preachers, pastors, teachers, and mission leaders. They should be blanketed with prayer.

10. Gary Collins, *How to Be a People Helper* (Santa Ana, Calif.: Vision House, 1976), 130–31.
11. It is worth noting that the category "Helping Behavior" was added to the listings of the *Social Sciences Index* (Bronx, N.Y.: Wilson) in the early 1970s.

This approach has application to successful pastors and older church workers as well as to the younger sons and daughters of the church. The work needs Pauls and Barnabases as well as Marks and Timothys! Might not some established pastor-teachers be divinely appointed to do the work of an evangelist in a new area? Where are the modern Pauls—divinely motivated to go to churchless vacuums rather than larger churches? And what about laypeople who are in a position to provide for their own while still moving out to help claim new territories for Christ?

ME-1 illustration: One of the greatest preachers America ever produced, George Truett, once said that he probably never would have become a preacher at all apart from the encouragement of the saints of God in his church back home. Encouragement is a part of the plan of God. It should be a part of our master plans. It need not be less spontaneous or sincere for being so.

Training Christian Workers for the Missionary Task

Biblical Principles and Precedents

Two types of training described in Scripture can and must be distinguished. Otherwise confusion will arise as to what the Bible teaches concerning the training of missionary-evangelists. While it is popular today to obliterate the distinction between laity and clergy, Scripture maintains the distinction. However, the biblical distinction is not the hierarchical one that some churches make today. Rather, it is in regard to the training of the workers that the true distinction is seen. It can be readily seen that Paul, Timothy, and Titus were not trained in the same manner as were the saints at Berea, Thessalonica, or any of the other churches which Paul founded. Likewise, the Twelve were not trained by our Lord in the same way as were the multitudes.

The reasons for this distinction are varied. First, the Lord taught that the disciple is not above his teacher. This indicates that the teacher must know more than does the disciple. Second, the gifts required by the various types of ministry differ. Logically, a person is trained according to one's gifts. Development of the gifts granted to the missionary-evangelist requires a training program distinct from that for a deacon. Third, the role of the missionary-evangelists and pastor-teachers is that of training laity for the work of the ministry. That is, the leaders must be trained to train others. Their purpose in the church is not so much to carry out the entire ministry as it is to equip others to minister. The training of the missionary-evangelist, then, must differ from that of the laity in profundity and intensity in accordance with the gifts which God has given.

While Scripture mentions only the school of Tyrannus as a place where disciples were instructed daily, one must not infer from this that the training given first-century workers was not profound. A cursory reading of the Pastoral Epistles shows that the two young missionaries trained by Paul had a profound grasp of the Word of God and could put it into action. Paul taught them both true doctrine and sound practice.

That doctrine was taught can be seen in Paul's command to Titus to make sure that the Cretans adorned the doctrine of God in every respect (Titus 2:1, 10). Timothy was told to disseminate that which Paul had taught him (2 Tim. 2:2). He knew fully the doctrine of Paul (2 Tim. 3:10 KJV). He was to pay attention to doctrine until Paul came (1 Tim. 4:13). Clearly the two young missionaries were taught doctrine.

But they were also taught practical theology. Titus had been schooled in financial matters and was entrusted with the mission of carrying the offering for the poor from Corinth to Jerusalem (2 Cor. 8:1–6, 16–21). Timothy knew about deacons and their qualifications (1 Tim. 3:8–14), and both he and Titus knew the qualifications for the office of elder (1 Tim. 3:1–7; Titus 1:5–9). The content of a course in practical Christian living can be seen in Titus 2:1–10. Paul even hints at pedagogical techniques in this passage. Titus was to speak *(laleō)* to the elders, have older women teach the younger women, and be an example to the young men (vv. 1, 3–4, 7).

Not only the substance of doctrine and practice, but also the manner in which they were taught can be seen in the New Testament. It was on-the-job training. For the younger missionary-evangelists this meant accompanying the apostle. John Mark, Timothy, and Titus were all required to leave home to be trained. This is one of the big differences in the training of the elder and the missionary. There is no evidence that the elder had to leave his home environment in order to receive training, but the missionary-evangelists who are described in Scripture did leave home.

Relevant Research

Of course, the approach of the New Testament to the training of Christian workers is of paramount importance. But it also is noteworthy that both sound pedagogy and church history confirm the validity of this approach.

It is often assumed that the preparation of the clergy in modern times has been much the same as the pattern with which we are familiar today. Such, however, is not the case. In the past the vast majority of the clergy in the United States, for example, were trained by the apprentice system. Notably, in a return to the past one of the most important recent trends in theological education in America is to emphasize internship as part and parcel of that education. And one of the most important recent trends overseas is theological education by extension—an approach designed to take at least some of the learning process out of the classroom and put it into the local areas where church leaders live, work, and serve. Educational and historical research upholds the validity of these approaches.

Practical Reflection

The time has come to rethink our programs of preparation for the various Christian ministries. In view of the rapid rise of educational standards all around the world there can be no doubt that thorough preparation is needed. The question is, "What kind of preparation is needed?"

Negatively, we can no longer afford to take young men and women, send them off to schools which effectively seal them off from both the church and the world for a longer or shorter period, and then thrust them into the work at home or abroad. Positively, we must find ways of bringing the church and the school closer together by providing training where churches exist and where they are yet to be established.

One of the priceless possessions of the church of Christ is her present and potential leadership—especially that kind of leadership that labors at the cutting edge where new territory is being claimed for Christ. Contrary to popular Christian opinion, it is this kind of pioneering that makes the greatest demands upon the Christian worker. That being the case, every local church should give special attention to directing and helping those who may be called of God for this task.

Part Four

The Emerging Church and the Christian Mission

The Audience Contacted 9

"God is no respecter of persons" (Acts 10:34 KJV). He loves all and "desires all men to be saved and to come to the knowledge of the truth" (1 Tim. 2:4). Our Lord reached all types of people—including a Matthew, a Zacchaeus, a Mary Magdalene, and an anonymous but disreputable Samaritan woman. The church knows no barriers. Not only has the distinction between Jew and Gentile been superseded, but the same is true of distinctions of race, sex, and social standing (Gal. 3:28).

We begin this chapter with these understandings. But they do not militate against selectivity in making contacts for Christ and his churches!

In the first place, it is manifestly impossible to reach all people simultaneously with the message of Christ. Therefore some must be contacted before others.

In the second place, our Lord was selective in his contacts!

In the third place, the privilege of hearing, believing, and being reconciled to God through Christ entails responsibility. Therefore, fairness is not an issue. Even the natural descendants of Abraham were chosen not simply with a view to their own blessing, but with a view to the blessing of all the nations of the earth (Gen. 12:1–3).

In the fourth place, our aim in any strategy of contact should be to reach all people with the gospel. Selectivity in initial contacts can contribute toward that goal.

In the fifth place, Paul had a strategy of contact that involved a degree of selectivity.

Whatever the actual method, the principle which we learn from Paul, not only from his time in Athens but from his entire missionary career, is that the way to reach people is not to expect them to come to us, but for us to go to them.

Being a pioneer made . . . demands upon him which are very different from what we expect of an evangelist today. There was no existing church or group of churches in Athens or most of the other cities he visited to invite him to come and conduct a series of meetings. Nor were there any local Christians to whom he could look to prepare for his arrival and

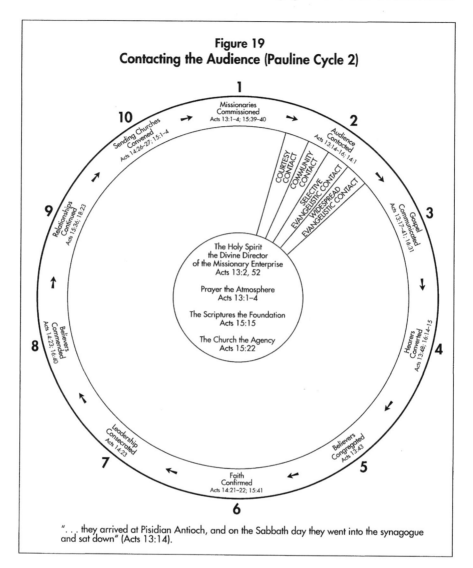

Figure 19
Contacting the Audience (Pauline Cycle 2)

". . . they arrived at Pisidian Antioch, and on the Sabbath day they went into the synagogue and sat down" (Acts 13:14).

invite their friends and neighbors to come and hear him. Rather it was the evangelist himself who was first on the scene and who had to go out and make his own contacts. And it was in the ability to do this, that the gifts of the evangelist largely lay.

Admittedly this is where our present society is not quite as pagan as the situation that faced Paul. . . . Yet . . . the really difficult task for which God's help is especially needed is not to find someone who can come and deliver evangelistic sermons—quite a number can do that—but to find those who can make effective contact with unbelievers wherever they are.

If we insist on having meetings addressed by an evangelist, the major task will still be to persuade people to come and hear him.[1]

Objectives

Of course, the initial objectives of the church planter will become more concrete and specific as acquaintance is gained with the target community. We can, however, mention four general objectives:

1. To gain as much understanding and goodwill of the local citizens (especially their leaders) as possible
2. To reach unchurched Christians and invite them into the church fellowship
3. To reach "prepared people" (those who might be favorably disposed toward the gospel)
4. To get as wide a hearing as possible for the gospel

When Christian workers go into a new community, they are armed with the information gained through preliminary surveys. They know whether the people can be expected to be receptive or hostile. They know the general class and ethnic composition of the community. On the basis of such information and their overall strategy they can make preliminary plans and establish objectives in relation to community contact. Clearly, they cannot assume that people owe them a hearing or that it will make no difference to whom and how they make their approach. They must win a hearing and should prayerfully determine a strategy of contact.

A Preliminary Consideration—
Social Structure and Response to the Gospel

Biblical Principles and Precedents

Perhaps the most difficult decisions facing the missionary-evangelist in coming up with a strategy relate to social structure. There are two absolutely basic sociological facts that come to the fore as one reads the biblical record of the Apostolic Age.

First, social distinctions arising out of racial, cultural, economic, and other differences were very much a part of the experience of the early Christians. At first Jesus commanded his disciples to go only to the lost sheep of the house of Israel (Matt. 10:6). Later he commanded them to

1. Kenneth F. W. Prior, *The Gospel in a Pagan Society* (Downers Grove, Ill.: Inter-Varsity, 1975), 33.

make disciples of all the nations (Matt. 28:19–20). One of the first great misunderstandings in the early church was occasioned by racial and social distinctions: the Hellenistic Jews complained that their widows were being discriminated against (Acts 6:1). Peter had to overcome his Jewish prejudice in order to help Cornelius (Acts 10:28). It was news of the conversion of a large number of Gentiles at Antioch that caused the Jerusalem church to send Barnabas to evaluate what was happening there (Acts 11:20–22). The presence of Jew and Gentile, masters and slaves (1 Peter 2:18), and rich and poor, was clearly a part of the record of the early church.

Second, just as certain is the fact that social distinctions were to be transcended in the preaching of the gospel and in the fellowship of the saints. For God "is not one to show partiality" (Acts 10:34) but is "abounding in riches for all who call upon Him" (Rom. 10:12). In Christ there is no male or female, Jew or Gentile, bond or free (Gal. 3:28). It is clear, therefore, that "whoever will call upon the name of the Lord will be saved" (Rom. 10:13). Accordingly, in the fellowship of the early church, masters were to realize that their servants were also brothers (Philem. 16); moreover, the rich were not to receive preferential treatment (James 2:1–4), but were to be generous (1 Tim. 6:17–18).

To sum up: the New Testament recognizes that certain tensions arising from social differences will exist as long as the church is in the world. Social distinctions which are a major part of human intercourse cannot be erased. But neither are they to be determinative of who will hear the Good News of Christ and how believers will be received into the fellowship of the church.

Social orientations arising out of race, wealth, and other such factors figured into Paul's strategy and into the way his hearers responded to the gospel that he preached. Thus the synagogue community was usually the first to be contacted, and though some Jews from that community believed in Christ, the majority of the converts were from the Gentile proselytes and God-fearers. Paul did preach and even dispute publicly, but he did not make a practice of preaching on street corners or in other public places to the "idle and curious crowd" or to "the loafers, the porters, the ignorant and degraded, the casual labourer on the street."[2] William Ramsay comments, "The classes where education and work go hand in hand were first to come under the influence of the new religion."[3] Roland Allen adds, "The majority of St. Paul's converts were of the lower commercial and working classes, labourers, freedmen, and

---

2. Roland Allen, *Missionary Methods: St. Paul's or Ours?* (Grand Rapids: Eerdmans, 1962), 22.
3. Quoted in Allen, *Missionary Methods*, 23.

slaves."[4] Allen emphasizes that within these groups there were people who had personal qualities and community contacts that lent strength and potential to the fledgling churches. Paul "so taught that no church of his foundation was without a strong centre of respectable, religious-minded people. These naturally took the lead and preserved the church from rapid decay."[5]

Relevant Research

Think of social structure as "those social relations which seem to be of critical importance for the behavior of members of the society."[6] It includes groupings and segments in society that tend to persist: classes, castes, clans, peer groups based on age, secret societies, and kinship groups.[7] When Donald McGavran refers to "homogeneous units" in society, he has these groups primarily in mind.[8] (Of course, more is involved than that. Ties of language, ways of thinking, value systems, and cultural preferences also tend to bind groups together.) As McGavran notes, people like to become Christians without having to cross the major boundaries that distinguish these groups from one another.[9]

Years ago, P. E. Kraemer claimed that American denominations are basically made up of "class churches."[10] He categorized denominations according to the class that predominated at the time of his study:

Upper class: Episcopalian and Unitarian
Upper-middle class: Presbyterian, Congregational, and Reformed
Middle class: Methodist, Lutheran, Baptist, Disciples, Evangelical–
    United Brethren, Evangelical Reformed, and Christian Reformed
Lower class: Sects

Essentially the same phenomenon can be found around the world. On a particular Sunday during a visit to India several years ago, the author visited three churches in Bombay. Not only were the three churches of different denominations, each one was made up of members of a particular caste (think of caste as congealed class), and the approach to worship in each church was appropriate to both the denom-

---

4. Allen, *Missionary Methods*, 24.
5. Ibid.
6. Raymond Firth, *Elements of Social Organization* (Boston: Beacon, 1963), 30.
7. Ibid., 31.
8. Donald A. McGavran, *Understanding Church Growth* (Grand Rapids: Eerdmans, 1970), 85–87.
9. Ibid., 289–91.
10. See Joel H. Nederhood, *The Church's Mission to the Educated American* (Grand Rapids: Eerdmans, 1960), 31.

ination and the caste of the members. There is no getting away from the fact that though there are many multiclass, multiethnic, multilingual churches, most churches tend to be class, caste, ethnic, or tribal churches in addition to being Christian churches!

Practical Reflection

Most churches today will feel the same tensions that were evident in the apostolic church. But insofar as they are Christian, they will also rise above those tensions. That does not preclude approaching a homogeneous societal unit when we plant a church. Nor does it mean that churches cannot pattern their corporate life and worship (we will call this "programmatic posture") to fit the preferences of a responsive segment of society within the target area. Indeed, sound strategy might dictate that the initial approach be made to members of one group and that the programmatic posture be such that members of that group will feel especially at home in the meetings.

On the other hand, sound sociological strategy must not be allowed to supersede spiritual reality. No one should be discriminated against because of color, class, caste, or tribe. And, once established, Bible-believing churches must find ways of demonstrating their essential oneness in Christ. With this in mind, four factors should be given preliminary consideration before actually establishing contacts in the target area:

1. Newcomers to a society may find it easier to relate to people of different classes (i.e., people of classes higher or lower than the class to which they belonged in their home culture) than will a person who is native to that society. In closed-class societies especially, this potential for increased contacts on the part of the newcomer (in comparison with the opportunity of the native) should not be overlooked.

2. One of the results of undifferentiated initial contacts in church-extension evangelism in many areas has been that the new churches have become identified with marginals and outcasts who attach themselves to the missionary-evangelist for purposes of self-aggrandizement. Another result has been that the churches become identified with people who because of disease, impairment, age, social standing, or the like have little power to persuade their fellow citizens to accept the gospel. Make no mistake. Every individual is equally precious in the sight of God. That is not in question here. What needs to be thought through (but rarely is) is the implications of the rather widespread nonstrategy of making initial contacts with those who are most easily approached.

3. It can be of great value if a core of solid citizens can be won to Christ and to the church. Not only does their conversion lend stability

to the work, it may well enhance the possibility of still others coming to Christ. If the first converts are from the lowest class, the conversion of middle- and upper-class people will be made more difficult. If middle- and upper-class people are won to Christ, the conversion of lower-class persons may be made easier. Missionary John Kemp won a Fijian chief by the name of Elijah Veronti to Christ. Thousands followed him into the faith. In general, however, the strategy of a prolonged delay in approaching potentially responsive people who are lower on the social scale while work continues among unresponsive higher-class people is questionable strategy.

4. The experience of many Pentecostal and some Baptist groups should cause us to give more consideration to reaching the lower-middle and upper-lower classes where "education and work go hand in hand." Biblical precedent and the success of these groups indicate that many denominations and missions may be missing an opportunity for great growth among a responsive people who obviously make good timber for building churches. This may necessitate a programmatic posture that would be difficult for more staid, formal, and intellectually oriented groups to evolve, however.

Preevangelistic Courtesy Contacts

Biblical Principles and Precedents

In our evangelistic zeal we sometimes have a tendency to forget two very basic biblical principles. The first one has to do with the integrity of humankind, all of whom are made in the image of God. This integrity is reflected in such commandments as "Love . . . your neighbor as yourself" (Luke 10:27); "Therefore, however you want people to treat you, so treat them" (Matt. 7:12); and "Do good to all men" (Gal. 6:10). The second has to do with the divine origin of legitimate human authority. It is reflected in such statements as "The powers that be are ordained of God" (Rom. 13:1 KJV), and in such commandments as "Render to Caesar the things that are Caesar's" (Matt. 22:21), and "Render to all what is due them" (Rom. 13:7). These principles are certainly relevant to preevangelistic contacts in a target area. We are not, however, suggesting that the Lord Jesus and Paul made a practice of heading for the home or office of the highest available governmental official upon entering a new province, town, or city. Indeed the most important factor in their identification with local citizens seems usually to have been a positive response to their message. More should be said, however.

The mission of Paul was, of course, to the Gentiles (Acts 9:15; 26:16–18). He was commissioned to this task (Acts 13:2) and was recognized by the apostles for his mission to the Gentiles (Gal. 2:7–9). At the same time he had a great concern for his fellow Jews (Rom. 10:1). In the light of this commission and concern, Paul's practice of visiting the synagogues (and the homes of certain citizens) can be seen as courtesy contacts of the highest order.

Relevant Research

Research in the areas of anthropology, sociology, and communication underscores the importance of the roles of formal leaders, sponsors, and mediators in society.[11] Under certain societal arrangements the newcomer may find it all but impossible to gain acceptance apart from a proper approach to such persons. Even in Western societies that emphasize egalitarianism, an initial contact with those who fill leadership roles will usually enhance the missionary cause.

Practical Reflection

Even if it could be successfully argued that missionary-evangelists have no sacred obligation to conform to local rules or protocol in entering a new community, nothing is to be gained by disregarding them out of hand. Even in the United States, a courtesy call upon certain local Christian leaders, government and school officials, and mass-media representatives may occasion goodwill and open doors for the new work. In other societies such contacts may be even more vital and rewarding than in our own.

ME-3 illustration: Missionary James Luckman has had outstanding success in opening new doors to the gospel in Ethiopia. Why? Because he made it a habit from his early days in that land to visit the highest officials, explain his business, and secure their goodwill upon first entering any new territory.

ME-3 illustration: John Ritchie established some two hundred churches among the Indians of Peru. It was his conviction that an unexpected and unsponsored evangelistic effort simply did not fit the Indian culture. So he never went to a village unless he had been invited by a sponsor (any outstanding member of the community). Often he would stay with the sponsor while carrying on his evangelistic effort.

ME-3 illustration: Some missionaries while on furlough at Trinity Evangelical Divinity School worked on a master plan for entering tribal villages in Kenya. They realized that although village elders (sitting as a group) were usually cordial to the missionary effort, they had been

11. Felix Keesing, *Cultural Anthropology: The Science of Custom* (New York: Holt, Rinehart and Winston, 1966), 403, 421.

thoughtlessly bypassed in most cases of pioneer evangelism. The missionaries then incorporated a courtesy contact with village elders into their master plan, and with good results.

ME-3 illustration: A missionary to Japan found that one of her most fruitful contacts in any new area was with the principals of the local schools. She would visit them with an offer of appropriate Christian books for their school libraries. Of course, the books themselves constituted a form of witness. Still more important, however, were the personal contacts made with leaders in the local school system.

One of the great failures of Christian evangelism at home and abroad has been in the area of preevangelistic contacts. It has often been true that the greater the concern for the lost and the greater the vision for a lasting work for Christ, the less the attention given to social amenities and the building of bridges of friendship and trust. This failure has been most conspicuous in Jewish evangelism at home. But it is apparent in almost every country and culture, whether in the United States or abroad. We should remember that there is a very real sense in which those who are not against us are for us. Even unbelievers oftentimes will in friendship open strategic doors for those who engage in the noble work of building the kingdom of God.

Christian workers, then, should make a simple list of courtesy contacts to be made as they enter the area of their new ministry. They should not assume too much at this point. Even within North American culture there will be significant differences between the subcultures of, for example, a city on the Eastern seaboard, a small town in the Midwest, and a mountain community in Kentucky.

Preevangelistic Community Contacts

For want of a better term, we will call wider preevangelistic contacts "community contacts." Getting to know the people in the community and allowing them to know us are part of the process. Participation in community life is still another aspect of it.

Biblical Principles and Precedents

Unlike present-day missionaries, Paul did not have to deal with the problem of isolation from the community. When he arrived in a town, he lived there. This involved not only residing in the town, but working in the community and staying in the homes of the people. Lydia invited Paul to stay at her home (Acts 16:14–15), and it is certain that he stayed with Jason (Acts 17:6–9) and with Aquila (Acts 18:2–3) as well as with Titius Justus (Acts 18:7). No wonder that he could ask the Thessalonians to remember his life among them (1 Thess. 2:8–9). He had lived with them. Jesus had taught that the good shepherd knows his sheep. Paul certainly qualified as a good shepherd!

Paul also knew the community from the business viewpoint. He plied his trade and sold his tents. While this enabled Paul to earn a living so that the young church would not have to support him, it also put him in contact with people of the business community. He knew those from whom he purchased supplies and those who purchased tents from him. It could be that these community contacts resulted in certain influential people coming into the fellowship of the young churches (Lydia, Jason, Philemon, Priscilla, Aquila, and Aristobulus, to name a few).

Relevant Research

All societies have certain expectations regarding newcomers. In some societies (e.g., the United States) it is expected that local people will visit the newcomer to their community. In other societies (e.g., France) it is expected that those taking up residence will visit their neighbors. When these expectations are met, lines of communication are opened and the groundwork is laid for continued relationships. By the same token, when these expectations are not met, communication becomes strained and the possibility of good relationships jeopardized.

Fulfilling what is expected of a newcomer is perhaps more important in the case of a church worker than in almost any other case. In our own culture the reason for this is obvious. People have so many preconceived ideas (many of them negative) about churches and church workers that the new work and worker stand prejudged unless one does something to dispel the preconceptions.

A study of the social organizations and roles in a culture will often reveal how the missionary and the new church will be understood. For example, previous to the coming of missionaries, the Tila Chol society of Mexico had no religious organization comparable to a church and no one in a religious role comparable to that of a missionary-evangelist. Naturally some significant preevangelistic contact was required to ensure that the missionary was not regarded as another medicine man (with bad medicine!).

Practical Reflection

It appears that the average church-planting missionary—national and expatriate—takes far too much for granted upon entering a new community for Christ. If we put ourselves in the place of the local resident whose community is invaded by some outsider who has come to preach to us and start a new religious organization in our area, perhaps we will understand what is involved. Ways should be found to break down prejudices, gain a hearing, and secure understanding. Classes in cooking, child care, and photography, for example, have been used to advantage in some areas. Of course, there is no substitute for living and working alongside local residents over a period of time.

In the initial stages of a work, a house-to-house survey may help to break the ice and monitor community attitudes. It must be recognized that this will not work everywhere, however. In metropolitan areas like New York, for example, apartments are all but inaccessible, and personal questions are not well received. On the other hand, missionaries and national workers in the Philippines found a quite different situation. So while surveys can be extremely helpful, this will not always be the case.

ME-1 illustration: Robert H. Schuller, pastor of the flourishing Garden Grove Community Church in Garden Grove, California, writes about ringing the doorbells of hundreds of homes in the area before actually starting the church. He advocates setting aside two weeks in order to call door to door in ever widening concentric circles from the location (or possible location) of the church. Suggesting that we listen to what people have to say about the churches with which they are familiar, he promises the education of a lifetime!

Allocate these two weeks *full time* toward the following project: begin by calling door-to-door in the immediate vicinity of your church. You have called on some of the homes before, but you are going to call now with a different purpose, a different motive, and a different question.

You are going to ask: "Do you attend our church regularly? Have you ever attended it? Do you attend any other church?"

If they give you a negative answer, you will reply by saying: "I'm delighted to hear this because I'm anxious to find out how I can improve this church and make it such an exciting church that intelligent and wonderful people like you will want to come. You are obviously an intelligent person, so you undoubtedly have good reasons why you don't attend the church. Would you please tell me what they are? And could you tell me what our church could possibly do to help in any area of your life? Is there any program that you would be interested in?"

Generally, after you have asked the first one or two questions, the answers will be forthcoming. I did this years ago and it was an eye-opening experience! I heard criticisms of "typical sermons." And I heard criticisms about other gaps in the church program. The criticisms of the unchurched persons in my community became a major learning experience!

If you will spend two weeks calling door-to-door in an ever-widening circle, beginning from your church property, and will listen with an open mind, then indeed you will have the education of a lifetime! Listen to the individuals you talk with—listen to them carefully.

Do not be defensive! In spite of all that you have ever been taught, assume—for one humble time in your life—that you may have been wrong about a lot of things! So, listen to what the unchurched are saying and you will find out where they are hurting, where they are frightened, where they are worried. Take careful notes. Keep a diary detailing your calls.

After two weeks you will know what kind of a church program you have to design to meet the needs of these people in your community. You will know what kind of messages to give in order to bring them into the church.[12]

What Schuller has to say is helpful though it must be remembered that we are building churches of Christ. Christ, not the community, must be allowed to determine both the program and message of the church.

ME-3 illustration: In the Philippines, Conservative Baptist pastors and missionaries found that a simple house-to-house survey and invitation can be a significant preparation for a church-planting evangelistic effort. They discovered that surveys are generally acceptable only in the larger urban centers, however. Out in the barrios, people are extremely suspicious of this approach. The difference, of course, grows out of the experiences and values of city dwellers as opposed to those of residents of the relatively isolated barrios.

ME-3 illustration: Many readers will be familiar with the video *Ee-Taow*, which tells the remarkable story of the conversion of the Mouk tribespeople of Papua New Guinea. Not many will know that Mark Zook, who with his wife Gloria evangelized the Mouk and planted the Mouk church, has written a little booklet in which he reflects on the church-planting process step by step. Looking back, Zook asks why the Mouk responded to the gospel as they did. And he concludes that they were actually being taught during the preevangelism period. They were observing such things as the obedience of the Zook children, the part that Gloria played in ministry, the evenhanded way in which the Zooks treated the Mouk irrespective of their status, and the importance they attached to the message they would eventually deliver. In answer to questions concerning that message, the Zooks responded that the message was so important that they did not want to respond to questions about it until they were sure that they understood the Mouk language and culture well enough to assure that the message would not be misunderstood! It was a time of preevangelism, but community contacts were being made that proved to be crucial to the planting of the church.[13]

12. Robert H. Schuller, *Your Church Has Real Possibilities* (Glendale, Calif.: Regal, 1974), 81.
13. Mark Zook, *Church Planting Step by Step* (Sanford, Fla.: New Tribes Mission, 1989), 2–9.

Selective Evangelistic Contacts

Entering an area without any plan other than to preach the Word to whosoever will is in itself a selection. It really means that those who have the most time, or are the most accessible, or are reachable by the particular media and modes of communication utilized, will constitute our selective contacts. This approach may result in initial conversions which in effect close doors of opportunity by identifying the new church with individuals who in the eyes of many others are undesirable. It is not likely that this approach will result in reaching those who are best prepared to understand the message and receive Christ. If, on the other hand, initial evangelistic contacts are prayerfully selected, the first converts may be the occasion for a much wider hearing for the gospel. Societal arrangements should therefore be taken into consideration before deciding on initial evangelistic contacts.

Biblical Principles and Precedents

Reaching Prepared People

In regards to selective evangelistic contacts, three principles can be enunciated from Scripture. We have alluded to the first one already. We might call it the doorway principle. The selective evangelistic contact should be a doorway to a wider audience. This principle can be seen in Paul's visits to the synagogue. His target group, the Gentiles, was represented in the synagogues by the God-fearers, the devout, and the proselytes. The utility of the principle can be seen in Paul's visit to Antioch in Pisidia. At the close of Paul's message "the Gentiles besought that these words might be preached to them the next sabbath. . . . And the next sabbath day came almost the whole city together to hear the word of God" (Acts 13:42, 44 KJV).

The second principle is the preparedness principle. A group of people or a single person selected for evangelism should demonstrate a degree of preparedness to accept the gospel. This principle can be seen at work in the case of the Ephesians. The record states that Paul found some disciples (Acts 19:1) who had not heard of the Holy Spirit (v. 2), but had been baptized into John's baptism (v. 3). Paul then preached about the Savior for whom John had prepared the way. These disciples demonstrated a degree of previous preparation and thus became key targets for evangelistic effort.

The Macedonian call could be considered an example of the same principle. The man in the vision cried, "Help us" (Acts 16:9). This is the plea of either a believer who was unable to evangelize his area effectively and thus was in need of aid, or of an unbeliever who realized his plight and called for help. Whichever might have been the case, the call for aid indicated that a preparatory work had been accomplished.

The third principle in selective evangelistic contacts can be called the confirmatory principle. It is seen in the case of the lame man from Lystra. Paul carefully scrutinized *(atenisas)* him and perceived *(idōn)* that he had faith to be healed (Acts 14:9). Then Paul commanded the man to stand on his feet (Acts 14:10). While the episode could be construed as a case of previous preparation, it can also be seen as a case of confirmation (Heb. 2:3). The message was to be confirmed with certain apostolic signs. Such signs confirmed the message preached.

Although some make the argument that there are no apostles today and thus confirmatory signs are not to be expected, the principle of confirmation stands. Paul later wrote to the Thessalonian converts, who of course were not apostles, that they were examples "to all the believers in Macedonia and in Achaia. . . . For they themselves report about us what kind of a reception we had with you, and how you turned to God from idols to serve a living and true God" (1 Thess. 1:7, 9). Here there is no evidence of physical miracles, but it is clear that the miracle of the transformed life was confirmatory evidence of the message preached.

Perhaps we should go one step further. Roland Allen states that conversions among the God-fearers were not in sufficient numbers to tip the scales in favor of Christianity.[14] Stephen Hsu, however, argues that Paul was following a strategy that led to an increased number of evangelists, not just converts. The people who frequented the synagogues—especially the Grecian Jews and Gentile proselytes—had ready access and entrée to the Gentile population that surrounded them. In a short time a whole region such as Asia (Acts 19:10) could hear the message from them. Hsu thinks that many proponents of church growth have overlooked this aspect of Pauline strategy. Paul was not thinking simply in terms of bringing many members of a responsive homogeneous group into the kingdom. Rather, "he saw any harvesting opportunity as a means to reap a greater harvest. . . . The principle of selective evangelistic contacts is, therefore, to select the group which has the greatest potential of response to the Gospel *and* the greatest potential of becoming effective evangelistic witnesses to the target area."[15]

Reaching People Related to Believers

A study of the kinships of the disciples of Jesus is informative. It reveals the principle of reaching those related to believers and the principle of working within the family relationship instead of breaking up the

14. Allen, *Missionary Methods,* 13.
15. Stephen Hsu, "Selective Evangelistic Contacts" (paper submitted at Trinity Evangelical Divinity School–School of World Mission and Evangelism, Feb. 1978).

family. Andrew brought his brother Simon Peter to hear the one whom he believed to be the Messiah. James and John, the sons of Zebedee, are (together with their mother) examples showing that Jesus worked within family relationships.

The principle of working with the family was so important to the apostle Peter that he gave special instructions in this regard to women married to unsaved husbands (1 Peter 3:1–6). This seems to be the only case in which Scripture speaks of winning an unsaved person without use of the Word. Here the transformed life of a family member is the factor that the Holy Spirit uses to gain an unsaved person.

Paul in all probability had this principle in mind when he urged believing spouses to remain with their unbelieving spouses. Whatever else the expression "the unbelieving husband is sanctified through his wife, and the unbelieving wife is sanctified through her believing husband" (1 Cor. 7:14), may mean, it indicates that the unbelieving spouse (or any other member of the family) of a believer has been set apart and thus is a candidate for salvation. At the same time we must bear in mind that the promise to the jailer in Philippi, "Believe in the Lord Jesus, and you shall be saved, you and your household" (Acts 16:31), does not mean that a believer can believe for another person. Rather, the promise indicates that kinship provides a favorable environment for evangelism.

Donald McGavran argues that Paul approached many individuals and groups who were related in some way to the Christians in Antioch, and that he planned to do so. They constituted people who were "on the bridge," to use McGavran's phrase. McGavran finds evidence of a movement of faith across these bridges, igniting a great "people movement" among Greeks even as people movements had started among the Jews and Samaritans after Pentecost.

> While Paul worked with that Greek-Hebrew Antioch community for a year, he must have come to know hundreds of relatives of Christians and to hear of thousands more. Some of these relatives from Cyprus, Pisidia, Iconium, Lystra and Derbe had quite possibly come to Antioch during Paul's year there and had joined in his hours of instruction. According to the record some of the Christians who had first spoken of the faith to Greeks in Antioch had come from Cyprus. They probably belonged to families who had connections on both the island and the mainland. Having won their relatives in Antioch, it was natural for them to think of winning their unconverted relatives, Jews and Greeks, in Cyprus. . . .
>
> How then did Paul choose fields of labour? To be accurate we must say that he did not choose fields. He followed up groups of people who had living relations in the People Movement to Christ.[16]

16. Donald A. McGavran, *Bridges of God* (New York: Friendship, 1955), 27, 31.

Relevant Research

Psychological Factors Relating to Preparedness for the Gospel

In addition to the sociological factors noted earlier in this chapter, certain psychological factors are important to the preparation of a people for the gospel.

1. The concept of worldview as developed by anthropologists is most relevant here. Put very simply, a worldview is simply the way in which a person sees the world. As Norman Geisler says, people do not see things as they are, but as they appear to be through glasses tinted by their worldview.[17] A naturalist or materialist, for example, sees no evidence of God's presence or power in the world. Such an individual will always look for psychological or scientific explanations of observed phenomena. An animist, on the other hand, sees gods and spirits everywhere. In this view, even natural phenomena must have spiritual explanations. People who share the monotheistic worldview of Christianity may be easier to win to Christ (e.g., nominal Christians) or more difficult to win (Jews and Muslims). But once won they often make good timber for the church because of the broad areas of commonality and consequent understanding.

2. Another important factor is that of timing. For example, if tribal people can be reached before they adopt some other developed religion or ideology, they will likely be much more responsive to the claims of Christ. Further, people who have been uprooted from their old communities, who have broken old ties, and have settled in a new area are often most receptive to new ideas and associations. Sociological barriers to conversion are no longer so high. New friendships are sought. Old patterns tend to break down; new ones are in the process of being established. In such a situation Christ and his church may well receive a favorable consideration.

3. A third factor closely related to receptivity is that of fit. When an innovation more or less matches the cultural values and social forms of a target community, the possibility that members of the community will adopt the innovation is enhanced. George Foster notes that in post-Reformation Europe the desire to read the Bible led to the world's first mass literacy movement. He predicts that in the future, as was the case in ancient Mesopotamia, economic needs will be more important than Bible reading as an incentive to literacy.[18] Perhaps so.

17. Norman Geisler, "Some Philosophical Perspectives on Missionary Dialogue," in *Theology and Mission*, ed. David J. Hesselgrave (Grand Rapids: Baker, 1978), 241–57.

18. George M. Foster, *Traditional Cultures and the Impact of Technological Change* (New York: Harper and Row, 1962), 145–46.

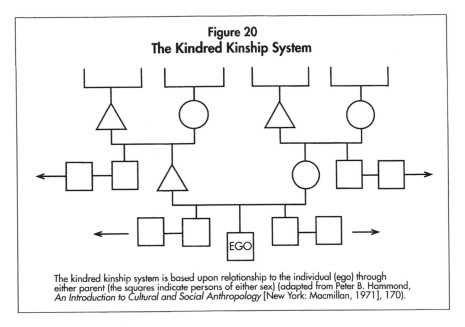

Figure 20
The Kindred Kinship System

The kindred kinship system is based upon relationship to the individual (ego) through either parent (the squares indicate persons of either sex) (adapted from Peter B. Hammond, *An Introduction to Cultural and Social Anthropology* [New York: Macmillan, 1971], 170).

But situations will vary, and can, in fact, be turned around. Whatever the motivation for learning to read might be, in numerous situations literacy has opened the door for missionary-evangelists. The ability to read, coupled with the lack of reading material and the Protestant emphasis on the message of the Book, has made for a fit that has been most significant.

Distinguishing Kindred Kinship and Lineage Kinship Systems

The family (nuclear or extended) is the basic social group in human societies. But as Francis L. K. Hsu has noted, "Though the family as the *first human grouping is universally important*, its importance to the individual varies enormously from society to society."[19] In old China the family was most important; in America the family is of lesser importance. We can see a pronounced difference between various societies when we examine the patterns in which relatives by blood or marriage interact.

Peter Hammond makes a distinction at this point between kindred and lineage.[20] The term "kindred" is applied to that group of people with whom an individual (ego) can establish a genealogical bond through one's parents and with whom one is reciprocally bound by cer-

19. Francis L. K. Hsu, *Clan, Caste, and Club* (Princeton, N.J.: Van Nostrand, 1963), 6.
20. Peter B. Hammond, *An Introduction to Cultural and Social Anthropology* (New York: Macmillan, 1971), 169–72.

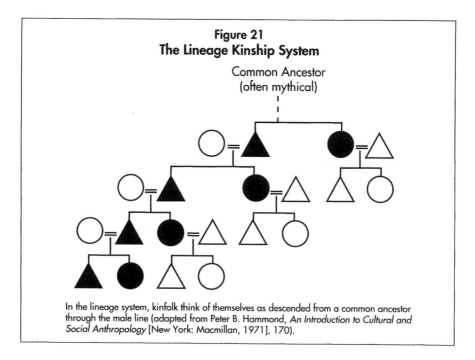

Figure 21
The Lineage Kinship System

In the lineage system, kinfolk think of themselves as descended from a common ancestor through the male line (adapted from Peter B. Hammond, *An Introduction to Cultural and Social Anthropology* [New York: Macmillan, 1971], 170).

tain conventions and obligations. Note that kindred is ego-focused and that the composition of the kindred group which is important to ego and with whom relationships are vital will vary according to age, situation, and interests (see figure 20).

The term "lineage" is applied to a group composed of all blood relatives to whom an individual is related through one or the other parent and bound in a system of conventions and obligations. Lineage is ancestor-focused. All descendants of an ancestor become members of the lineage upon their birth and grow into a set of relationships with (and responsibilities toward) the other members which is predetermined and constant. The composition of the group does not change according to the needs and wishes of ego, but only as new members are born into it and as the older members die. Even after death it is likely that the ancestor will continue to occupy an important place in the lineage and will remain bound to the living in a very real sense (see figure 21).

The social system of the United States is basically of the kindred type. The kinfolk of both parents are included among our relatives. Only rarely, however, do we give consideration to those who are more distant than second cousins. Since the system is ego-focused, every individual will have one's own concept of one's kindred (a concept shared only with full siblings). This concept will change for the individual according to age and situation. When a child, the individual relates to the nuclear family and such other kinfolk as are important to the parents (proximity being a key factor). On growing older, ego may become interested in establishing a relationship with various other relatives, especially at times of childbirths, christenings, graduations, weddings, funerals, and so on. When ego grows old, the composition of the kindred grouping may change dramatically because of the death of others of one's own generation, the multiplication of descendants, and, in many cases, the rather general disregard for the very old in our society.

The lineage groups of traditional China, Japan, and literally scores of tribal societies are at the other end of the continuum. In those societies the bloodline (either of the father or of the mother, but not both) may well determine an individual's entire life pattern—education, vocation, marriage, the care of elders and younger members of the lineage, religious obligations, and much more. Ego has comparatively little to say. Lineage members are bound together not simply for the sake of convenience and fellowship, but in order to sustain life, secure the good of all the relatives, and perpetuate the ancestral line.

Because of the overemphasis on ego (the individual) in much of Western—and particularly North American—society, the family and relatives of contacts and potential contacts in evangelism have been largely overlooked. It is true that in kindred societies such as the United States the potential of reaching relatives of Christians is not as great as elsewhere. (In fact, individualism has produced a situation in which numerous people are [or feel] abandoned by even their own family and relatives. This is especially true among older citizens. These potential contacts should not be neglected.) But even in kindred societies family contacts should not be overlooked.

In societies where lineage patterns prevail (as they do in much of the non-Western world), the missionary-evangelist must view potential prospects in an entirely different light. Family contacts will present a whole new set of problems and potentials to the church. The most important of these can be defined rather easily once one is in the society. Neglect of them will be a great loss to the work of Christ.

Practical Reflection

We have often overlooked the fact that God has prepared people in our target areas, and that he will prepare people as we pray. As a consequence, we have neglected many people whom Jesus and his apostles, and Paul and his team, never would have passed by.

Unchurched "Church People"

People who have had an association with churches in other areas may be unchurched after moving. Such people may or may not be genuine Christians, but if they have been in a church in the past, we can expect that they will be understanding and appreciative of the Christian worldview and faith.

ME-1 illustration: An American denomination has inaugurated a commendable program of church extension in Florida. One key to the success of the program has been that initial contact is made in each target area with a significant number of retirees who have left denominational churches in the North and have not yet been churched in their new communities.

Newcomers and Other Responsive Segments of the Society

Newcomers to a target area can be singled out as being potentially receptive. Of course there may be other responsive segments in any given area. All such should have special attention.

ME-3 illustration: There are some 150,000 Antilleans in France today—many of them in the Paris area. They have come mainly from Martinique and Guadeloupe. They are French citizens, but similarity to their native French neighbors ends at that point. Among the differences is that they constitute a subgroup that is far more responsive to the gospel than are the French. Their responsiveness is occasioned by several factors. No viable plan for church-planting evangelism in the areas where the Antilleans live would be possible without taking these people into consideration.

Classes with Matching Characteristics

The characteristics and interests of some classes in the target area will more closely match the programmatic posture of the projected church than will those of other classes. Let's face it. Churches are tied in to class in that they appeal to the members of certain classes. In closed-class societies such as India, churches rarely cut decisively across class (caste) lines. Even in open-class societies such as the United States, churches usually have a primary appeal to certain class segments. With that in mind it may be wise to match the primary target audience with the programmatic posture. This approach is not calculated to preclude wider contact. It simply acknowledges social realities, especially in the beginning stages. It is true that we have thought of the differences between churches and denominations as being historical and theological. But there can be little doubt that the differences are psychological and sociological as well.

ME-1-2-3 illustration: An outstanding example of a programmatic posture that fits the values and patterns of the target area is that of the Pentecostal churches in Latin America. In general, the Pentecostals have had unusual success in reaching people of the lower-middle and upper-lower classes in a number of areas around the world. Donald Palmer's study on the success of the United Pentecostal Church in Colombia emphasizes that their program and approach have a special appeal to the mentality of certain segments of that society.[21]

Kinship as a Bridge

Missionaries from highly individualistic, ego-focused kindred societies have hardly begun to avail themselves of the opportunities that are theirs for reaching the immediate families and other relatives of those who have already decided for Christ. Increasingly—East and West—church planters must think of Christians as links and bridges to the unsaved. It may well be that the relatives of believers constitute the largest single group of prepared people in the world today.

ME-3 illustration: After three terms of planting churches in Japan, a missionary redirected the strategy. Instead of making initial evangelistic contacts with children, young people, and a few interested mothers, and stopping there, the strategy was directed toward using these individuals to make contacts with whole families, including fathers whose working hours and misconceptions of Christianity had kept them aloof from the church. The result? Whole families were won and a new church was established in half the time it had required to establish other churches.

Widespread Preaching and Teaching

Biblical Principles and Precedents

The Bible clearly states that God desires all to come to repentance (2 Peter 3:9). The principles of selectivity which we have discussed do not in any way negate this divine desire. They represent an attempt to accomplish the task in the most efficient manner. But it is clear that if the church is going to comply with the desire of God for the salvation of all, it will have to follow the biblical mandate and use biblical methods. It will have to sow abundantly if it is to reap abundantly (2 Cor. 9:6).

How did Paul engage in widespread evangelism? First, he used his fellow workers wisely. Seldom was Paul found working alone. He

---

21. Donald Palmer, "Jesus Only: The United Pentecostal Church," in *Dynamic Religious Movements*, ed. David J. Hesselgrave (Grand Rapids: Baker, 1978), 234–35.

worked with teams. Timothy, Luke, and Titus were often sent on missions of varying types. While the coworkers often carried instructions from the apostle, they were not just messenger boys. Titus was to rectify the problems in the church on Crete (Titus 1:5). Timothy was sent to strengthen and to comfort the Thessalonian saints (1 Thess. 3:2), and upon his return he was to give a report of the work (1 Thess. 3:6). All of this freed the apostle Paul for his work and at the same time enlisted others in the task of evangelism.

Second, Paul encouraged and used in the task of evangelism the churches which he had begun. Often it is asked how the Colossian congregation was formed. It is fairly certain that Paul did not visit the area; thus he was not the founding missionary. Donald Guthrie suggests that Epaphras, a convert of Paul, was the human instrument involved in founding the Colossian church. It is noteworthy that Paul had a Bible training school in Ephesus (Acts 19:9), and that to the Ephesians he wrote that gifted men are granted to the church for edification and increase of the body (Eph. 4:7–16). Paul stressed that the work of the ministry is the responsibility of all the saints and not the work of just a few. The result of the efforts of the saints at Ephesus is seen in the Book of Revelation—the seven churches singled out include Ephesus and six others in the general area. Note also that Paul commended the Thessalonians because from them "sounded out the word of the Lord . . . so that we need not to speak any thing" (1 Thess. 1:8 KJV).

Third, Paul withdrew from growing congregations. While in some cases his withdrawal was forced by persecution, in other cases it was not due to either human or satanic opposition. It was in the midst of revival that Paul and Barnabas left Antioch to engage in extension work (Acts 13:1–3), and it was after a tremendous victory that Paul left the island of Cyprus to go to Perga (Acts 13:6–13).

What, then, was the pattern Paul used in order to maximize evangelistic teaching and preaching? He engaged in evangelism himself, he trained others to do the same work, and he left others to do the work for which they had been trained.

Relevant Research

It seems trite to mention the sales principle that the more doorbells the salesperson rings and the more contacts made, the more success will be achieved. Preliminary consumer surveys determine the sales potential of given products. After the survey a great part of sales technique is simply to contact as many people as possible in the knowledge that, on an average, one out of seven (or ten or fifteen) contacts represents a sale. Rapidly growing religious movements such as the Mormons and the Jehovah's Witnesses are well aware of this principle.

Practical Reflection

The gospel is for everyone. The invitation is, "Whosoever will, let him come." This has been one of the guiding principles of evangelicalism at home and abroad. Mass meetings, radio, television, tracts, advertising, correspondence courses—all have been used to contact entire populations. In fact, the emphasis on innovative methodologies to reach anyone and everyone (except the next-door neighbor!) prompted Joe Bayly's satirical *The Gospel Blimp*.[22] While that book teaches us an important lesson, we should pray that we not neglect the use of as many means as are honorable to reach as many people as possible.

Churches must find ways of penetrating all classes of society. In North America, Protestantism has traditionally been linked primarily to the middle class. Howard Snyder seems justified, then, in giving special attention to "the gospel to the poor" in his book *The Problem of Wine Skins*. He is probably correct in saying that "renewal in the church has usually meant the church's rebirth among the poor, the masses, the alienated."[23] The masses must be reached and won if the churches are to experience unusual growth.

Formation of a Master Plan

There are a number of basic considerations to be kept in mind as we prepare a strategy for entering a target area with a view to making contacts for Christ.

1. The whole church-extension enterprise must be bathed in prayer as we enter a new area. It is not to be forgotten that whenever we enter a churchless community we are, in a real sense, walking on Satan's ground. Therefore, the Christian workers involved, any believers in the community, the public officials, the general populace—all must become the subjects of special prayer.

2. A basic analysis of the target area and peoples must be carried out. We must know, for example, which classes are represented, their characteristics and distinctives. Ideally, the implications of these findings will have been taken into account in the selection of our target area. In-

22. Joe Bayly, *The Gospel Blimp* (Grand Rapids: Zondervan, 1960).
23. Howard A. Snyder, *The Problem of Wine Skins: Church Structure in a Technological Age* (Downers Grove, Ill.: InterVarsity, 1975), 51.

formation that might have been overlooked previously must be taken into consideration at the contact stage.

3. We will select our evangelistic team on the bases of their essential qualifications and their ability to relate to the target peoples. They must not be chosen simply on the basis of availability.

4. We will take cultural differences into account while working on our plan for making contacts in the target community. The cultural context may compel us to modify our ideas or even abandon and replace them with culturally appropriate ones.

5. We will keep reviewing and updating the information we have garnered, realizing that it may be incomplete or even incorrect, and remembering that careful discipline will be required if we are to avoid slipping back into old, familiar patterns and routines. With these basic considerations attended to, we can proceed with a master plan for entering the target community.

Preevangelistic Courtesy Contacts

Review the section in this chapter on courtesy contacts. With that as background, two basic questions must be answered in forming the master plan: (1) What people in the community should be contacted in order to conform to societal expectations? and (2) What additional courtesy calls can be made with a view to making the proper contacts in the target area? To produce a list of potential contacts it will be helpful to answer a few more-detailed questions:

1. What do the people in the target culture expect newcomers in the community to do?
2. Who are the people in the various social segments of the target area whose understanding and goodwill would be of special importance?
   a. Governmental community
   b. Business community
   c. Educational community
   d. Religious community
   e. Others
3. Are there any persons in this society who would especially benefit (in money, prestige, etc.) by association with the missionary-evangelists and whose influence (at least in the initial stages of the work) might therefore prove detrimental?
4. Besides understanding and goodwill, what do we desire from the various persons upon whom we will call (for example, introductions to still other people, information on community life and needs, the opening of doors for ministry)?

Figure 22
Suggested Letter to Pastors of Churches
in the Target Area

Dear Pastor_____,

Please allow me to introduce myself. I am (missionary's name) representing (name of the church organization). In the near future, representatives of our church will be contacting people in this community with a view to establishing a local church of our denomination. In the process of conducting a community-wide survey it is likely that some members of your congregation will be contacted. Be assured that it is not our objective to influence members of other churches to leave their respective churches. Rather, we desire to discover what the needs of the community are and to minister to those needs.

If you have any questions about our church and its place in the community, please feel free to contact me. Our aim is to become better acquainted with you and the members of the larger community, and to be good representatives of our Lord and Savior, Jesus Christ.

Sincerely yours,

Under some circumstances members of the religious community may merit special consideration. It may be wise to send a letter or, better yet, call on the pastors (and priests) of churches in the target area. (For a sample letter see figure 22.)

Preevangelistic Community Contacts

A primary type of preevangelistic community contact is through normal everyday interaction with individuals in society. People we frequently encounter in daily life have potential as evangelistic contacts in the community.

Another way of establishing preevangelistic contact is to join civic organizations or special-interest groups in the target area that aim at community improvement or individual growth and furnish opportunities for future evangelistic contacts. We should also consider whether there are any important services or ministries that need to be performed in the community and that require the organization of a new group.

Taking an area survey is another means of making contact. It should be carefully planned, and the participating personnel should be carefully selected, instructed, and prepared. A survey should not be used as

Figure 23
Suggested Interview in an Area Survey

*

To be filled out in the presence of the respondent:

Name of Respondent _____

Address _____

Telephone _____

Members of household:

Husband _____ Wife _____

Children _____ Sex ___ Age ___ School _____

_____ Sex ___ Age ___ School _____

_____ Sex ___ Age ___ School _____

Occupation of husband and/or wife _____

Length of residence in the area _____

Religious affiliation (if any) _____ Active? _____

**

How could our kind of church serve your family? _____
_____

Do you desire a visit from the missionary/pastor? _____

Do you need a Bible? _____ Christian literature on any subject?
_____

May we send you information concerning our church periodically? _____

Do you have any friends or relatives who might have a special interest in a church such as ours? _____

***

Notes:

*Church representative introduces self and explains the reason for the survey.
**The representative introduces the church and its beliefs, objectives, and program, being sensitive to the interests and needs of the respondent.
***The representative leaves printed information concerning the church, including an invitation and the name of someone who can be contacted in case of a question or need (as appropriate).

To be filled out by the representative after the interview:

What degree of interest was evidenced by the householder? _____
_____

Any item of special interest or concern? _____

Any recommendations? _____

Figure 24
A Checklist of Available Media

MEDIA	COST	AUDIENCE	RESPONSE
1. Radio or Television			
a. Spot announcement			
b. Identification with existing programing			
c. New program			
d. New coverage			
2. Newspaper			
a. Advertisement			
b. Inserts			
c. News coverage			
3. Public signs			
a. Church signs			
b. Gospel signs			
c. Billboard advertising			
4. Telephone			
a. Directory advertisement			
b. Telephone survey			
c. "Dial-a-Message"			
5. Other			

At the contact stage it is usually sufficient to note the cost per potential individual or household contact, the composition of the audience (age, education, class, etc.), and the actual response received.

a pretense to gain admittance to a household. It should represent an honest attempt to gather information and should be carried out in conjunction with definite plans to utilize that information in a ministry to the community. Anything less than this is unworthy of the kingdom (see figure 23).

Finally, we can make use of the media in the community. Of course the availability and effectiveness of media for making contacts will vary greatly with the area of the world and the characteristics of the local

Figure 25
Questionnaire: Prospective Contacts

We would greatly appreciate your assistance in our evangelistic church-planting endeavor here in _____. After prayerful consideration, please fill in the following information concerning any person who you feel would be a likely prospect for contact by representatives of our church.

(Please fill in a separate form for every such prospect.) Thank you.

Name _____

Address _____

Relationship (to the undersigned): Friend _____ Kin _____

    If kindred, specific relationship _____

Other members of household _____

Spiritual condition (as far as you know):

        Unbeliever and unchurched _____

        Unbeliever and churched   _____

        Believer and unchurched   _____

        Believer and churched   _____

Information important in making contact with the prospect (who should contact; when contact should be made; cautions in making contact, etc.):

_____

_____

_____

Are you in communication with this person? _____

        Your name _____

        Date _____

community involved. That being the case, it is wise to study the various possibilities and their potential, and then settle on those media that seem to hold the greatest promise given the situation. (Media should be used in ways that complement personal contacts. Careful records should be kept so that proper follow-up is possible.) (See figure 24.)

Selective Evangelistic Contacts

From the very outset of a new work, wise stewards of the gospel will want to direct a special witness to individuals and groups who may be unusually receptive and who will be bridges to still other people in the target community. At first, efforts to identify and reach those people who might serve as bridges will be the responsibility of the individual or team that is pioneering the new work. Wise use of the data gathered through community surveys and other means will serve to augment and correct initial information.

In identifying responsive and potentially responsive people, effective church-planters will solicit a continuous inflow of information in addition to the survey already suggested.

1. The preliminary and community surveys should be analyzed with a view to identifying responsive individuals, families, and segments of the community.

2. Some denominations and fellowships of churches provide missionaries and pastors in an unchurched area with the names and addresses of newcomers who have in the past been associated with member churches in other areas. Denominations which do not provide this service are shortsighted, and missionary-evangelists who do not take advantage of such a service are even more so.

3. Obviously, a primary method will be to ask believers who live in the target community if they have any relatives or friends in the area who might be interested. This will tend to be a haphazard investigation unless some specific instrument is developed. Figure 25 gives an example of a simple questionnaire to be filled out by believers (and persons who become believers) who reside in the target community.

4. As soon as meetings for the general public are scheduled (whether for Bible study, evangelism, worship, or whatever), missionary-evangelists should make sure that a record of attendees is kept. People who evidence enough interest in the gospel and the new church to attend such meetings should have priority in the program of evangelistic follow-up. Such people should be contacted in their homes within a few days of their visit (see figure 26).

Figure 26
Registration Card for Visitors

We welcome you to the _____Church today. We are grateful for your presence and want to do everything possible to make you feel at home in our church. We also want to serve you and your family in any way we can. In order to make this possible, would you be so kind as to supply us with the following information and place this card in the offering plate as it is passed?

Thank you very much.

Name_____

Address_____

Telephone_____

Home church (if any)_____

Location_____

How did you become acquainted with our church?

_____Family member   (Name: _____)

_____Church friend   (Name: _____)

_____ Advertisement   (_____)

_____Other   (_____)

How can we serve you or your family?

_____ Information concerning the biblical teaching on salvation

_____ Information concerning the biblical teaching on the Christian life

_____ Information concerning the program of the church

_____Information concerning church membership

_____ Other

Widespread Evangelistic Contact

Ultimately, faithful Christian workers in church-planting evangelism will want to contact just as many citizens of the target community as possible with the message of Christ. The timing and type(s) of such large endeavors will be matters for prayer and determination in each locality. Plans (at least tentative ones) should be made at the initial contact stage. For example, the involvement of future believers in a program of visitation evangelism, the utilization of mass media in gospel outreach, and the scheduling of special evangelistic campaigns should be considered very early in the planning process.

In this chapter we have addressed ourselves to another of the great challenges confronting Christian churches. Peter says Christians constitute a holy nation. Paul likens Christian workers to soldiers. But all too often the nation is too holy to contact the world. All too often the soldiers train and periodically go on parade but never really engage the enemy. Meanwhile, non-Christian and sub-Christian sects are out in the front lines in hand-to-hand combat. Or, to come back to the terminology of this chapter, they are making vital contacts. Think! Who rings our doorbells to invite us into their faith? Who sells the religious magazines in our cities? Who engages us in the airports?

We conclude with three very simple but crucial admonitions.

1. Make contacts—consider the possibilities, devise the means, motivate others—and follow through by making those contacts.

2. Keep meaningful records. Whether contacts are made by a church-planting individual or team, keep records. Adequate records will indicate who made the contact, identify and locate the contacts, note their relationship with believers, and otherwise serve the follow-up process.

3. Ask the question, "Why will people come here?" Among the forty-four questions Lyle Schaller directs to church planters, this one is perhaps the most elusive and subjective. It is also one of the most urgent.[24] It must be asked and answered from the perspective of the contacts. The church planters know why they should come, but why would the contacts think they should come? It is up to us to pray, plan, preach, and program in ways that enable them to answer that question.

---

24. Lyle E. Schaller, *44 Questions for Church Planters* (Nashville: Abingdon, 1991), 84.

The Gospel Communicated   10

Probably no subject has been the focus of more attention, discussion, and inquiry in the evangelical wing of the church in recent days than has the subject of evangelism. Rightly so. The Good News must be proclaimed. Need any more be said here? We think so. Here is the place for the missionary-evangelist to ask, first, "What more can be learned about effective communication of the gospel?" and, second, "What can we do to communicate the gospel effectively in the target area?"

Objectives

The ultimate objective in evangelistic communication is clear and persuasive presentation of the gospel to every person we can possibly reach within the area of our responsibility—to those whose hearts have been specially prepared by the Holy Spirit, to those to whom there are inbuilt channels of communication, but also, to all who will hear us. We want them to respond with repentance of sin, faith in Christ, and commitment to his cause.

Although our ultimate objective is clear and persuasive presentation of the gospel to all the unsaved in the target area, the practical problems that stand between us and the achievement of that objective often may be great. That being the case, it is better to draw up a short list of more humble and immediate objectives:

1. To mobilize as many believers as may be available and can be effectively deployed in evangelizing the target area
2. To relate the Good News of Christ to the audience(s) in a way that will be clear, convincing, and compelling
3. To employ the most appropriate methods of evangelism
4. To utilize the potential of various communication media within the target area
5. To reach the unevangelized in the target area in the order set during the contact phase of the Pauline Cycle

142

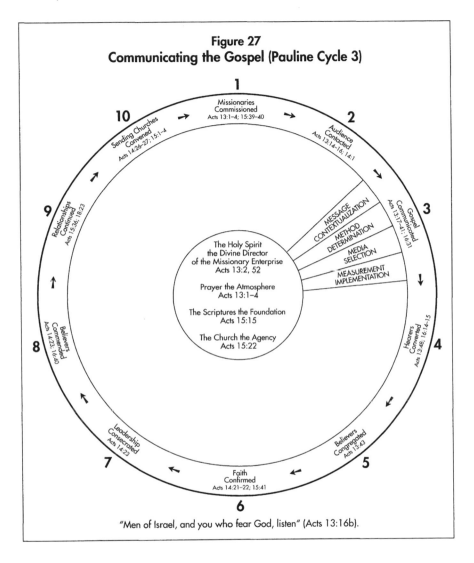

Figure 27
Communicating the Gospel (Pauline Cycle 3)

1
Missionaries
Commissioned
Acts 13:1–4; 15:39–40

10
Sending Churches
Convened
Acts 14:26–27; 15:1–4

2
Audience
Contacted
Acts 13:14–16; 14:1

9
Relationships
Continued
Acts 15:36; 18:23

MESSAGE
CONTEXTUALIZATION
METHOD
DETERMINATION
MEDIA
SELECTION
MEASUREMENT
IMPLEMENTATION

3
Gospel
Communicated
Acts 13:17–41; 16:31

The Holy Spirit
the Divine Director
of the Missionary Enterprise
Acts 13:2, 52

Prayer the Atmosphere
Acts 13:1–4

The Scriptures the Foundation
Acts 15:15

The Church the Agency
Acts 15:22

8
Believers
Commended
Acts 14:23; 16:40

4
Hearers
Converted
Acts 13:48; 16:14–15

7
Leadership
Consecrated
Acts 14:23

5
Believers
Congregated
Acts 13:43

6
Faith
Confirmed
Acts 14:21–22; 15:41

"Men of Israel, and you who fear God, listen" (Acts 13:16b).

The biblical message is normative for all people in all places. Some naively believe that nothing more need be said. Perhaps nothing more would be required if God had decided upon some vehicle other than words, and some agents other than humans, to communicate his message. But such is not the case. So gospel communication—perhaps above all other steps in the Pauline Cycle—will require thoughtful investigation and planning.

Preliminary Consideration: The Basic Content of the Gospel

Biblical Principles and Precedents

New Testament evangelism was full-orbed. It reflected the emphasis of the Great Commission: "Teaching them to observe all that I commanded you" (Matt. 28:20). According to Mark, there is indeed a "beginning of the gospel of Jesus Christ, the Son of God" (Mark 1:1). But Mark immediately refers his readers to Old Testament prophecies concerning Christ's coming (Mark 1:2–3). That is part of the gospel. There is good news in the Old Testament as well as in the New Testament. The good news of Jesus Christ is found in both Testaments! The prophecy and the fulfilment are not to be divorced from one another. According to the record, Jesus' contemporaries—believers and unbelievers alike—did not really understand his claims and cross because they did not know the Scriptures. So Jesus commanded his contemporaries to "search the Scriptures" precisely because they testify of him (John 5:39).

Evangelism must be based on biblical theology rather than our systematic theology. Why? Because, as the New Testament scholar D. A. Carson points out, even in the United States one cannot be at all sure that "God loves you and has a wonderful plan for your life" will be understood in terms of biblical meanings. Which God, after all, are we talking about? The God of the Bible or the god of Shirley MacLaine? And as for the "wonderful plan," what exactly is it? Does it mean that we will be healthy? wealthy? have great sex and perfect children? Carson goes on to find deficient even the much more elaborate, but still systematic theology–based approach of John Frame:

> In short, the good news of Jesus Christ is virtually incoherent unless it is securely set into a biblical worldview. . . . I have no fundamental objection [to Frame's approach]. However, to establish such a framework while simultaneously tracing out the rudiments of the Bible's plot-line strikes me as wiser, more strategic. One is simultaneously setting forth a structure of thought, and a meta-narrative; one is constructing a worldview, and showing how that worldview is grounded in the Bible itself. One is teaching people how to read the Bible. *For these reasons, evangelism might wisely become, increasingly, a subset of biblical theology.* [italics added][1]

Not only is Carson's point well taken, it is shared by an increasing number of theologians, missiologists, evangelists, and missionaries.[2]

---

1. D. A. Carson, *The Gagging of God* (Grand Rapids: Zondervan, 1996), 502.
2. See David J. Hesselgrave, *Scripture and Strategy: The Use of the Bible in Postmodern Church and Mission* (Pasadena: William Carey Library, 1994).

Of course at the stage of evangelism the plot line or larger story of Scripture cannot be communicated in detail. Of necessity there will be certain gaps. But there will also be significant gains because the meta-narrative of Scripture is essential in its own right and can be further elaborated and explained over time.

Relevant Research

Two aspects of contemporary inquiries and research are especially pertinent here. One has to do with semantics, with words and meanings. The other has to do with worldview, with the way that people view themselves and the world around them.

As we learn from semanticists, communication of meaning is not a simple process. Research indicates that communication is only about 80 percent effective in the most ideal circumstances.[3] What is communicated is not necessarily what the speaker says. What is communicated is what the audience hears. Hearers (and readers) will put their own meanings into our words!

As we learn from anthropologists, at the core of any culture is its worldview. We can define worldview as the way people see themselves and the world, and as their basic ideology or belief system. For practical purposes it can be analyzed in terms of basic beliefs about supernature (God and the spirit world), nature (the cosmos and the world around us), humans (their nature and destiny), and time (past, present, and future).[4]

Christian anthropologist G. Linwood Barney thinks of culture as being something like an onion. At the core is worldview. Growing around and out of worldview comes a layer of values—the value system of the culture. Then comes the institutional layer—education, law, marriage, and so forth. Finally, there is the outer layer comprising material artifacts and observable behavior. Barney draws our attention to the need for communicating the gospel in such a way as to effect a change in worldview, not just a change in some behavioral patterns, religious affiliation, or even in some values. To be Christian is to have a biblical view of God, the world, oneself, and others—a biblical understanding of the plan and purpose of God in the world and in history.[5]

---

3. Martin Joos, "Semiology: A Linguistic Theory of Meaning," *Studies in Linguistics* 13 (1958): 53–72.

4. For an elaboration of the meaning and importance of worldview see David J. Hesselgrave, *Communicating Christ Cross-Culturally: An Introduction to Missionary Communication*, 2d ed. (Grand Rapids: Zondervan, 1991), 193–285.

5. G. Linwood Barney, "The Supracultural and the Cultural: Implications for Frontier Missions," in R. Pierce Beaver, ed., *The Gospel and Frontier Peoples: A Report of a Consultation, December 1972* (Pasadena: William Carey Library, 1976), 48–57.

So once again we are brought back to the Scriptures, to both Old and New Testaments, to biblical theology, to the larger story. Why? Because a worldview is not formed by adding up a number of facts, even though those facts may be true. A worldview is formed by hearing and learning a big story with a beginning, a middle, and an end. A Christian worldview is formed by hearing and learning the big story of Scripture and seeing how all the little stories, whether of the men and women of the Bible or of ourselves and our neighbors, fit into that big story.

Practical Reflection

Whether home or abroad, church planters will need to rethink some common evangelistic approaches. One area that needs reflection is our love for the word "gospel," and our disaffection for words such as "teaching," "doctrine," and "theology." Let us remember that according to our Lord teaching is the means whereby disciples are made (Matt. 28:19–20)! And according to Paul the inspired Scriptures are profitable for teaching and much more (2 Tim. 3:16).

Also in need of rethinking is the practice of reducing the gospel to topics such as God, sin, and salvation, or to paradigms such as the "Four Spiritual Laws" and "Six Things God Wants You to Know." While they have their place, they hardly qualify as teaching "all that [Christ] commanded." They are, in fact, overly simplified forms of systematic theology. Moreover, as conservative theologians like B. B. Warfield have always made clear, valid systematic theology is built-up biblical theology. And biblical theology is not just theology that is biblical, but theology that gives priority to Scripture itself as progressive revelation—to its authority, unity, narrative, chronology, and teachings.

Finally, we need to remember that the words most intimately related to the gospel of Jesus Christ ("God," "Christ," "sin," "cross," "blood," "redemption," "salvation," and "eternal life"—to say nothing of "atonement" and "propitiation"!) communicate little or nothing of the gospel to an ever increasing percentage of the world's population. Biblical meanings must be put into these words, or other words must be used! Otherwise true communication will not occur.

Preliminary Consideration: Elenctics

Biblical Principles and Precedents

For some strange reason the subject of elenctics is neglected in contemporary theological studies, although some aspects of it are dealt with in the study of apologetics. The word comes from the Greek word *elenchein*, which originally meant "to bring to a sense of shame," but later came to mean "to bring to a sense of guilt." The latter meaning is found in the New Testament. For example, in promising the Holy Spirit, our Lord said, "And He, when He comes, will convict [*elenxei*] the world concerning sin, and righteousness, and judgment" (John 16:8). This verse raises a basic question regarding evangelistic communication. That the Holy Spirit is the subject in John 16:8 is without doubt. Only he can convince the world of sin, righteousness, and judgment. And therein lies our problem. What role, then, do Christian communicators play? What about their strategies? In short, what implications does elenctics hold for evangelism?

While the answer to this problem is far too complex to probe in depth here, there are some facts that require emphasis. First, note that the areas of conviction are given in John 16:8. The Holy Spirit convicts of sin, righteousness, and judgment. It is as if our Lord is saying to the evangelist, "Preach along these lines because the Holy Spirit will deal with your audience in these three areas."

Second, sin, righteousness, and judgment are defined. There can be little doubt as to the meaning of these words in the context. The "sin" our Lord is talking about is the sin of not believing on the Lord Jesus Christ (v. 9). "Righteousness" is the sufficient righteousness of the Lord—the righteousness with which the Father was well pleased and which Christ alone can give to us (v. 10). "Judgment" is that of Satan, the head of the world system under whose authority every human being is born and from whom Christ saves (v. 11).

We conclude that only the Holy Spirit can bring the sinner to the place of repentance and faith; that human instruments are, nevertheless, used of the Holy Spirit (2 Cor. 5:11); that the great themes to be specially emphasized are sin, righteousness, and judgment; and that this Good News of God's provision for sinners is to flow out of, and lead into, the whole counsel of God.

Relevant Research

Classical rhetoricians maintained that there are three kinds of communication. Some modern theorists have added other types, but all communication can basically be reduced to three or perhaps four types and purposes:

1. Entertaining communication
2. Instructive communication
3. Persuasive communication
4. Expressive communication

The first three are self-explanatory. Expressive communication is communication which is primarily designed to meet the psychological needs of the source rather than to accomplish something for the recipients.

Most of the new rhetoricians maintain that pure instances of the four types of communication are impossible to achieve. For example, they would argue that it is impossible to instruct without persuading. They insist that all communication is in some sense persuasive. Even the common greeting "How are you?" they say, is not motivated so much by the desire to gain information as by the desire to communicate the idea that the speaker is a tolerably cordial and jolly fellow. When it comes right down to it, even from a secular point of view, persuasion does seem to be the name of the game.

Practical Reflection

As we review our past record in evangelism, and what we learn from revelation and research, some soul searching is in order in at least two areas:

1. Could it be true that, as Eugene Nida contends, a considerable proportion of Christian preaching is expressive, designed to fulfil the need of preachers to erase their own guilt, achieve a sense of self-worth, perform their duty, or increase their prestige?[6] Gospel communicators should practice introspection periodically. God tries the hearts of his servants (2 Cor. 5:11).

2. Do we sometimes tend to manipulate the audience rather than persuade them in the power of the Spirit? It would almost seem so. Some approaches in personal and mass evangelism seem perilously similar to the selling techniques elucidated in manuals for salespersons; they seem to be designed to get people to accept Christ before they realize what has happened. This analysis may seem unfair, and it may be untrue. But it is worth pondering.

The Christian faith is a reasonable faith though it is not the product of human reason. There are compelling reasons for becoming a believing member of the body of Christ. Let these reasons be articulated fervently and forcefully, but always humbly in the realization that we stand on holy ground where divine fire will reveal the deepest motives of speaker and hearer alike.

---

6. Eugene A. Nida, *Message and Mission: The Communication of the Christian Faith* (New York: Harper and Row, 1960), 4.

The Contextualization of the Gospel

Biblical Principles and Precedents

Obviously, the whole of God's revelation to humans, whether general (nature) or special (Christ and the Scriptures), cannot be delivered on any one occasion. Some parts must be selected, others omitted. However, we should not jump to a conclusion at this point. Jesus and the apostles did not always and everywhere communicate what we might think of as the heart of the gospel, even though Jesus did so in the case of Nicodemus. Nor did they always take note of the special interest and concerns of their audience and begin at that point, even though Jesus did so in the case of the Samaritan woman. What they seem to have done in most cases was to take note of the level of understanding possessed by their audience and start communication at that point. Moreover, and especially after Christ's resurrection, they most often related part of the big story of God's dealings with humankind as it is revealed in Scripture and culminates in Christ.

1. On the Day of Pentecost, Peter spoke to those who had gathered at Jerusalem for this special Jewish celebration. His design was to persuade them that the Holy Spirit had been given in accordance with the prophecy of Joel and that Christ was both crucified and raised from the dead in accordance with the plan of God and the testimony of David (Acts 2:14–36).

2. Stephen's apology before the Sanhedrin began with the calling of Abraham and ended with an indictment of the "betrayers and murderers" of the Righteous One, the Lord Jesus (Acts 7:2–53). The apology was an altogether remarkable rehearsal of God's dealings with his people throughout Old Testament times.

3. Philip had played a leading role in spiritual awakenings in Judea and Samaria. Then the Holy Spirit orchestrated a meeting with an Ethiopian official who was riding along a desert road south of Jerusalem. Spiritually the official was headed in the wrong direction, but he was reading just the right passage in the right book—Isaiah 53! Beginning from this Scripture, Philip preached Jesus with the result that the Ethiopian believed and was baptized (Acts 8:26–38).

4. Evidently Paul took a big-story approach when communicating the gospel to Jews and God-fearing Gentiles in the synagogues of Damascus (Acts 9:20–22), Pisidian Antioch (Acts 13:16–41), and Thessalonica (Acts 17:2–3). This is made crystal clear in the extended summary of his message at Pisidian Antioch.

5. It is instructive to compare Paul's approach to Jews and God-fearers with his approach among the polytheists of Lystra (Acts 14:15–

17) and the pantheistically inclined philosophers of Athens (Acts 17:22–31). The message at Lystra was undoubtedly an abbreviated one, but Paul had enough time to contrast the idol gods of Lystra with the Creator God, to overview the history of God's dealings with the world's peoples, and to make it clear that the apostles were but ordinary men with an extraordinary message. With more time at his disposal on the Areopagus, Paul painstakingly began by quoting a Greek poet, proceeded to speak of the nature and workings of the Creator God and the resurrection of Christ, and concluded with a call for repentance and faith.

It would be instructive at this point to examine those passages in the Epistles where the apostles speak most pointedly of their message and its delivery. Especially illuminating are those passages in which Paul affirms the authority of his message, summarizes its essential features, and explains how, as a gospel communicator, he became like a law-abiding Jew, a law-less Gentile, a weak individual, or whatever—all in order to win people to Christ (see 1 Cor. 9:23). Even apart from that more thoroughgoing examination, however, our cursory review of specific cases of gospel communication in Acts reveals at least four distinctive features:

1. Gospel communication was set in the context of the nature of God and the history of God's dealings with humankind.
2. When the audience had knowledge of Scripture, special revelation provided the context for Paul's proclamation of Christ. When they were without Scripture, general revelation provided the context for the message about Christ and his work.
3. Further adaptations allowed the gospel proclaimer to better communicate with his audience.
4. The divine insistence upon repentance and faith was part and parcel of gospel communication.

Relevant Research

Reflecting their situation, ancient Greek rhetoricians tended to analyze communication in terms of speaker, speech, and audience. They were sensitive to the importance of the context in which communication occurred, but it remained for modern scholars with experience in a wide variety of cultural settings to give context the attention it deserves. In the forefront of research and writing on the interanimation between cultural context and communication, students of mission concentrated primarily on ways in which gospel communication is affected by cultural differences and on means of enhancing understanding between cultures. Then, in the 1970s, they coined the word "contextualization."

As proposed by its initiators, contextualization had to do with encouraging Christian theologians and communicators (especially foreign nationals) to allow a much larger place for cultural traditions in the determination of even the content of the gospel. Evangelicals took exception and tended to redefine contextualization in terms of making the biblical gospel more understandable, meaningful, relevant, and effective in the various cultural contexts.

It goes beyond our present purpose to sort out the many and varied issues that have attended discussions on contextualization in recent years. But in our multicultural and fast-changing world it should now be clear to Christian communicators that it will not do simply to turn up the volume or enlarge the print. The old gospel must be communicated, but it must be communicated in new ways that engage the attention, employ the thought forms, enhance the understanding, and merit the consideration of people enculturated in systems very different from our own.[7]

Practical Reflection

Christian missionaries have always given attention to the need for adaptation to the language and cultural orientation of the people to whom they are sent. In a world of ever increasing intercultural contact—especially since the inauguration of discussions on contextualization—this need has become more and more apparent not only to missionaries but to all Christian communicators. Don Richardson's thrilling account of the way in which he employed the West Irian ritual of the Peace Child to communicate Christ has inspired many a missionary to search out similar redemptive analogies within the culture of their target people.[8] Alan Roxburgh urges evangelists and pastors at home to consider the worldview shift that is taking place in Western cultures and to undertake a thoroughgoing contextualization of the Christian message by discovering themes of interest in their target communities and addressing people in those terms.[9] The themes he suggests in his book have to do with ecology ("mind and nature on a new frontier"), community ("making the world whole again"), and the new spirituality ("the quest for transcendence").

No doubt about it, the books of Roxburgh and Richardson speak volumes to evangelists and church-planting missionaries wherever they

7. For an extensive treatment of contextualization issues see David J. Hesselgrave and Edward Rommen, *Contextualization: Meanings, Methods, and Models* (Pasadena: William Carey Library, 1998).

8. Don Richardson, *Peace Child* (Glendale, Calif.: Regal, 1974).

9. Alan J. Roxburgh, *Reaching a New Generation: Strategies for Tomorrow's Church* (Downers Grove, Ill.: InterVarsity, 1993), 31.

might be! Roxburgh is right when he insists that evangelists need to change their approach as surrounding culture changes. He is also right when he suggests that it would be advantageous to dialogue on themes suggested by cultural interests. Richardson is right in realizing that a standardized approach exported from North America will not communicate to pagan Sawis. He is also right when he draws attention to the value of redemptive analogies as entering wedges and eye openers to the gospel.

Nevertheless, in both cases a caveat is in order. More must be said. Perhaps the eye-opener idea is the key to understanding both the strengths and weaknesses of the various contextualization strategies. Roxburgh's use of themes and Richardson's use of analogy are effective ways of winning a hearing and gaining entrance for the gospel. But in the final analysis God has already set the agenda, chosen the themes, and provided the analogies that must be heard, understood, and embraced if sinners are to repent and believe, and saints are to mature and serve. He has done so in his Word, the Bible. And so we are brought back to the importance of biblical theology and of "teaching them to observe all that [Christ] commanded."

ME-1 illustration: A number of years ago Harry Wendt journeyed from his native Australia to the United States in order to study theology. Being Lutheran, Wendt became acquainted with a number of Lutheran congregations during the course of his studies. Challenged by the lack of overall Bible knowledge even among older Christians, upon his graduation Wendt set about the task of developing an illustrated Bible study on the larger plan of God in the Old and New Testaments. Ultimately, that course of study was developed at three different levels in a series of books (including *The Divine Drama* and *See through the Scriptures*). Wendt's seminars and materials continue to be offered across North America and worldwide.[10] In fact, though originally developed for Christians in North America, Wendt's approach and materials are being adopted by various Third World schools and missions for use in evangelizing and church planting overseas!

ME-3 illustration: Another Australian, Trevor McIlwain, went to the Palawano people of the Philippines with New Tribes Mission in the 1960s. There had been something of a people movement to Christ among the Palawanos after World War II. Numerous Palawanos had converted to Christ, and a number of churches had been planted. Over the years, however, it became apparent that, in spite of the sincerity of the believers, neither they nor their churches were growing spiritually.

---

10. Harry Wendt, *The Divine Drama: A Study of the Christian Faith in Word and Diagram* (Minneapolis: Crossways International, 1983).

Christians would fall back into the old ways, experience revival and re-newal, and, after a time, fall into the old ways again.

This cycle kept repeating itself in spite of the prayers and efforts of the missionaries. McIlwain himself met with discouragement until he realized that the Palawanos' understanding of Scripture was distorted because it was based on piecemeal instruction. In short, they had never developed a truly Christian worldview. It was then that McIlwain began teaching chronologically, starting with the Old Testament and going right through the Bible. The results were so amazing that New Tribes Mission charged McIlwain with the responsibility of putting his studies in a form that has now become the basic pattern for New Tribes church-planting strategy worldwide.[11] Unlike Wendt's approach, which was developed in North America for Westerners and is now being used in missions, McIlwain's approach was developed on the mission field and is now widely used among churches in North America! Perhaps all of this has come about because both employ the ap-proach God himself utilized in inspiring the Scriptures and ordering their use![12]

The Varied Methods of Gospel Communication

Biblical Principles and Precedents

In the New Testament the gospel message is given in a variety of ways:[13]

1. Privately to individuals (John 3; 4; Acts 8) and to family or household groups (Acts 10; 16; 20:20); publicly to gathered groups (Acts 13:14–41; 19:8–9) and to crowds in public places (Acts 17:17, 22–33)
2. By means of preaching (Acts 2:14–40), teaching (Acts 10:34–43), and witnessing (Acts 26:1–23)
3. Sometimes in the form of a monologue (Acts 2:14–36), but often in the form of a dialogue (Acts 17:16–17)
4. In a manner that sometimes entailed simple proclamation and exhortation (Acts 13:14–41), but often was apologetical and po-lemical (disputational) (Acts 17:16–31; 19:8–9)

11. McIlwain's Building on Firm Foundations series and a variety of related materials are available from New Tribes Mission, 1000 East First Street, Sanford, Fla. 32771-1487.

12. See Hesselgrave, *Scripture and Strategy*, esp. chs. 3, 6, and 7.

13. For an informative statement on the diversity and depth of the evangelistic ap-proach of the early church, see Michael Green, *Evangelism in the Early Church* (Grand Rapids: Eerdmans, 1970), 160.

Figure 28
The Comparative Advantages and Limitations
of Interpersonal versus Mass Communication

	Interpersonal Communication	Mass Communication
Reaching a Large Audience		
Speed	Slow	Fast
Cost per individual reached	High	Low
Influence on the Individual		
Ability to attract attention	High	Low
Accuracy of message communicated	Low	High
Probability of selective screening	Relatively Low	High
Clarity of content	High	Moderate to Low
Feedback		
Direction of communication	Two-way	One-way
Speed of feedback	High	Low
Accuracy of feedback	High	Low

From James F. Engel, Hugh G. Wales, and Martin R. Warshaw, *Promotional Strategy,* rev. ed. (Homewood, Ill.: Richard D. Irwin, 1971), 27. Copyright by Richard D. Irwin, Inc. Used by permission.

Note that all of these methods involve interpersonal (face-to-face) communication. Our Lord and the apostles did not have recourse to the vast resources of communications media that we have today. However, the relative lack of mass media in Bible times had its advantage because, in some ways, interpersonal communication is superior to mass-media communication.

Notice also that New Testament methods of communication seem to have allowed for a significant degree of interaction between the speakers and their audience. Over and over again we read that the listeners asked questions, raised objections, or verbally reinforced the message. This is to say that much of New Testament gospel communication was dialogical even though that precise word may not be used. The word *dialegomai,* which literally means to "discuss" or "conduct a discussion," was used "of lectures which were likely to end in disputation" (e.g., Acts 17:2, 17; 18:4, 19; 19:9; 20:7, 9; and 24:12).[14] There is little

14. Gottlob Schrenk, διαλέγομαι, in *Theological Dictionary of the New Testament,* ed. Gerhard Kittel and Gerhard Friedrich, trans. Geoffrey W. Bromiley, 10 vols. (Grand Rapids: Eerdmans, 1964–76), 2:94.

room to question that the gospel communication of the Apostolic Age was characterized by much more personal interaction than is generally the case today.

Relevant Research

1. Reason and research indicate that, as compared to mass communication, interpersonal communication has some very real advantages as well as limitations (see figure 28).

2. Research carried on by psychologists Albert Dabba and James Dabba Jr. at the University of Michigan yielded some rather surprising results. In an experiment designed to test the extent to which a speaker's distance from the listener affects the ability to persuade, speakers and listeners were observed at a variety of distances from each other: one or two feet, five or six feet, and about fifteen feet. The Dabbas hypothesized that the speakers would be most persuasive at the middle distance because they would not be invading the personal space of the listeners and thus causing discomfort on the one hand, or losing the listeners' attention because of being placed too far apart on the other. To the experimenters' surprise, the speakers proved to be most persuasive at the greatest distance.[15]

It may not be too far-fetched to say that this experiment gives some support to the biblical practice of preaching to an audience with a view to their conversion. From the word "preach" we cannot infer that it is necessary that there be a distance between speaker and audience. But in a day when preaching—and perhaps evangelistic preaching especially—is under attack in some quarters, it is well to remind ourselves that much of the preaching in Bible times (as today) of necessity involved an appropriate spacing between the preacher and his audience. There is a time for the more personalized witnessing, counseling, and small-group teaching with which we are so familiar today. But there is also a time for the more public proclamation of the Word of God.

3. The limitations of preaching of the more formal, one-way kind are indicated by research such as was carried on by Kurt Lewin. In an assignment which has received considerable attention since it was carried out, Lewin was asked to assist the Red Cross during World War II in an effort to overcome negative attitudes toward eating animal hearts and other internal organs. When lectures on the subject produced no significant effect, he substituted group discussions, with the result that 32 percent of the participants responded favorably.[16]

---

15. "Behavior," *Time*, 7 September 1970, p. 27.
16. Kurt Lewin, "Group Decision and Social Change," in *Readings in Social Psychology*, ed. Theodore M. Newcomb and Eugene L. Hartley (New York: Henry Holt, 1947), 330–44.

Practical Reflection

Innovation is needed in communicating the gospel today, but of first priority (methodologically) is the need to get back to basic New Testament evangelistic methods. If our abilities to innovate are not exhausted in exploiting the potential of biblical models, we can go on to attempt new methods for communicating Christ. But why not give special consideration to didactic, apologetic, and visitation methods (which are quite often overlooked today), especially in the dialogical pattern? Experience seems to indicate that they are still effective.

ME-3 illustration: An arresting example of sound strategy that actually combines a number of principles (didactic evangelism, extended-family evangelism in a lineage society, group communication, the use of a team) comes from the Sevav area of Nigeria and the evangelistic outreach of the Fellowship of the Churches of Christ in the Sudan. Missionaries Eugene Rubingh and Ralph Baker took note of the fact that not one person from that area had been baptized into the Tiv (tribe) church in thirteen years. A special strategy was devised:

1. In the social structure of the Tiv the smallest unit or segment is called the "ipaven u ken iyou." This normally consists of from nine to twelve extended-family compounds. The segment head lives in the central compound. Mr. Rubingh determined as a pilot project to evangelize one segment.
2. This plan was explained to the leaders of the local church, and a team of men enlisted who would give one day a week for fourteen weeks to work in the chosen segment. Mr. Baker prepared a syllabus of fourteen lessons that explained the way of salvation.
3. The team on the first of the fourteen days went to the segment and there divided so that in each compound one man taught the assigned lesson, preached the assigned sermon, and told the assigned story.
4. At the close of the fourteen weeks, a three-day conference was held in the compound of the clan head. Decisions for Christ were called for.
5. Those who responded were organized into a catechumen class and began regular weekly worship. They continued working to enlist other catechumens. While not an organized church they carried out many functions of a church congregation.
6. Definite plans for another visit were made previous to the team's leaving.[17]

17. John B. Grimley and Gordon E. Robinson, *Church Growth in Central and Southern Nigeria* (Grand Rapids: Eerdmans, 1966), 213–21.

The results of the very first attempt of this type of segment evangelism (1962) were most gratifying. Three teams had worked among three segments with a total of 350 people. The number of catechumens enrolled as an outgrowth of the effort was 60! Remember, this was in an area that had not had one baptism in thirteen years.

Selecting the Appropriate Media for Gospel Communication

Biblical Principles and Precedents

When approaching the target area the modern church-planter must make the decision as to what media will be used to reach the community. In Bible times the task was not as complicated as today because, of course, modern techniques of reaching the masses had not been developed. Nevertheless, there were choices to be made and at least two primary media were used to reach people.

Luke states that when persecution had scattered the Jerusalem congregation, "they . . . went every where preaching the word" (Acts 8:4 KJV). This person-to-person, face-to-face activity was the usual approach to communication, but it was not the only approach. Letters and books were also used, and thus the New Testament came into existence. Written materials were widely used to communicate the gospel to unbelievers and also to give assurance and instruction to believers (see John 20:31).

Relevant Research

Research indicates that there are good, solid reasons for carefully evaluating the media by which we communicate the gospel:

1. The various media have different degrees of effectiveness as channels of suasive communication.[18] Research indicates that at all social, economic, and educational levels (in the United States at least) people are more inclined to believe news reports on television than those in the newspaper.[19] A study made in isolated towns in the Andean mountains of Ecuador revealed that while both radio and audiovisual media were effective, they differed in respect to the influence they had on the audience.[20]

18. Joseph T. Klapper, *The Effects of Mass Communication* (Glencoe, Ill.: Free, 1960), 129–32.

19. A Roper study cited in Louis Hausman, "Measured View: The Public's Attitude toward Television" (speech to the Advertising Club of Philadelphia, 8 Feb. 1962).

20. Cited in J. B. Haskins, *How to Evaluate Mass Communication* (N.p.: Advertising Research Foundation, 1968), 56–57; and in G. Ralph Milton, "Media Integration—A Fad and a Fact: The Church and the Media," *Asia Focus* 6.3 (1971): 37.

2. Despite the unchallenged potential of the mass media for reaching large audiences rapidly and efficiently, their persuasive potential is more limited than some suppose. *The mass media can help only indirectly to change strongly held attitudes or valued practices.* Mass communication has never proved very effective in attacking attitudes, values, or social customs that are deep-set or strongly held."[21] Indeed, "enough research has been done . . . to enable us to be certain that a person's communication with family and friends is more significant in terms of attitude change and formation than any or all of the media. In fact, this result is reported with almost monotonous regularity. This is especially true of deep-rooted attitudes and beliefs such as religious conviction."[22]

3. Studies indicate that the various media should be used to complement one another. In 1955 the United States Department of Agriculture made a study of more than 1,100 homemakers in five states. These homemakers had been exposed to messages communicated by a variety of media and calculated to influence them to change their housekeeping practices. The results were most revealing. Of those who had been exposed to one or two media, about 46 percent were influenced to make the suggested changes. However, of those homemakers who had been exposed to two or three media, 68 percent were motivated to change. And of those who had been exposed to eight or more media, over 97 percent were influenced to change![23]

The implications are clear. While in any given cultural situation a certain medium may prove to be superior to others when it is properly employed, overall the church will greatly enhance the effectiveness of its communication if the various mass media are used in such a way that they complement each other. In general, no one medium should stand alone.

Practical Reflection

The use of the media both in planting local congregations and in completing the Great Commission worldwide gives us much cause for encouragement. Never before has the world witnessed such an explosion of information. Never before has the church possessed such a variety of means and methods—and expertise—for communicating the Christian gospel. Not a few Christian workers of the generation now passing stand almost aghast as media they used extensively and effec-

21. Wilbur Schramm, *Mass Media in National Development* (Stanford, Calif.: Stanford University Press, 1969), 132.

22. Milton, "Media Integration," 41.

23. Wilson and Gallup, Extension Service Circular 495, U.S. Department of Agriculture, Washington, D.C., 1955.

tively have become outmoded and even ancient. I recall a lecture in which a fellow professor of church planting and growth explained how he had used a mimeograph machine to produce hundreds of copies of a little church newspaper in order to acquaint an entire community with the new church in their midst. Some of us could identify with him as he spoke of the patience required to produce unsmudged and readable copies. Others did not even know what a mimeograph machine looked like. Today's exploiters of the potential inherent in E-mail, the Internet, and web sites will smile. But they should bear in mind that before long the technology of the electronic age may pass them by as well.

Nevertheless, it is incumbent upon church planters to keep abreast of contemporary media that can be utilized to enhance gospel communication and church growth. They should take advantage of the writings of Viggo Sogaard and others who continue to study and report the latest thinking in this area.[24] They should employ media that are both available and effective. And they should employ them wisely, remembering that the person is more important than the method, and the message is more important than the medium.

ME-2-3 illustrations: I recall two conversations regarding the use of radio to spread the gospel overseas. In one conversation shortly after the fall of communism, a Russian Christian told how he and some of his Christian friends had listened frequently to a certain missionary radio station. At first he spoke appreciatively but then he said, "We were so grateful that the gospel was being made available to the Russian people, but at the same time we often wished that there would have been more solid Bible teaching to help us believers really grow in the faith."

The other conversation sounded a similar but even more pointed note. Donald McGavran was responding to the inquiries of a small number of missionaries and missiologists concerning the need to evangelize India. Among them was a missionary who was involved with an Asian radio ministry. He commented that millions of otherwise unreached Indians had the opportunity to hear the gospel by means of Christian radio. In his quiet and thoughtful way McGavran replied, "Yes, and for that we should always be thankful. But have you ever considered how effective it would be if the presentation of the gospel were attended by the kind of teaching that would help believers find one another, organize themselves into local congregations, and grow as Christians?" Most of those present had never given a thought to using radio as a means of actually organizing churches!

---

24. See, for example, Viggo Sogaard, *Media in Church and Mission* (Pasadena: William Carey Library, 1993).

ME-3 illustration: Undoubtedly, the *Jesus* film has been translated into more languages and shown to more people than has any other Christian film in history. Few will question its potential to attract large audiences in almost any culture. However, two vital and closely related questions have been, and continue to be, asked. One has to do with the relationships between the life and teachings of Jesus on the one hand, and the rest of Scripture on the other. The other question has to do with the best way to use the film so as to enhance the growth of the local church.

As to the former question, our prior discussion makes it clear that the *Jesus* film must somehow be linked to instruction in the Old Testament and also the rest of the New Testament. The latter question has been answered at least in part by Cathy Lee Mansfield, who carefully tested the results of showing the film to people in Zambia. Her study revealed that the degree of its effectiveness depended on a variety of factors and especially on how the film was used. She concluded that "one isolated showing is not likely to be followed by permanent impact unless succeeded by careful teaching about God's entire plan of salvation from the Bible."[25] This conclusion is what we would anticipate, but is easily overlooked in our zeal to reach more and more people.

Measuring Audience Understanding and Response

Biblical Principles and Precedents

There is a reluctance on the part of some church planters and other Christian workers to measure results; to do so is thought to be unspiritual. Others overemphasize results. In view of this state of affairs it is important to see how the apostles measured response to their message.

1. The apostles measured response numerically. On the Day of Pentecost 3,000 souls were added to the 120 (Acts 2:41). Later it is reported that 5,000 believed (Acts 4:4). "Churches [were] established . . . and increased in number daily" (Acts 16:5 KJV).

2. The apostles measured response qualitatively. For example, Paul knew that the Thessalonians had been chosen by the Lord for salvation. This knowledge came from his awareness that the Holy Spirit was present in his preaching to them and that they first became imitators of him and then examples to others (1 Thess. 1:4–8). After this initial measurement Paul sent Timothy to Thessalonica. When Timothy returned, he reported that the Thessalonian believers had faith and love, but that

25. Cathy Lee Mansfield, "Cognitive and Attitudinal Changes following Viewing of the *Jesus* Film among the Gwembe Tonga of Zambia" (M.A. thesis, Trinity Evangelical Divinity School, 1984), 72.

they did not understand the second coming of the Lord (1 Thess. 3:1–7; 4:13–5:10).

Epaphras apparently took the same kind of reading in respect to the spiritual state of the Colossians; Paul in response expressed a desire that they might be "filled with the knowledge of His will" (Col. 1:7–10). And it was news from the house of Chloe about the spiritual state of the Corinthian church that prompted Paul to write a corrective letter (1 Cor. 1:11).

We conclude that the apostolic preachers took a rather careful measurement of how many people were becoming believers and how well believers were doing spiritually. They wanted to know if the message had been accepted, and by how many, and whether or not believers were progressing from the elementary to the exemplary stage of Christian understanding and conduct.

Relevant Research

Research findings in the area of Christian communication are most revealing:

A church of 650 members seems to be successful from all external measures. But a survey of the congregation revealed that only 20 percent attempted to share their faith in the past month; 21 percent had family devotions; 70 percent confined their church involvement to Sunday services; 10 percent knew their spiritual gift; and 50 percent claimed they are not being fed spiritually in this church.

A Christian-owned radio station offers both secular and Christian programming. It was discovered that programs designed to evangelize the non-Christian are listened to almost entirely by Christians.

Bibles were given to every inmate in a large United States prison. A few days later it was discovered that 90 percent of these found their way into the trash cans, thus causing the unnecessary expenditure of more than $250,000 when this program was prematurely spread to other prisons.

Fewer than 8 percent of the Christians in the seven largest cities of Brazil ever bother to tune in to the many hours of teaching programs directed at them weekly by two major shortwave missionary broadcasters.

The plan of salvation was prominently displayed in a magazine directed toward non-Christians on the college campus. It was largely ignored, whereas several articles focusing on a Christian perspective on pertinent issues were both read and positively evaluated.[26]

Citing these examples, James Engel comments:

26. James F. Engel, *How Can I Get Them to Listen? A Handbook on Communication Strategy and Research* (Grand Rapids: Zondervan, 1977), 14–15.

This list of examples could be extended for many more pages. Notice the common denominator in each: a reliance on one-way communication. Messages are sent from the pulpit, door-to-door, over the airwaves, or in print. But what is the response? Real communication does not occur until the message is both comprehended and acted upon by the recipient as intended. Communication, in reality, is a two-way process. All too often we ignore the audience.[27]

Practical Reflection

It is imperative that we determine the audience's interest in, understanding of, and commitment to the gospel message. In the secular sector there are organizations whose sole purpose is to measure public opinion and audience reaction in forms like Gallup polls and Nielsen ratings. Christian radio broadcasters often use such devices as "letter week" and mail pulls to determine the size and (to a certain extent) reaction of the listening audience. At the local level few efforts are made to secure this type of feedback until some members of the target audience reach the conversion stage, which is often signified by raising hands, coming forward to the altar, or signing a decision card. The advantage of such methods as visitation evangelism, family-centered evangelism, and small-group Bible study is that they allow for true dialogue in which the audience has the opportunity to state their opinions and ask questions, and the missionary-evangelist has a chance to relate the gospel to their specific needs.

It is crucial that we think of new ways to measure the attitudes and understanding of those to whom we direct the gospel message. Evangelistic methods that move quickly to the decision stage without taking stock of whether the audience really understands the gospel run the risk of measuring response only on the basis of how many actually follow through. Wise stewardship dictates that gospel communicators at every level give more consideration to measuring listener understanding and response. Especially in a day in which methods for taking such measurements are widely known and readily accepted, it is irresponsible to disregard them.

Master Plan Formation

A knowledge of the audience is absolutely essential in planning for effective communication. Fortunately, the pioneer worker will have a store of previously gathered information concerning the audience. Particularly helpful are the data included in figure 10 (pp. 68–70), which

27. Ibid., 15.

Figure 29
Audience Orientations
vis-à-vis the Christian Message

A. Religious Orientation:_____ (naturalist, nominal Christian,
    Hindu, etc.)
B. Percentage of Target Community:_____
C. Basic Beliefs

Biblical Doctrines of Central Importance	Predominant Beliefs of the Target Audience
1. **God:** Creator and Sustainer of the universe, God is a personal being who has will, is moral and holy, reveals himself to humans, demands worship, condemns idolatry. . . .	God:
2. **Humans:** Created by God in his image, humans are fallen creatures yet the objects of God's redeeming love. . . .	Humans:
3. **Jesus Christ:** Preexistent and both fully God and fully human, Jesus underwent incarnation and as the Lamb of God gave himself over to substitutionary death. . . .	Jesus Christ:
4. **Sin:** Rebellion against God's will, sin is true moral guilt entailing judgment and resulting in estrangement and death. . . .	Sin:

---

were collected with a view to selecting the target area. Those data will likely need to be augmented and refined. This task accomplished, they will serve well in the devising of a communication strategy.

Contextualizing the Christian Message

Gigantic chasms often separate people of the various religious traditions. If our audience is composed largely of Hindus, for example, a study of their worldview will be required in order to contextualize the

How?	To Whom?	When?	Where?
Figure 30 **Methods of Gospel Communication** **Target Audience:** _____			
1. Private Public 2. Preaching Teaching Witnessing 3. Monological Dialogical 4. Proclamational and exhortational 5. Apologetical and polemical			

Christian message. Even when religious traditions are not so different from ours, however, it will be most helpful to take time to characterize the dominant beliefs of target audiences. (Most target areas are home to a variety of religious orientations. Hence the use of the plural.) This exercise may seem altogether too time-consuming and, perhaps, ivory-towerish. We will come to recognize its importance, however, if we reflect on the prevailing attitudes of various audiences toward the gospel and the need to tailor the message accordingly.

By gathering information on how the target community feels about the Christian message (see figure 29) the gospel communicator will be aided in contextualizing that message and putting biblical teaching into language the audience can understand. In the process a number of questions call for attention:

1. At what points are the hearers most likely to misunderstand the gospel?
2. Which of the religious beliefs held by the audience are similar to the Christian worldview and can thus be expected to provide conceptual bridges for communication? Which are decidedly different?
3. To what special concerns of the target audience does Christ speak with authority and clarity?
4. What adaptations have successful Christian communicators used in addressing this or similar audiences?

Figure 31
Evaluation of Potential Media for Gospel Communication

Type	Local Use Overall (high, medium, low)	Subgroup Preference (high or low appeal to the following groups)	Suitability for Church Use (taboos, etc.)	Special Considerations
1. Printed media a. Newspapers b. Magazines c. Journals d. Books e. Pamphlets and tracts f. Mailings g. Billboards h. Others _____				
2. Electronic Media a. Radio b. Television c. Movies d. Slides e. Records f. Cassette tapes g. Others _____				
3. Other Media a. Drama b. Puppets c. Chalk talks d. Others _____				

Determining the Methods of Communication

Once we have identified and characterized our target audience, it is natural to ask how we will communicate the (contextualized) message to them. The key to successful gospel communication is to utilize as much variety as possible, with special attention to biblical principles, the gifts of the missionary-evangelist, and the preferences of the audience.

Much Christian communication is, and should be, spontaneous. But there is much communication that should be carefully planned. Insofar as it is planned, completing the form in figure 30 should prove helpful.

Selection of Communication Media

What media do the members of the target audience use in communicating with each other? This is an important question. Missionary-evangelists may import new media and introduce innovations in media use, but they will be wise to give attention to indigenous media first. These may range from simple chalkboards to television sets. Local availability and usage should be carefully studied. Then the process of media selection can begin. (A small group of two or three informed residents can provide the needed data for an initial projection—see figure 31.)

Measurement Implementation

Three questions are paramount in evaluating how well the gospel is being communicated: (1) Is the message actually getting through to the intended audience? (2) Is the message we intend the message that is actually being received? (3) Are the methods and media serving their intended ends, and not becoming ends in themselves? The means of answering these questions range from personal conversation and observation to thorough community surveys employing advanced statistical methods. The means should fit the size and nature of the audience. Proper stewardship demands that we take positive steps to determine whether the five or ten talents entrusted to us are earning five or ten more, or are simply being buried in those messages, methods, and media which are most familiar to us as communicators. Evaluation requires serious effort, but is well worth the information it can provide to guide us as we consider ways to improve our communication to a lost world.

Increasingly, the messengers of Christ are becoming concerned with the quality of Christian communication. But quality means far more than employing the best talent and the most up-to-date technology. It also has reference to the content of the message, the method of its presentation, and the kind of media chosen to convey it.

The Hearers Converted   11

Concerning conversion Michael Green says: "We normally use the word, in a religious context, in one of two ways, either to indicate that a man has left one religious position (or, indeed, none) for exclusive attachment to another. Alternatively, we speak of conversion in a man who up till a certain period had been a mere nominal adherent of his faith, but had then awoken to its significance and importance with enthusiasm and insight."[1] Quite probably this represents what most church people regard as conversion. And it is correct as far as it goes. Much more must be said, however, if church planters are to solve problems such as the lack of conversions and the frequency of reversions today.

Objectives

Our objectives in relation to conversion should be:

1. To secure a response to the gospel that grows out of understanding.

2. To secure a response to the gospel that is in keeping with the cultural patterns of decision making.

3. To secure a response to the gospel that will be genuine and lasting, and result in spiritual fruitfulness.

4. To secure a response to Christ that will heighten the possibility of others becoming Christian.

Instruction as to the Meaning and Importance of Conversion

Biblical Principles and Precedents

The Definition of "Conversion"

It is popular in contemporary theology to use the term "conversion" in a loose sense to describe salvation. Certainly there is a close connection, but the Bible usually does not use the words that signify conversion in this fashion.[2]

---

1. Michael Green, *Evangelism in the Early Church* (Grand Rapids: Eerdmans, 1970), 144.
2. David F. Wells, *Turning to God: Biblical Conversion in the Modern World* (Grand Rapids: Baker, 1989), 30–44.

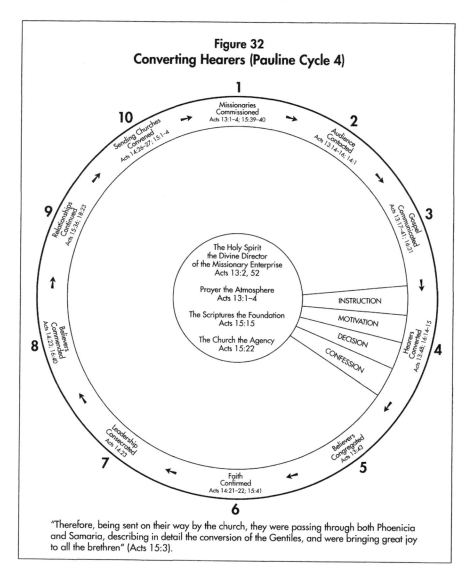

Figure 32
Converting Hearers (Pauline Cycle 4)

"Therefore, being sent on their way by the church, they were passing through both Phoenicia and Samaria, describing in detail the conversion of the Gentiles, and were bringing great joy to all the brethren" (Acts 15:3).

The closest single-word equivalent for conversion in the Old Testament is *šûb*, a common term that means "turn" or "return." Most often it is used of the covenant people: they "turn away" from false gods and evil, and "return" to the God of Israel. In a few instances the word is used of noncovenantal people, as in the case of the Ninevites, who are called upon to "turn away" from their wickedness (Jon. 3:8, 10).

The New Testament uses the word *epistrephō* (or, occasionally, just *strephō*) in a general sense to describe a "turning around" (Matt. 9:22;

Mark 5:30) or a "turning back" or "returning" (Matt. 10:13; 12:44). When describing spiritual conversion, it is used of both Jews and Gentiles becoming Christians—that is, turning or returning to God (e.g., Acts 3:19; 9:35; 11:21; 14:15). But other words are used as well, notably *metanoeō* ("change one's mind, repent") and *pisteuō* ("believe"). These words are sometimes used together to denote what we might call a complete conversion. For example, on Pentecost Peter exhorts his hearers to "change their minds" and "return" (Acts 3:19). And Paul reminds the Ephesian elders that he had solemnly witnessed to Jews and Gentiles about repentance *(metanoian)* toward God and faith *(pistin)* in Jesus Christ (Acts 20:21).

Conversion, therefore, has to do with a turning from evil and false gods and a turning or a returning to God. As such it has implications regarding behavior, membership in an institution, and value system. But fundamentally it has to do with a change of heart and mind, with obedience and trust, with one's basic beliefs and worldview.

Insider and Outsider Conversion

Drawing upon Scripture and a consultation on conversion held in Hong Kong in 1988, David Wells makes an illuminating distinction between what he calls insider conversion and outsider conversion.[3] For those in a covenant relationship with God, conversion entails coming to a fresh understanding of what it means to be God's people. This is the predominant sense in which the prophets, John the Baptist, and also the Lord Jesus called for conversion. For those outside the covenant, however, conversion means to discover the true God and enter into that relationship with him for which all people were created in the first place. This evangelistic sense of conversion is often referred to in the Book of Acts and also the New Testament letters. For example, writing to the Thessalonians, Paul specifically states that they turned from idols and to the service of God (1 Thess. 1:9). Whether among the pantheists and polytheists of the Third World or the materialists and naturalists of the Western world, this is the sense in which we most often refer to conversion today.

The Importance of Conversion

Those passages which are central to the definition of conversion also reveal the importance of conversion.

1. Conversion is important because it is related to understanding the law. Paul states that the Israelites had a veil over their hearts when the law was read. "But whenever a man turns to the Lord, the veil is taken

---

3. Ibid., 33–39.

away" (2 Cor. 3:16). Charles Ryrie explains that this veil is over our hearts "as long as [we] consider the law as permanent and do not turn to Christ, who takes away the veil."[4] In other words, the law cannot be understood apart from a turning to Christ. Conversion is essential to understanding the Old Testament.

2. Conversion is important because it is related to forgiveness of sins (Acts 3:19; 26:18). Peter links conversion and forgiveness in his first epistle: his readers have returned to the Shepherd and Guardian of their souls—Jesus Christ who bore their sins on the tree (1 Peter 2:24–25). Thus conversion is a return to the God who offers forgiveness. Paul argues in the same vein in the letter to the Colossians. Forgiveness of sin is more or less synonymous with redemption. Redemption is in the beloved Son of God, into whose kingdom the believer has been transferred (Col. 1:12–15).

3. Conversion is important because it is a prerequisite to blessing (Acts 3:19).

4. Conversion is important because it naturally precedes service to God (1 Thess. 1:9–10).

Relevant Research

History reveals that conversion of the New Testament variety was utterly foreign to the Hellenistic world of the first century. Michael Green adduces several reasons for this. In the first place, Hellenistic society did not consider belief to be a requirement for belonging to a cult. In the second place, ethics was not regarded as part of religion. In the third place, Christian conversion made an exclusivistic claim upon adherents, a notion that was startling to the Hellenistic world.[5]

Conversion, therefore, should not be looked upon as something that was quite acceptable (or even fashionable) in the first century but is outmoded in the twenty-first. In the face of society's antipathy Christian conversion was, and is, necessary by divine requirement. This is part of the believer's cross.

Practical Reflection

Contemporary evangelism often leads to a hurried decision for Christ with but scant attention to repentance and inadequate explanations of faith and conversion itself. That the Holy Spirit may bring a person to repentance and faith on the basis of minimal knowledge

4. Charles C. Ryrie, *Ryrie Study Bible—NAS: New Testament* (Chicago: Moody, 1976), 318.

5. Green, *Evangelism in the Early Church*, 144–46.

should not be used as an excuse for inadequate instruction. It is imperative that potential converts be instructed in the gospel and concerning the meaning and significance of conversion. To ask anyone to make such an important decision on the basis of minimal understanding or misunderstanding is ethically indefensible.

ME-3 illustration: John L. Nevius, the great missionary statesman of China and Korea, writes that the majority of missionaries in the China of his day gave "chief attention" to evangelizing the "middle or more illiterate class."[6] This they did by going to relatively unreached areas and by visiting the fairs that were a striking feature of country life in China. Curiosity assured great crowds and, when an appeal was made, good response. But Nevius warns against assuming that in such cases the people understand what is being preached. He advises missionaries that the important objective in such cases should be to leave an impression of goodwill and to create a sense of expectancy for future visits. That is good advice. The world has an overabundance of "converts" whose curiosity has been satisfied but whose hearts have not been transformed!

Motivation and Conversion

Biblical Principles and Precedents

In the previous chapter the subject of elenctics was treated briefly. That subject is intimately related to motivation. It is abundantly clear that no one comes to the Son unless one is drawn by the Father (John 6:44). The Holy Spirit was sent into the world precisely for the purpose of convicting the world of sin, righteousness, and judgment (John 16:8). Our Lord's explanation makes it clear that in this context sin is unbelief in Christ, righteousness is Christ's righteousness, and judgment is the judgment of Satan in Christ's triumph over sin and death. Indeed, the Holy Spirit alone can convince the world of these things. That unbelief in Jesus is heinous sin is not easy to accept. With Christ in heaven instead of on earth we humans tend to compare ourselves with our neighbors rather than with the righteous Christ. And to the natural self the idea that the struggle against evil is already a lost cause seems preposterous. Accordingly, the motivation to convert must come from the Holy Spirit. However, this does not mean there can be no other motivational factors connected with conversion. Within the potential convert there may be at least three types of motivation.

6. John L. Nevius, *The Planting and Development of Missionary Churches* (Philadelphia: Presbyterian and Reformed, 1958), 81–82.

A first set of motivational factors can be described as being God-oriented. There are some people who already comprehend something of the majesty and holiness of God. Paul was in this category. He saw the light, heard the voice, and was blinded. Only upon inquiring, "Who art Thou, Lord?" (Acts 9:5), did he come to recognize the lordship of Christ. Paul's conversion was instantaneous. It came as a result of his being God-oriented.

Second, there is a self-oriented set of motivational factors. There are several illustrations of this in the New Testament. A leper went to Jesus and asked to be cleansed. His motive was personal—"Thou canst make me clean" (Mark 1:40 KJV). Then there was blind Bartimaeus, who requested, "Lord, that I might receive my sight" (Mark 10:51 KJV). Both men were motivated by the desire for a better life in the here and now. The rich young man also evidenced a personal motive by asking, "What shall I do to inherit eternal life?" (Luke 18:18 KJV). Notice that Bartimaeus and the leper were concerned about the present while the rich young man was concerned about the future. But even more interesting and important is the reaction of the Savior. He did not declare the motives of any of these men to be unworthy. He recognized self-oriented motives as having a certain legitimacy.

A third type of motivational factor can be termed society-oriented. This is evident when an individual does not seek something for self, but seeks the good of another person or of a social group. In the New Testament, society-oriented motivation was apparent when the people brought the sick and afflicted to the Lord and the apostles for healing. It was also apparent in Zacchaeus, who, at the time of his conversion, evidenced a new concern for the poor and for anyone whom he might have wronged (Luke 19:8–10).

There is a crucial question related to these motivations: Is the preacher justified in appealing to self-oriented and society-oriented motivations? Perhaps our Lord resolved the problem when he said, "Seek ye first the kingdom of God, and his righteousness; and all these things shall be added unto you" (Matt. 6:33 KJV). He was speaking to a nation that was actively seeking a better life. The words "these things" definitely referred to food and raiment (v. 25). But the Lord did not demean his hearers by telling them their motives were unworthy. Rather, he told them that by seeking for the kingdom and the justice of God they could have the other things as well. In other words, Jesus appealed to the non-spiritual self- and society-oriented motivational factors. But in doing so, our Lord did not pass over the conditions necessary to their fulfilment.

Paul and the other apostles emulated the Lord in this respect. That an appeal to self- and society-oriented motivations was inherent in their preaching the kingdom did not cause them to desist. They continued to preach the kingdom (Acts 8:12; 28:31), and they explained the necessary conditions (Acts 8:22; 14:22).

Our discussion has brought us to another question. Can we today preach the kingdom in the same way that Christ and the apostles preached it? Can today's missionary-evangelist promise fulfilment of personal and social desires on the basis of changing allegiance from Satan to God? The answer to these questions seems obvious. A converted sinner is not exempt from social injustice. Suffering is the lot of the believer (2 Tim. 1:8, 12; 2:11–13; 3:12). No one has the authority to promise the absence of suffering. Nevertheless, the kingdom is to be proclaimed. It is part of the "teaching . . . all that I commanded" of the Great Commission. All believers will participate in it when the Lord establishes his reign on earth. Believers will reign with Christ (2 Tim. 2:12). However, salvation is not for the future alone. The personal blessings of peace with God, true freedom in Christ, absence of guilt, and victory over vices can be promised to those in any age who make Christ Lord.

Relevant Research

Obviously, conversion is closely related to motivation—a subject that has proved difficult for researchers and theorists. Out of the vast literature on the subject, several items are of special interest in the present context:

1. Following Abraham Maslow's publication of various works on the "motivational pyramid" and the "hierarchy of human needs" in the 1950s and 1960s, people in general and scholars in particular became increasingly interested in human needs, their relative importance, and their fulfilment.[7] Much could be said about the impact of Maslow's ideas on Christian believers for good and ill, especially his ideas concerning self-fulfilment and self-actualization. In the present context, however, it seems most important to distinguish between real needs and felt needs. Real needs arise out of what we are by virtue of creation. Created a biological organism, the human needs food, rest, sleep, exercise, and so forth. Created as sentient beings, we, whenever we make choices, require reasons which are grounded in our intelligence or sense of well-being. Created social beings, we need fellowship with, and the approval of, other humans. Created spiritual beings, we need fellowship with God. Understanding this, missionary-evangelists, by the very nature of their calling, must give attention to the real needs of the whole person, and especially to essential spiritual needs. Those needs which are merely felt may well serve as points of contact, but they should not be confused

7. See Abraham Maslow, *Motivation and Personality,* 2d ed. (New York: Harper and Row, 1970).

with real needs, nor should they be allowed to divert the missionary from ministering to real needs or delivering the whole counsel of God.

2. Another area of interest here has to do with the relationship between personality types and traits on the one hand and religious conversion on the other. David Wells very briefly reviews some of the relevant research of William James, J. H. Leuba, Sigmund Freud, Gordon Allport, and L. B. Brown. He believes that there probably is some relationship between, for example, the suggestible personality and instances of sudden conversion. However, he warns against elevating the conclusions of psychologists to the level of finality. Those conclusions tend to reflect the preoccupations of some of the prominent schools of psychology—psychoanalytic, empirical, psychophysiological, behaviorist, and cognitive. The research does not suggest that there is a particular kind of person from whom we can expect a conversion experience. Rather, "people come into a relationship with Christ from an array of life experiences, and from within the whole diversity of personality and culture, and this fact should be neither minimized nor misinterpreted."[8]

3. A classic research project conducted in India by J. Waskom Pickett indicated that purity of motive may not be a decisive factor in conversion.[9] His careful study of Indian converts of a previous generation categorized their primary motives for becoming Christians:

a. Spiritual motives (34.8 percent)
b. Secular motives; e.g., a better job, a better life (8.1 percent)
c. Social reasons; e.g., others were becoming Christians (22.4 percent)
d. Natal influences (34.7 percent)

The study concluded that there was an unexpectedly high degree of spiritual attainment among those who became believers for other than strictly spiritual reasons; 70 percent of those who became Christians for other than spiritual motives, and 75 percent of those who became Christians because others of their family or caste had done so, went on to attend church regularly.[10] Obviously, other factors were at work.

Practical Reflection

From a practical point of view, at least three considerations should be borne in mind when we urge conversion to Christ.

8. Wells, *Turning to God,* 71.
9. J. Waskom Pickett, *Christian Mass Movements in India* (New York: Abingdon, 1933), 165.
10. Ibid., 168.

1. Conversion motives that are not strictly spiritual are not necessarily unworthy. There is nothing wrong with the desire to become a Christian in order to have warm fellowship with the people of God or to live a more meaningful life, for example. The fact that great Christians still wrestle with lesser motives should be enough to indicate that God accepts something less than pure converts and takes considerable time (a lifetime?) and trouble to make them into pure saints. This does not mean that our Lord lowers the standard. He did not keep the believer's cross a secret in order to gain disciples. On the other hand, he said that those who are pure in heart will see God (Matt. 5:8). Ultimately, we can bear our crosses only because he walks with us, and we can be pure in heart only because in his grace he makes us so.

2. As a result of Western individualism, missionary-evangelists are likely to overlook the high value which many cultures place upon group identity. The new emphasis being given to family life, communal living, and group dynamics in our society is a reaction against individualism which has been carried too far. One can only imagine the loyalties that were involved in the conversion of the household of Cornelius, the jailer's family in Philippi, and other people groups in the New Testament. These examples are not to be confused with the large numbers responding to the invitation at a mass evangelistic crusade. The latter are still individualistic, almost to the core. We need to consider approaches to conversion that encourage homogeneous units to become one in Christ and individual members of unbelieving units to be true to Christ, not only with a view to their own salvation, but also with a view to the salvation of their fellows. Notice again what a high percentage in the Pickett study were motivated to receive Christ by social and natal influences, and then went on to become productive Christians.

3. Finally, let us remember that the missionary-evangelist is always called upon to be faithful. Success is not promised. Jesus wept over Jerusalem. Great hosts were not converted on Mars' Hill. But Jerusalem had heard words from the lips of the Son of God. And those Athenian inquirers had listened to the greatest apostle of them all.

The Decision to Convert

Biblical Principles and Precedents

1. The biblical record is clear that both privilege and responsibility are involved in hearing God's Word. It is not the hearer but the doer who is justified (James 1:22). The gospel is not only a message to be proclaimed, but also an invitation to be received (John 1:12) and a com-

mandment to be obeyed (2 Thess. 1:8). A. R. Tippett calls this "verdict theology."[11] By whatever name, it is biblical.

2. As we have seen, conversion in the New Testament sometimes involved only one individual, but often it involved groups of people. There are instances in the New Testament where individuals came to accept Christ without apparent relationship to anyone other than an evangelist. The Ethiopian eunuch is a case in point (Acts 8:30). Sometimes individuals were called upon to decide for Christ in the face of opposition from friends and even family. When sending out his disciples, Christ warned that faith would sometimes bring a sword between members of the same family (Matt. 10:34–36). It is also true that whole households were converted in Bible times (Acts 10:24, 44; 16:30–33). And on one occasion so many came to Christ simultaneously that the historian could write, "All who lived at Lydda and Sharon saw him [i.e., the paralytic Aeneas arise], and they turned to the Lord" (Acts 9:35).

3. The call to repentance and faith was addressed to those capable of making the decision. Fully responsible people especially were called upon to convert to Christ. Care must be taken not to place too much weight on an argument from silence. Children were undoubtedly present on many occasions when the gospel was preached and its claims were presented. That children followed Christ is clear from narratives such as that of the loaves and fishes (John 6:9–13). Christ made it clear that children have a special place in his kingdom (Mark 10:14). But the record is specific as to the identity of those who were commanded to repent and believe the gospel: it was basically adults (including young adults) who were in view.

Relevant Research

1. Societies differ in their attitude toward decision making. Some societies are decision-oriented (e.g., the United States). Any decision is considered to be better than no decision. Other cultures avoid decisions as often and as long as possible (e.g., traditional China). When decisions do become necessary, one does not burn the bridges behind oneself, but leaves the door to reconsideration as wide open as possible. The Chinese (and people of similar orientation) are acting according to the values of their culture when they do not follow through on a decision that is no longer to their liking. In their view, when it becomes difficult to live with a decision made previously, the intelligent person does not abide by it! Inasmuch as this approach to decision making does not lessen the responsibility of the Chinese to follow Christ, mis-

11. A. R. Tippett, *Verdict Theology in Missionary Theory* (Lincoln, Ill.: Lincoln Christian College Press, 1969).

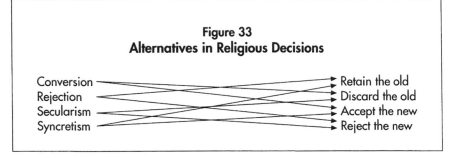

Figure 33
Alternatives in Religious Decisions

Conversion ——————————————→ Retain the old
Rejection ——————————————→ Discard the old
Secularism ——————————————→ Accept the new
Syncretism ——————————————→ Reject the new

sionary-evangelists who are called of God to work with them should be mindful of it.

2. There are various possibilities when we are called on to make a decision. We usually think of a decision vis-à-vis any proposed change in attitude or action as involving only two possibilities: acceptance or rejection. This, of course, is an oversimplification, for there are actually four possibilities:

a. We can retain the old.
b. We can discard the old.
c. We can accept the new.
d. Or reject the new.

In terms of these four possibilities, it is evident that conversion means to discard the old (unbelief, sin, idolatry) and accept the new (faith in and obedience to Christ). Both elements are vital. There are other scenarios, however. It is possible to retain the old and discard the new. This is rejection. It is possible to discard the old faith without accepting the new. The result is secularism. It is also possible to accept the new without discarding the old. The result is syncretism. (See figure 33.)

3. Decision occurs at a specific point yet also as a process. Numerous scholars have pointed out that the process of decision making needs careful study. We should be aware, for example, of the various steps in the process (though, of course, they can be elaborated differently):

a. Discovery: "Possibility X exists for me."
b. Deliberation: "Should I choose possibility X?"
c. Determination: "Yes, I will accept X."
d. Dissonance: "If I had not chosen X, I would not be having this trouble."
e. Discipline: "The implications of choosing X must be accepted."[12]

---

12. David J. Hesselgrave, *Communicating Christ Cross-Culturally,* 2d ed. (Grand Rapids: Zondervan, 1991), 18–19.

These steps in the decision-making process are self-explanatory, with one exception—dissonance.[13]

Dissonance refers to the state of unsettledness that often occurs after one has determined to take a certain course of action—be it to purchase an automobile, to attend a particular school, or to change one's religious faith. Dissonance arises when one experiences problems connected with the chosen course of action (e.g., low gas mileage in the case of the automobile, inordinate educational requirements on the part of the school, unexpected opposition to conversion).

What we do when we experience dissonance depends on the kind of people we are. It also depends on the kind of situation in which we find ourselves. Once a down payment has been made on a new car, the buyer will probably not be able to return it no matter how low the gas mileage is! But we do not lose our freedom when we make a decision for Christ. We can revert. (See figure 34.)

A much more elaborate outline of the decision-making process as it relates to the Christian mission at home and abroad has been attempted by James Engel and H. Wilbert Norton in their book *What's Gone Wrong with the Harvest?*[14] The authors' basic contention is that Christian communicators have erred greatly in failing to ascertain their audiences' level of understanding of, and response to, the Christian message.

4. Who can make decisions? Societies vary considerably as to who can legitimately make certain kinds of decisions and the circumstances under which they can be made. In many societies (e.g., Japan) decisions by children and even young adults will not be taken very seriously. Only at the time of economic independence and the establishment of a separate household are one's decisions accorded proper respect. As a result, Westerners should keep two matters in mind when they try to convert people in such societies: (a) those who press for a decision by young people without conferring with their elders may be thought of as disrupters of family life and flouters of proper authority; (b) the real test of a younger person's resolve may not come at the time of religious decision, but on entering an occupation or marriage.

5. Group decision is sometimes possible. In general, cultures with lineage kinship patterns, rural (village and especially tribal) orientations, and closed-class (caste) stratification will tend to stress group unity and the need for group decision. Cultures with the kindred kin-

13. See Leon Festinger, *A Theory of Cognitive Dissonance* (Stanford: Stanford University Press, 1957), 446–52.

14. James F. Engel and H. Wilbert Norton, *What's Gone Wrong with the Harvest? A Communication Strategy for the Church and World Evangelism* (Grand Rapids: Zondervan, 1975).

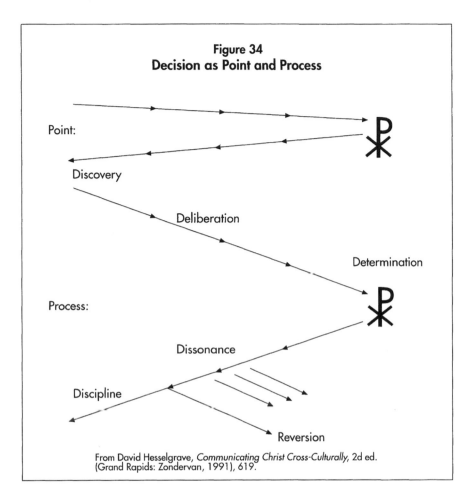

Figure 34
Decision as Point and Process

Point:

Discovery

Deliberation

Determination

Process:

Dissonance

Discipline

Reversion

From David Hesselgrave, *Communicating Christ Cross-Culturally,* 2d ed. (Grand Rapids: Zondervan, 1991), 619.

ship system and a significant degree of heterogeneity and openness will tend to stress individual decisions and the need for maintaining the integrity of individual convictions. Group decisions, of course, obviate the problem of social dislocation. Accordingly, it has been demonstrated that even in the West, group decision is more lasting. Once a group arrives at a decision to act, the members are likely to carry it through.

In the context of Christian mission, group conversions may be called people movements or multi-individual conversion.[15] Group decisions do not necessarily mean that individuals have been overlooked. They

15. Donald A. McGavran, *Understanding Church Growth* (Grand Rapids: Eerdmans, 1970), 296–305.

usually mean that individuals make choices in consultation and concert with others rather than independently of them.

Practical Reflection

A review of the biblical and research data on conversion and decision making reveals a number of areas where some adjustment could bring present-day evangelical understanding and practice much closer to the New Testament ideal. There is perhaps no single area in which we are more circumscribed by traditional thinking and practice. Our practice has not always been faithful to New Testament teaching, nor has it kept pace with contemporary understanding. This is apparent enough within the North American context, but it becomes even more pronounced when we cross cultural boundaries. The practice of missionary-evangelists in settings very different from our own reveals an insensitivity to basic cultural differences that is often appalling. As a consequence we often needlessly arouse antagonism. We sometimes make syncretists or secularists instead of Christians. We often resort to approaches that result in reversions and then think of those who revert as being fickle. We go to target areas with great potential for group conversion and still resort to methods conceived for individualistic cultures. It is to be hoped that we have now entered a time of transition during which missionaries and evangelists will become increasingly aware of sociocultural factors.

It should be remembered that in conversion we are dealing with humans, not machines, and with souls, not statistics. If there are to be actual decisions for Christ among a target people, we must take into consideration what they experience as individual persons and as persons in society. Calls for decision should be not only Christ-centered, but also culturally related and person-oriented.

The Culture-Sensitive Call for Decision

Decision is to be called for in every society because the gospel demands response. But, as we have seen, cultures differ so widely that cultural awareness is needful if missionary-evangelists are to elicit a proper response.

1. Missionary-evangelists must plan regular, frequent, and culturally appropriate opportunities for unbelievers to receive Christ. The time and place of such occasions will vary significantly. What is essential is that there be a general understanding that invitations to receive Christ may be given at any time and will be given regularly.

ME-1 illustration: O. S. Hawkins, pastor of the rapidly growing First Baptist Church of Fort Lauderdale, Florida, has implemented a lay-witness training program in which literally hundreds of believers have been trained in the methods of James Kennedy's Evangelism Explosion. In that context the lead question "If God were to ask you, 'Why should I let you into my heaven?' what would you reply?" has proved to be an effective appeal in personal evangelism. However, every Sunday Hawkins extends a public appeal that is carefully crafted to invite unbelievers to come to Christ, to encourage recent converts to make their commitment public, and to help those who are hurting as they travel the pathway of obedience. The culture-relatedness of Hawkins's overall approach becomes apparent when one studies the "30 practical principles" he proposes for public and personal evangelism.[16]

2. A great effort should be made to approach those leaders who are regarded by their respective cultures as being capable of making decisions as important as religious conversion. Even when they do not accept Christ, the understanding and goodwill that may be gained by recognizing their authority may make it easier for other members of the group to become Christians. Christian workers whose evangelistic efforts are directed primarily to children, students, and women (those who in some cultures are regarded as lacking authority to make decisions) would do well to give special attention to this advice.

ME-3 illustration: After years of evangelism in Kenya, a master plan for reaching new villages was prepared. The small planning group represented many years of missionary experience in Africa. They unanimously concluded that their previous strategy of going first and directly to those who were immediately accessible had been a mistake. They determined that in new areas an initial presentation would be made to the village elders in order to secure their understanding and goodwill, or even their conversion and cooperation. Subsequent experience proved the validity of this approach.

3. Group decisions should be encouraged. For altogether too long, Western individualism has determined our conversion patterns. Even in North America attention is now being given to approaching couples and whole (nuclear) families with the gospel. The possibility of encouraging group decisions should not be overlooked.

ME-3 illustrations: Some of the most outstanding examples of group conversion in recent times have occurred in West Irian, where whole tribes have burned their fetishes and come to Christ. An illustration with a wider applicability is the Sevav plan explained in some detail in the previous chapter. In Sevav there was a deliberate attempt to reach entire extended families as units, and to encourage group decisions for

16. O. S. Hawkins, *Drawing the Net: 30 Practical Principles for Leading Others to Christ Publicly and Personally* (Nashville: Broadman, 1993).

Christ. The relatively large number of those who decided for Christ and followed through, witnesses to the viability of the approach.

The Process-Sensitive Call for Decision

By using the phrase "process-sensitive call," we direct attention to the fact that in dealing with those for whom Christ died, we are dealing with people who have numerous questions, frustrations, and trials. We should plan, therefore, to counsel some potential converts concerning the issues of repentance and faith over a period of time. Do not minimize the importance of the decision point. But come to grips with the spiritual and psychological realities of the situation.

"Process decision," in the sense in which we use the phrase, has special reference to group decisions. However, it is also important to keep the nature of process decision in view when we are dealing with individuals who run the risk of ostracism as a result of conversion to Christ. To help these people counter dissonance is vital. Satan is not a good loser!

ME-3 illustration: Conservative Baptist missionaries in Kalimantan (Borneo) were interacting with a group of natives who were considering conversion to Christ. Many questions were asked and answered— seemingly to the satisfaction of all. Finally one elderly man found the courage and words to express a problem that was probably on the minds of all. He said, "We want to believe and follow your God, but tell us, can he make a rice field?"

How easy to give glib answers in such a situation. After all, our God made fields, rice, sun, and rain! By contrast, those offerings and prayers which have traditionally attended farming in that part of the world add up to superstition and idolatry! But these were responsible people with growing children to care for. They were sincere. And, given their view of the world up to that time, the question was entirely legitimate. Blessed are such a people when those who bring God's Word into their midst understand their worldview, and when they have ministers who refuse to leave them in idolatry or lead them into secularism, but who instead lead them to Christ.

Baptism and Confession of Faith

Biblical Principles and Precedents

In New Testament times, anyone who accepted Christ was expected to confess Christ. This was done in three ways: (1) in verbal confession of Christ as Lord; (2) in symbolic confession by water baptism; and (3) by good works and a changed life. None of these in and by itself was sufficient for salvation. All were the accompaniments of saving faith.

1. The importance of verbal confession is evident in the solemn words of the Lord Jesus that he will confess before the Father those who confess him before others, and deny before the Father those who deny him before others (Matt. 10:32–33). It is also evident in the oft-quoted words of the apostle Paul in his letter to the Romans: "If you confess with your mouth Jesus as Lord, and believe in your heart that God raised Him from the dead, you shall be saved; for with the heart man believes, resulting in righteousness, and with the mouth he confesses, resulting in salvation. For the Scripture says, 'Whoever believes in Him will not be disappointed.' . . . For 'Whoever will call upon the name of the Lord will be saved'" (Rom. 10:9–11, 13).

The content of the confession is the lordship of Christ. But what is confession? Literally, it is a "saying of the same thing"—that is, saying the same thing about the Son as the Father says about him. But in the context of Romans 10 confession is explained in a somewhat different way. There is a parallelism of sentence structure which can be seen by grouping similar statements:

    a. "believe in your heart that God raised Him"
    b. "with the heart man believes, resulting in righteousness"
    c. "Whoever believes in Him will not be disappointed"

and

    a. "confess with your mouth Jesus as Lord"
    b. "with the mouth he confesses, resulting in salvation"
    c. "Whoever will call upon the name of the Lord will be saved"

It becomes clear that confession is equivalent to calling upon the name of the Lord. Confession of Jesus as Lord is an act which is based on faith in Christ as Lord and in which the believer calls upon his name.

2. The importance of water baptism is evident in the place that it is given in the Great Commission and in the experience of the early church. The grammatical construction of Matthew 28:19–20 indicates that the basic imperative to "make disciples" is to be accomplished by "going," "baptizing," and "teaching" (in ascending order of importance). That Paul seemed to denigrate his role as a baptizer vis-à-vis the planting of the church in Corinth (1 Cor. 1:13–16) should not be interpreted as undercutting the importance of baptism. He did baptize the household of Stephanas and perhaps others as well, but baptizing was not his first priority, and he did not want his role as baptizer to contribute to pride on the part of those he baptized.

At any rate, the close relationship between conversion and water baptism is readily seen in Acts. People were called upon to repent, believe, and be baptized. And accounts of individual and group conversions from the three thousand on Pentecost (Acts 2:41) to the Ephesian Christians (19:1–6) make it clear that the outward ritual of baptism both accompanied and symbolized entrance into the life of faith.

Few matters having to do with the conversion stage of the Pauline Cycle will elicit more varied opinions and practices than will baptism. This is not the place to even attempt to resolve the issues. On this matter let each person be persuaded in one's own mind. But let us also at least agree that baptism is not a doctrine to be treated cavalierly or a practice to be carried out indiscriminately. Too much is at stake.

3. A third type of confession in the New Testament is apparent in the requirement that the believer perform "deeds appropriate to repentance" (Acts 26:20). This type of confession is underscored in Titus 2, where the believer's conduct is described as adorning the doctrine of God (v. 10). Good works were to be done because "the grace of God has appeared" (v. 11). The works of the believer were a testimony to the grace of God. So essential were good works that James could affirm that their absence was a sign of dead faith (James 2:17) and their presence an evidence of saving faith (James 2:18).

Relevant Research

1. Researchers speak with a united voice on the intimate relationships that exist between knowledge and words on the one hand, and between communication and behavior on the other. It is difficult—perhaps impossible—to think without words. To articulate one's beliefs is not only to convey them to others, but also to clarify and reinforce them for oneself. As for nonverbal behavior, which is now widely referred to as silent language, people are thereby constantly communicating their ideas, attitudes, feelings, and values without saying so much as a word.

2. Research also indicates that it would be unusual if some kind of rite did not accompany so important an event as Christian conversion and the identification of the new believer with a new family and another way of life. Analogies to Christian baptism are to be found in most religions and pseudoreligious organizations—from Jewish circumcision, bar mitzvah, and priestly ordinances (see Num. 19:7), to Babylonian and Greek (especially Eleusinian) rituals, to the rites of modern Freemasonry. In fact, initiation rites which signify taking on the obligations and privileges of adulthood are common in many areas of the world. Christ did not overlook the significance of that kind of symbolic act in establishing his church.

Practical Reflection

Obviously not all believers are called to be missionaries, evangelists, or pastors. But all are called to be witnesses. And witness begins with one's first open confession of Jesus Christ as Savior and Lord, whether by words, deeds, or the rite of baptism. For a variety of reasons it is easy for church planters to err in this area, especially in ME-2 and 3 contexts. Accordingly, most of our illustrations will come from cultures very different from our own.

1. The evangelist and church planter bear the responsibility to encourage converts to confess Christ, but converts bear the responsibility to actually make such a confession. Situations vary. In one case the convert may be an extrovert, the conversion very dramatic, and the culture conducive to individual decision-making. In another case the convert may be an introvert, the decision to become a Christian may be the result of a long process, and the culture may exact a tremendous toll for conversion. Toledo, Tokyo, and Tunis represent very, very different challenges to the Christian convert. Biblical teaching is constant, but people and places differ. Sensitivity is required.

ME-1 illustration: Pastor O. S. Hawkins of Fort Lauderdale knows that many, if not most, conversions take place in the privacy of the home. To encourage public confession he designs the Sunday service invitation in such a way as to make it clear that those who have accepted Christ during the previous week should now step forward in order to bear public witness to Christ.

ME-3 illustration: Early on in our church-planting ministry in Japan it became apparent that an unusually large proportion of converts would be high school and university students who were still responsible to their parents and extended family. Using well-known Scripture passages as reinforcement, we encouraged young converts to be strong and to confess their allegiance to Christ immediately and decisively. Time, study, and experience resulted in a very different approach. We learned to encourage young converts to seek out an early but appropriate time and then to testify of their new faith in a very humble way:

> Father and Mother, I have something important to tell you. First of all, I confess that I have not been the obedient, dutiful son [daughter] that I have tried to make you think I am. Often I have disobeyed when you did not know it. And even when I have obeyed I have often been resentful in my heart. But I have repented of all of that before God. And I ask your forgiveness too. From now on I want to be a more obedient and loving son [daughter]. One thing, however; I will not be able to pray or bring offerings to the ancestors and god-shelves. I hope you will understand. You see, I have become a Christian. That is why I love you more than ever before. And I hope that you will come to Christ someday as well.

2. Both repentance and, especially, acts of repentance are often neglected aspects of conversion today. Why? Not because they are unbiblical, but because they seem odious. There are other reasons as well. One of them may be that we have misconstrued the meaning of grace. Etymologically and theologically grace is more than God's unmerited favor. To be full-orbed, it includes a proper response on the part of the one who is favored. To appreciate this we need to study the word *charis*, rethink passages like Romans 1:16–25 and Titus 2:11–12, and recall that our believing forebears "said grace" before they ate their food.

ME-3 illustration: The wife and daughter of a wealthy but abusive and dissolute Japanese businessman became Christians. Their home situation became more and more intolerable until, finally, they went to their pastor for counsel. It seemed that they would have to leave their home. After speaking to the pastor they faced the husband and father in one of his more reflective and sober moments. Mother and daughter issued an ultimatum that unless he, though an unbeliever, also sought counsel from the pastor, they would leave. Humbled and desperate, he relented. The counseling took but a short period of time and an unexpected turn. The pastor made it clear that the true and living God would in his Son Jesus accept and change the businessman, but first he had to truly repent of his many sins. This involved listing known sins and injustices, and actually seeking forgiveness and making restitution where possible! This was done; the man was transformed by grace. So were his home and his business. Today he is a model Christian husband, father, grandfather, businessman, and churchman. He is also a Christian philanthropist. This in a land no more than 1 percent Christian!

3. Christian baptism presents a special opportunity, but also some very special problems to the church planter. Christians differ theologically when it comes to baptism. These differences lead to differences in practice. They also lead to inertia or reactive extremes. Cultures differ also. In some societies Christian baptism is desirable and tantamount to salvation. In certain others to be baptized is to invite ostracism and even death. So questions concerning baptism range from the deeply theological to the basically cultural to the primarily practical. Every case calls for prayerful study. In the author's experience in postwar Japan, the practical question of the timing of baptism was a matter of great concern because of an unusually large number of reversions.

ME-3 illustration: Shortly after World War II some Southern Baptist church-planting missionaries in Japan became distressed concerning the number of converts who reverted. In order to determine if there was any relationship between the time of baptism and the frequency of reversion, they carried out a limited test. In some evangelistic campaigns converts were baptized very soon after profession of faith. In other campaigns converts were asked to take a prescribed course of Bible study before baptism. The missionaries concluded that the time of baptism was not a crucial factor in the incidence of reversion. Such factors as the quality of instruction received by the converts and their acceptance by older Christians seemed to be more important.

Master Plan Formation

Instruction concerning Conversion

It is to be expected that non-Christians will not understand what is involved in true Christian conversion. The very concept of religious conversion is absolutely foreign to some cultural contexts. As a matter of fact, when we call for conversion, any given group will entertain some misconceptions which should be faithfully dealt with from the Word of God, whether in our preaching and teaching or in our witnessing and counseling.

A relatively easy way to deal with the situation is to note the most likely misconceptions (which can be surmised from study and interaction with locals) and then to counteract those misconceptions with preconversion biblical teaching. When we do this much, we can depend upon the Holy Spirit to do the rest (see figure 35).

Analyzing Possible Motives for Conversion

The motives for conversion are best analyzed by putting matters in proper perspective. The results of sin will be evident in every culture: poverty, slavery, hunger, strained relationships, broken homes, greed, drunkenness, violence, ill health, ignorance, and many more. Conversion to Christ may or may not, depending upon a number of factors, result in the resolution of these problems, which for some is the motive for conversion. But the first responsibility of the messenger of Christ is to speak to those spiritual needs which, on the authority of God's Word, are known to be absolutely basic. The second responsibility is to take stock of the other needs of the audience and to deal with them in biblical ways, whether by word or deed. It would be unworthy of the servant of Christ to ignore the feelings and desires of the audience. It would be illegitimate to appeal to those feelings and desires without regard to God's response to them!

To analyze the various possible motives for conversion, look at figure 36 and then answer the following questions:

1. Which of the needs constitute legitimate motives for conversion? legitimate but insufficient? clearly illegitimate?

Figure 35
Audience Attitudes concerning Conversion

Misconception (check or rank)	Required Biblical Emphasis
_____ **Opposition:** "Conversion is unnecessary."	"Repent and be converted."
_____ **Syncretism:** "We have been _____ (Hindus, Buddhists, etc.), but we want to be Christians too."	"You shall have no other gods before me."
_____ **Reversible Decision:** "We can always change our minds again if things don't work out."	"If any man, having put his hand to the plow, turns back . . . ."
_____ **Cheap Grace:** "Pray a prayer. That's all there is to it."	"Count the cost."
_____ **Private Matter:** "Religion is not something one talks about."	"With the heart man believes, . . . but with the mouth confession is made."
_____ **Other:** _____	

2. Do the legitimate felt needs tend to obscure the real but unfelt needs? (For example, does the desire for acceptance in a Christian group cloud the need for forgiveness of sin?)
3. Do illegitimate motives for conversion (e.g., expectation of instant happiness or wealth) indicate that the gospel has been miscommunicated?
4. Will the convert tend to revert if the felt needs are not satisfied after conversion?
5. What adjustments might be made in our evangelism and counseling?

Encouraging Meaningful Decisions

Once we understand what the Bible teaches concerning the decision to convert to Christ, it remains for us to determine local understandings and practices relative to decision making. This can be done in several simple analytic steps.

Step One. Determine where the target group fits in on the continuum of the decision process (see figure 37).

Step Two. Determine whether different target subgroups should be placed at different points on the continuum. In generations past, for example, adult Americans were at (a); they now are closer to (b). Not a few adolescents are at (c) or even (d).

Figure 36
Analysis of Potential Motives for Conversion

Motives (check or rank)	Overall	Subgroup 1	Subgroup 2	Subgroup 3

1. Self-oriented Motivations
  a. To be able to cope with personal problems
  b. To obtain peace with others
  c. To gain prestige or power
  d. To escape the obligations of another religion
  e. To procure employment or material gain
  f. To obtain health or medical benefits
  g. To gain happiness
  h. Other _____				

2. God-oriented Motivations
  a. The awareness of God's love
  b. A sense of sin and the need for forgiveness
  c. The desire to be at peace with God
  d. The desire for personal holiness
  e. A need for freedom from evil and satanic powers
  f. The desire to know God
  g. A conviction that the Christian message is true
  h. Other _____				

3. Society-oriented Motivations
  a. Natal influence (Christian parentage)
  b. The desire for acceptance by the Christian group or church
  c. Desire to marry a Christian
  d. Compliance with the decision of a converting group
  e. A reaction against the religion (or irreligion) of an oppressing person or group
  f. Desire to gain entrance to a socially superior class or group
  g. Other _____				

Step Three. Determine who is capable of making decisions of the magnitude of religious conversion and who will participate only through their clan head, husband, parents, or some other authority figure. (In America, for example, a woman is considered competent to choose a religion independently of her husband, but a very young child may not have the same freedom.)

Step Four. Using the data which we have just determined, answer the following questions:

Figure 37
The Continuum of the Decision Process

Once the group understands the gospel and individuals want to convert, they will . . .

Decide by themselves, without regard to peers or community.	Decide by themselves, but with careful consideration of the views of peers and community.	Deliberate and decide in concert with peers or community, but with no sanctions against those who do not concur.	Deliberate and decide together and apply sanctions against those who do not join in the group's consensus.
a	b	c	d

---

1. Shall we place a higher priority on individual or group decisions?
2. Shall we give priority to certain segments (e.g., older people) of society in calling for decisions for Christ?
3. How much time will ordinarily be required in order to secure meaningful decisions?
4. Is it advisable for the evangelist to create a peer group (e.g., a study class) whose members can deliberate a decision together?

If the evangelist follows the steps outlined, decisions for Christ will tend to be more meaningful and genuine.

Determining Appropriate Forms of Confession and the Time of Baptism

In regard to the crucial steps of confession and baptism the missionary-evangelist would do well to consider certain questions:

1. What does baptism signify to most members of the community? (a means of grace? renunciation of one's heritage?)
2. In what ways might converts confess Christ and renounce their former religion without renouncing their culture and people?
3. Should the confession of faith be oral, written, or both?
4. Should confession and baptism occur in a private or public place?

Figure 38
Cultural Factors Relating to the Timing of Baptism

	Implications		
Factors (check those that apply)	Early Baptism	Short Delay	Extended Probation
1. Delay would encourage group decision. _____			
2. Delay would discourage the convert. _____			
3. Converts are generally knowledgeable about the Christian faith and its requirements. _____			
4. There are established practices in the locality that are important to timing. _____			
5. Other _____			

5. What are the cultural parallels to baptism (e.g., graduations, initiations, rites of passage)?
6. What do we learn from the cultural parallels? (E.g., should baptism serve as a functional substitute for an initiation ceremony that is widely practiced but unchristian?)

Closely related to these questions is the perennial problem of when to baptize converts. Unless the matter is dictated by the mission or denomination, or unless the church planter feels strongly that biblical precedents dictate early baptism, cultural factors may be important in deciding the question. If so, the kind of reflection suggested in figure 38 may be helpful.

While conversion is thought to be vital, the steps leading to and from conversion receive very little thoughtful planning by many missionary-evangelists. This is a most unhappy state of affairs. In faithfulness to God and in all fairness to potential and actual converts, they should be handled delicately and biblically. If the foregoing considerations aid us in doing this, they will serve an important function.

The Believers Congregated 12

Once people have been converted, it is imperative that they feel themselves to be a part of the divine family, that they faithfully gather with other members of the family, and that they regularly participate in the activities of the family. Only in this way will they become strong, mature, fruitful members of the body of Christ. The present chapter is concerned with making this happen.

Objectives

1. To establish times and places for the assembling of believers which will be in line with Christian practice and local customs and circumstances.

2. To make meetings of believers (scheduled and unscheduled) as spiritually meaningful and helpful as possible.

3. To introduce new believers into the fellowship and discipline of a local family of believers as soon as possible.

4. To provide as many ways into the fellowship of the family as possible.

5. To adjust the program of evangelism so as to encourage both converts from the world and converts from nominal Christian backgrounds to enter the new fellowship.

Believing Communities

Biblical Principles and Precedents

In the Old Testament Era, God was concerned for his people, so he determined that they should be together and that he would dwell among them. We have a picture of the New Testament church in the Old Testament gathering of the people of God around the tabernacle. Furthermore, God and his people lived and moved together (Num. 9:17–23).

In the New Testament, Jesus said, "Where two or three are gathered in my name, there am I in the midst of them" (Matt. 18:20 RSV). With the advent of the Holy Spirit, believers were baptized into the new body in

192

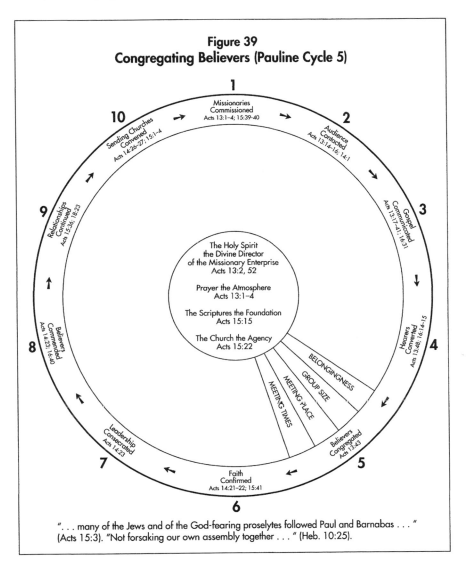

Figure 39
Congregating Believers (Pauline Cycle 5)

1
Missionaries
Commissioned
Acts 13:1-4; 15:39-40

10
Sending Churches
Convened
Acts 14:26-27; 15:1-4

2
Audience
Contacted
Acts 13:14-16; 14:1

9
Relationships
Continued
Acts 15:36; 18:23

3
Gospel
Communicated
Acts 13:17-41; 16:31

The Holy Spirit
the Divine Director
of the Missionary Enterprise
Acts 13:2, 52

Prayer the Atmosphere
Acts 13:1-4

The Scriptures the Foundation
Acts 15:15

The Church the Agency
Acts 15:22

BELONGINGNESS
GROUP SIZE
MEETING PLACE
MEETING TIMES

8
Believers
Commended
Acts 14:23; 16:40

4
Hearers
Converted
Acts 13:48; 16:14-15

7
Leadership
Consecrated
Acts 14:23

5
Believers
Congregated
Acts 13:43

6
Faith
Confirmed
Acts 14:21-22; 15:41

" . . . many of the Jews and of the God-fearing proselytes followed Paul and Barnabas . . . "
(Acts 15:3). "Not forsaking our own assembly together . . . " (Heb. 10:25).

which Jew and Gentile were one and Christ was the head (1 Cor. 12:13).
Believers constituted the household of God (Eph. 2:19); all of them were
accepted irrespective of ethnic background or social position. Believers
were part of a supportive community called the church and were to
"bear one another's burdens, and thus fulfill the law of Christ" (Gal. 6:2).

The believing community in New Testament times bore certain similarities to ordinary unbelieving organizations, of course. They met together regularly; they accomplished certain objectives together; they
encountered certain difficulties within the group; they sought out new

members. But at the same time they were different. Luke writes that on the Day of Pentecost Peter urged his hearers to save themselves from their corrupt generation. Accordingly, those who accepted the message and were baptized gave themselves to:

1. Study—"devoting themselves to the apostles' teaching"
2. Fellowship—meeting together in the temple and homes
3. Worship—breaking of bread, praying, and praising God
4. Stewardship—giving themselves and their substance to one another as there was need
5. Witness—"having favor with all the people" so that the Lord added to their numbers (Acts 2:41–47)

As time went on and as Christian communities multiplied, pagan culture and the unbelieving community became arrayed against the early believers. What made them suspect was not that they were bad, but that they were different! Follow the apostles, for example. Wherever they went there was trouble! Cyprus, Iconium, Lystra, Ephesus, Philippi, Thessalonica, Berea, Corinth—in all of these places the story was similar. Heathen temples lost their attraction, idol-makers lost customers, diviners lost their livelihood.

The Christian families of the first century were composed of people of different social class and, most likely, color. The believing community at Colossae included both Philemon and his slave Onesimus as brothers in Christ (Philem. 16). Certainly there were other masters and many slaves. Simeon Niger of Antioch was probably black (Acts 13:1). The apostle Paul made it clear that in Christ "there is neither Jew nor Greek, there is neither slave nor free man, there is neither male nor female" (Gal. 3:28a). That does not mean that such distinctions were totally disregarded among early Christians. It does mean that chromosomes, color, and class did not bring those communities together. Nor were they allowed to keep the believers of those communities apart.

In time, Caesar himself expressed opposition to the believing community. Even as the opponents of Jesus had accused him of sedition and treason, the enemies of the early Christian communities charged that believers acted contrary to the decrees of Caesar by undermining the imperial cult.

A hostile culture, differences of class and color, the antagonism of Caesar—none of these could ultimately divide the believing communities or destroy their fellowship. Why? There are two basic reasons. First, they were united in Christ. "For you are all one in Christ," the apostle wrote (Gal. 3:28b). Theirs was a common creed. It was expressed in various ways and in greater or lesser detail. But its essence was "Jesus Christ is Lord." So John could write very simply: "Anyone who goes too far and does not abide in the teaching of Christ, does not have God; the one who abides in the teaching, he has both the Father and the Son. If anyone comes to you and does not bring this teaching, do not receive him into your house, and do not give him a greeting" (2 John 9–10).

Second, the early believers were attracted to one another by common concerns. They had real problems in their relationships. Nevertheless, they voluntarily gathered together in order to worship, pray, fellowship at the table of the Lord, be instructed in the faith, give of their substance, help one another, and carry out their mission. And these concerns so motivated them—and Christ so captivated them—that in spite of the antagonism of their culture, the differences of class and color, and the opposition of Caesar, they gathered together to worship and went forth to witness. And God caused the churches to grow (1 Cor. 3:7).

Relevant Research

The Church as Structure and Organization

Raymond Firth distinguishes between social structure and social organization. He points out that persons relate to each other in order to preserve traditional ways and values (social structure) and also to effect change and accomplish ends that would not otherwise be achieved (social organization).[1] The church (and, therefore, the local churches, including embryonic local churches) is ordained by God to preserve and transmit his truth. In this sense it is a divinely ordained structure. Unfortunately it sometimes becomes entrenched and intertwined with particular Caesars and cultures in such a way that people born into a nation are automatically born into its church as well. When that happens, the church becomes a culturally determined structure!

Basically, however, churches begin as organizations. This means that individuals and families voluntarily align themselves with one another in order to change people (themselves included) and circumstances, and to achieve certain other purposes and goals. That being the case, a certain amount of antagonism or, at the very least, disdain, can usually be expected from the larger society. Research shows that cultural disapproval does not mean that a religious organization cannot grow, however. In fact, Dean Kelley has shown that religious organizations which are more or less like the larger culture of which they are a part tend not to grow. Groups such as the Assemblies of God, Mormons,

---

1. Raymond Firth, *Elements of Social Organization* (Boston: Beacon, 1963), 29–40.

Jehovah's Witnesses, Seventh-Day Adventists, and Black Muslims, on the other hand, grow rapidly while being out of step with the larger society.[2]

Differences in the Degree of Cooperation and Integration

Firth's distinction is not the only one that is important to an understanding of believing groups. There are at least two other well-known categorizations that emphasize the degree to which group members interact and cooperate with each other.

First, there is the *Gemeinschaft/Gesellschaft* distinction of the German sociologist Ferdinand Tonnies.[3] In *Gesellschaft* (association) the members are bound together by a system of exchanging goods and services, but they do not live and work in intimate relationship with each other. In *Gemeinschaft* (community) the members of the group are intimately related to each other much as is the case, for example, in nuclear or extended families.

Second, there is the distinction between integrated and nonintegrated groups. Integration here does not have to do with ethnic background, but with the degree of commonality of concerns and goals. Nonintegrated groups such as concert audiences and crowds at the ball park exhibit little by way of commonality. Integrated groups such as the faculty of a school or shareholders in a company exhibit a much higher degree of commonality.

If churches are to measure up to the New Testament standard, leaders and believers should pray and plan for warm personal relationships and a high degree of integration from the first. Believers are ordained to glorify God and promote the cause of Christ. Above all other groups they should evidence a united community and a common cause.

Homogeneous Units in Society

In the Church Growth movement there is special focus on the so-called homogeneous unit.[4] A rather nebulous term, it refers to a body of people who form a cohesive unit because of a common denominator such as ancestry, language, or lifestyle. Nuclear and extended families, clans and castes, ethnic and linguistic groups qualify as homogeneous units. Such units or groupings of people like to decide, work, play, and worship together.

2. Dean M. Kelley, *Why Conservative Churches Are Growing: A Study in Sociology of Religion* (New York: Harper and Row, 1972), 20–25.

3. Ferdinand Tonnies, *Community and Society*, trans. and ed. Charles P. Loomis (East Lansing: Michigan State University Press, 1957).

4. Donald A. McGavran, *Understanding Church Growth* (Grand Rapids: Eerdmans, 1970), 85–87.

This being the case, Donald McGavran believed that church planters should focus on individual tribes, castes, and language groups, even though such a policy seems to be in conflict with the biblical principle that Christians of all languages, classes, and colors are one in Christ.[5] Roger Greenway, agreeing with McGavran, says that this holds true even in the great cities of the world:

> Cities are "melting pots," but this aspect of urban life must not be over-estimated. Beneath the surface there are still many differences. Much of the loneliness and frustration which rural-urban immigrants experience stems from their inability to communicate freely in the official language and from the foreignness of much of the urban culture. Religious services in their own language or dialect will attract them, and sermons and hymns they can understand will get through to their hearts. As tribe and caste distinctions break down in the course of time, the shift can be made away from ethnic congregations to "all peoples" churches. But until that time comes, it is best to recognize and accept the cultural heterogeneity of the city and proceed to multiply as many tribe, caste, and language churches as possible until all parts of the urban community have been leavened by the gospel.[6]

Practical Reflection

It is apparent that cultural understandings, preferences, and ties on the one hand, and Christian ideals and requirements on the other hand, may be very much in conflict when believers congregate (as well as at the conversion stage of the Pauline Cycle). Just as the unbeliever is tempted to follow the crowd or stick with the clan and not convert to Christ, so the new believer, after an initial break, is tempted to return to the crowd or clan rather than following through and fully identifying with the believing group. The individual who does follow through is apt to seek out Christian fellowship among believers of the same cultural background. In either case, Christ and culture seem to be in conflict. What shall we do in congregating believers? Shall we capitalize on the ties of natural homogeneous units in order to avoid reversions and en-courage growth? Or are such ties to be disregarded in view of the much more important bond that believers have in Christ? Certain consider-ations can aid in the resolution of this problem:

1. There should be no question of ultimate authority. We must con-form to Christ, not to culture. However, the fact that in the divine Christ there are no distinctions of class, color, or sex does not mean that such

---

5. Ibid., 289–91.
6. Roger S. Greenway, *Guidelines for Urban Church Planting* (Grand Rapids: Baker, 1976), 16–17.

distinctions in human culture are obliterated. It simply means that they are transcended. They remain significant but they do not reign supreme. Every local family of believers need not evidence the full, variegated social and cultural richness that characterizes the larger family or body of Christ. Furthermore, no social or cultural distinctive should be significant enough to exclude a believer from any family of believers, nor to alienate local church families from each other or the larger body of Christ.

2. Choices that have already been made at the contact, communication, and conversion stages act in connection with cultural factors to determine to a large extent the composition of the initial believing group. Those choices will tend to include some people and exclude others. It is important, then, to recognize homogeneous and heterogeneous factors and develop complementing and compensating strategies accordingly.

ME-1 illustration: Lyle Schaller says that in the United States homogeneous units are defined in terms of common affiliations rather than familial lines. Church structures, he also notes, have three components: the pastor at the center, a membership circle, and a larger fellowship circle. Churches desiring to grow will seek on the one hand to increase friendship ties between individual members and outsiders who are not members of any worshiping congregation, and on the other to erase the line between the membership and fellowship circles. Schaller believes that one of the best strategies for accomplishing this is the development of small groups (homogeneous units) based on common affiliations.[7]

ME-3 illustration: By way of contrast consider the initial growth of a church among the Tzotzil Indians in Mexico. Out of a total of eighty early believers, seventy-nine were kinfolk. The lone exception was associated with one of the other believers through what we would call a farmers' cooperative. Marian Cowan, who reports on the formation of the Tzotzil church, does not focus on strategies for continued growth; but we can be relatively sure that, had that been her purpose in writing, she would have emphasized strategies for capitalizing on kinship loyalties.[8]

3. When we speak of growth, it is always necessary to think in terms of spiritual as well as numerical growth, even though the author of any given piece of writing may have only one type in mind. In considering Greenway's suggestion that in the city context we begin with homoge-

7. Lyle E. Schaller, *Assimilating New Members* (Nashville: Abingdon, 1978), chs. 4 and 5.

8. Marian Cowan, "A Christian Movement in Mexico," *Practical Anthropology* 9 (Sept.–Oct. 1962): 193–204.

neous congregations that will eventually become "all peoples" congregations, we do well to remember this tension. "All peoples" churches could have primary reference to churches that exhibit spiritual unity among otherwise diverse people or to churches that grow numerically because their strategy is designed to reach everyone. In any event, we should keep the biblical ideal before us and find meaningful ways to express and experience oneness in Christ, both in the local group and between believing groups.

4. Alan Harre has written an unusually helpful book concerning the problem of dropouts. He not only underscores the magnitude of the problem, but also devotes several chapters to measures for preventing dropout and ways in which to reclaim and minister to those who have dropped out. He notes a study by David Roozen on the dropout rate of the various age groups: among preteens—2.6 percent; teens—15 percent; people in their early twenties—9.1 percent; from twenty-five to fifty-four—4.6 percent; over fifty-five—preteen level.[9] Of course, statistics that are valid for one church, denomination, or culture would not necessarily be valid for others. But the study does suggest that reversion and dropout problems are significant in the United States, and that those in their teens and early twenties merit special attention because of their vulnerability.

Belongingness: The New Believer and the Believing Community

Biblical Principles and Precedents

According to Scripture, the plight of the unsaved is complete separation from God and his family. They are "excluded from the commonwealth of Israel, and strangers to the covenants of promise, having no hope and without God in the world" (Eph. 2:12). In eternity they are consigned to "the eternal fire which has been prepared for the devil and his angels" (Matt. 25:41). Lack of belongingness was so evident everywhere that Karl Marx used the term "alienation" to describe the desperate situation of the proletariat. To an even greater extent, the unsaved are alienated.

Believers, on the other hand, "are no longer strangers and aliens, but . . . fellow citizens with the saints, and are of God's household" (Eph. 2:19). In other words, *they belong!* Relevant to this truth are two important facts presented in Scripture.

9. Alan F. Harre, *Close the Back Door: Ways to Create a Caring Congregational Fellowship* (St. Louis: Concordia, 1984), 17–18.

The first fact is that humans are social beings. When Adam was created, God declared that it was not good that man should be alone (Gen. 2:18). Eve was created and the first society was formed. But they fell, and God made a new creature (2 Cor. 5:17; Gal. 6:15; Eph. 4:24; Col. 3:10). This new self is also a social being, that is, made for fellowship with God and with others. To recognize the social responsibilities of the new creature, one has only to observe the way the apostle Paul immediately plunges into a discussion of social relations when he speaks of the new self (Eph. 4:24–32; Col. 3:10–14). Redeemed or fallen, humans by nature are social beings. This truth cannot be ignored.

The second fact is that God has created a new society for the redeemed. This new society is the church. Belonging to the church is not optional for believers. By divine action they are united to the body of Christ. No believer is excluded nor exempted on grounds of race or social class (1 Cor. 12:13–14). All believers are part of the new society.

The early church understood these truths. To the embryonic new society of 120 believers, 3,000 were added in one day (Acts 2:41). There was no waiting period while the new converts learned basic doctrine or attained to a certain state of holiness. A part of the miracle of Pentecost was the fact that the 3,000 became like the 120 and not the other way around! This pattern was repeated again and again (Acts 4:4; 6:7; 11:21; 16:5). New converts were not left alone. The Spirit joined them to the body of Christ, and members of the early church identified the newcomers as their own.

In belonging to the church new believers had identity. They were Christ-followers. In the new society they received spiritual nourishment through the action of the believing group (Eph. 4:11–16). They were loved and were taught to love in return (Heb. 10:24–25). All the security and stability which come from belonging to a group were theirs. This sense of belongingness was so intimate that the group was called a body and each person was a body part. When one part suffered, all parts suffered. When one member was honored, all members were honored (1 Cor. 12:26).

Identification with the group, however, did not destroy individuality. As an individual the new believer had been given special abilities to make unique contributions to the body (Rom. 12:3–8; 1 Cor. 12:7–11; Eph. 4:7–16). These spiritual gifts gave status. New believers were needed by the group, for the group could not function properly without their abilities. At the same time the new believers needed the group since they could not function apart from it. Each person's individuality contributed to one's "social beingness," and each person's social nature contributed to one's individuality. In the new self and the new society alienation is completely overcome. The believer belongs!

Relevant Research

From a scientific point of view also, we are communal creatures. We live in the context of community. Not only is this in accord with human nature, but it also leads to our predicament: cooperation is essential to our existence. Therefore human beings relate to each other—especially to those of the same race, language, class, upbringing—in order to meet psychological and sociological needs. Throughout the literature there is emphasis on the need of the individual for belongingness and acceptance in the community. We will briefly look at three concepts which relate to this need.

1. Incorporation

Incorporation refers to the acceptance of new members into the group of which they are to become a part. Incorporation is of two kinds. Informal incorporation is accomplished by simply making new members feel that they are indeed part of the group. Formal incorporation involves some kind of ritualistic reception of new members into the group, usually in the presence of all or most of the members.

The activities and rites of incorporation are so important that almost every organization, including churches, has them in some shape or form. Nevertheless, we Christians are liable to err in this regard. In the first place, we might put so much emphasis on the decision point that we forget that the decision process involves incorporation into the new group and the acceptance of its discipline. In the second place, we place such an emphasis on accepting Christ and being accepted by him that we may take it for granted that the new believer feels accepted by the believing group. If the new believer has a responsibility to join the believing group, the believing group has a responsibility to do everything possible to incorporate and integrate the new believer into the family of faith!

2. Anomie

Perhaps more than any other sociologist, Emile Durkheim stressed the role of society in human life. In fact, he went so far as to suggest that religion is important primarily as a supporter and interpreter of the social order. It goes without saying that we cannot wholly agree with Durkheim at that point. Nevertheless, we can learn much from him.

Durkheim elaborated three very different types of relationships that exist between an individual and the moral order represented by society.[10] In the first type of relationship individuals are made to see them-

10. Emile Durkheim, *Suicide: A Study in Sociology* (New York: Free, 1951).

selves as separate and responsible for their own affairs. They do not have recourse to the community when things go wrong. The result may be "egoistic suicide." In the second type of relationship the individual is bound to society in an intense way, even to the point of being willing to give one's life for the community in an act of altruism. In the third type the individual is transferred from one social pattern or order into another and thus suddenly acquires a new social character. For example, one may become rich overnight; the result is that one is alienated from one's impoverished friends without being accepted by the established wealthy. Durkheim called this condition anomie—the state which results from being put into a place where norms are ill defined, contradictory, or absent.

If Durkheim's position seems extreme, it should be remembered that he was reacting against Charles Darwin, who saw everything from a biological perspective. In spite of our quarrel with Durkheim's position, it is important to view his concept of anomie from a Christian perspective. How often do new believers come into the company of believers without receiving clear signals as to what is expected of them and what it means to be a member of a Christian group or church? What may seem clear to us may well be altogether unclear to the new believer! Spiritual anomic suicide may be just another name for reversion or, to use the older term, backsliding. But when it occurs, at least part of the onus falls upon more mature believers.

3. Conformity

Analyzing the adaptation that individuals must make in relating to one another in order to achieve group goals, Robert K. Merton stresses that members must accept both the goals of the group and the means of attaining them.[11] If the individual member accepts the goals but not the means of attaining them, the result will probably be innovation. Accepting the means but not the goals will result in ritualism. Accepting both the goals and the means results in conformity.

Building upon Merton's ideas, Lawrence Richards believes that churches tend to give priority to means rather than to goals. As a result, Christians become ritualists, going through the motions of worship and service, but not really maturing as fellow believers in Christ.[12] The concept of conformity is usually frowned upon (in American society at least); but when conformity means adherence to true faith and practice,

---

11. Robert K. Merton, *Social Theory and Social Structure*, rev. ed. (New York: Free, 1957), 139–40.
12. Lawrence O. Richards, *A New Face for the Church* (Grand Rapids: Zondervan, 1970), 50–51.

when it means becoming more Christlike, when it means that the believing group can go forward in the plan and program of God—then it is a positive concept!

It seems that Richards himself is advocating innovation, for he accepts the goals of the churches but not the means that are being used to attain them. In any case, his observation merits consideration when we are planning for the first meetings of new believers as well as for the ongoing ministry of the churches. Though worship, service, witness, and fellowship are long-term goals, new believers must from the very first be introduced to them and to the biblical means for attaining them. Otherwise either ritualism or innovation may result, and innovation for the new believer may also spell reversion!

Practical Reflection

1. In many (though certainly not all) situations, church planters will need to rethink issues having to do with the relationship between evangelism, conversion, and baptism on the one hand and incorporation into the body of believers on the other. They might well do the kind of analysis that David Wells did:

> Evangelism today, especially mass evangelism, is usually not church-based. The evangelists minister apart from church connections and usually are unable to care for new converts. Furthermore, since baptism is an ordinance for churches to administer, it would be inappropriate for evangelists to begin baptizing randomly and promiscuously. The unintended result of this is that new converts are not put in touch with churches and so are left organically severed from the body of believers.[13]

Of course, recognition of the problem does not solve it. But it is a necessary beginning. Gaps between the converting and congregating stages of the Pauline Cycle need to be narrowed and, if possible, eliminated.

2. Once believers have come together in a new spiritual fellowship, it is imperative that that fellowship be carefully nurtured and maintained. The need for belongingness is universal, though the ways to enhance it may vary somewhat with the culture or subculture.

ME-1 illustration: With reference to American churches, Harre notes Lyle Schaller's conclusion that as many as one-third or even one-half of all Protestants do not feel that they belong or fit in the congregation of which they are members![14] With reference to those who drop out, he ac-

---

13. David F. Wells, *Turning to God: Biblical Conversion in the Modern World* (Grand Rapids: Baker, 1989), 45.
14. Harre, *Close the Back Door,* 25.

cepts John Savage's observation that dropouts allow the local congregation a period of only about six to eight weeks to visit them. After that they reinvest their interest and efforts in other pursuits.[15] Harre then goes on to suggest specific measures for retention of members, and specific attitudes toward and methods of ministering to any who do drop out. His suggestions are particularly applicable to the North American congregation but have wider applications as well.

ME-3 illustration: In the author's specific church-planting experiences in Saitama prefecture in Japan, probably the greatest single hurdle had to do with congregating believers. Large numbers of people were quite ready to try Christianity but, by the same token, they were quite ready to revert as soon as they felt that it did not work for them. There was no easy solution because the overall problem had to do with contextualizing the gospel communication on the one hand and building new and meaningful relationships on the other. A partial solution, however, lay in helping to establish an immediate relationship between the new convert and recent but secure converts. One might speak of the "buddy system," although that term would hardly be appropriate to the Japanese situation.

Group Functions and Optimum Size

The notion of optimum size will be new to most readers. We are referring to the proper size of a group given its goals and functions. The notion is somewhat analogous to so-called normal body weight. Obviously, every human body should not be the same weight. Normal weight depends upon one's height, body frame, and, to a certain extent, the kind of activities in which one engages. Similarly, the activities and aims of a group have a bearing on its optimum size.

Biblical Principles and Precedents

The Bible does not give all the information that we might like when it comes to the number of believers present in any given situation. But it does give some significant information in this regard:

1. Three disciples had a special relationship to Jesus—Peter, James, and John.
2. Our Lord chose twelve disciples to be with him as he went about his ministry. When one betrayed him, another—Matthias—was chosen to take his place (Acts 1:26).

15. Ibid., 20.

3. After sending out the Twelve on a mission, the Lord sent out seventy (or seventy-two) to go ahead of him to towns and places he was about to visit (Luke 10:1).
4. After his resurrection our Lord appeared to a group numbering in excess of five hundred (1 Cor. 15:6).
5. There were some 120 believers in the Jerusalem church at the time of Pentecost. After Pentecost the number of believers swelled to 3,000 and then 5,000 (men) and probably more (Acts 1:15; 2:41; 4:4).

It would be interesting to know exactly how many believers there were in those churches mentioned in the New Testament. The number must have varied greatly. We know that all in Lydda and Sharon turned to the Lord (Acts 9:35). Some scholars have conjectured that the congregation at Antioch numbered between three hundred and five hundred souls. On the other hand, the number of believers in some other places, such as Athens, must have been very small indeed. The early churches were modeled somewhat after the synagogue; thus the requirement that there had to be ten adult men in order to organize a synagogue may have had some significance for church practice. That believers often met in private homes (as well as in public places) meant that many of the gatherings were necessarily small.

Relevant Research

1. We cannot present firm figures for the optimum size of various types of groups, but there are some general indications in the literature. For example, core leadership groups such as those which run corporations and lead military campaigns seem to number in the range of three to twelve members. Edward T. Hall writes, "Eight to twelve persons can know each other well enough to maximize their talents."[16]

2. The small group, which is so prominent in sociological literature, is usually defined as a group of such a size that (a) its members can establish a face-to-face relationship, and (b) the absence of any member from a meeting would be noticed. The small group seldom numbers more than twenty-five or thirty members, and usually fewer. It is well suited to effect group learning, fellowship, and corporate action. Howard Snyder notes the importance of small groups in church history:

> Early Pietism was nurtured by the *collegio pietatis*, or house meetings for prayer, Bible study and discussion. The small group was a basic aspect

16. Edward T. Hall, *Beyond Culture* (Garden City, N.Y.: Doubleday, 1977), 203.

of the Wesleyan Revival in England, with the proliferation of John Wesley's "class meetings." Small groups undergirded the Holiness Revival that swept America in the late 1800s and led, in part, to the modern Pentecostal movement. More significantly, the road to Reformation was paved by small-group Bible studies. If nothing more, these facts surely suggest that small groups are conducive to the reviving ministry of the Holy Spirit.[17]

We have emphasized elsewhere that the extremely rapid growth of Soka Gakkai Buddhism in Japan is related to the prominence given to small discussion groups.[18] In a lecture at Trinity Evangelical Divinity School, George Cowan of Wycliffe Bible Translators emphasized that the Mexican government officially recognizes only groups of forty members or more.[19]

3. One definition of community is the "maximum number of people who can maintain face-to-face relationships." This is usually taken to be about 1,000 people. In his study of nativistic movements in Africa, David Barrett suggests that the number 1,000 may be very significant. He notes that at the time of his study the average size of some 600 Protestant mission churches or dioceses in Africa was 36,000 members; 300 Catholic dioceses averaged 97,000. But the independent churches which have been mushrooming in Africa tended to be considerably smaller—the overall average was 1,400, and only about 1,000 in Ghana, South Africa, Nigeria, and other long-involved nations. Barrett suggests that the size of a true Christian community may be smaller than the Western world has realized, and that the size of some of our church groupings may have to be scaled down in order to reintroduce *philadelphia.*[20]

Practical Reflection

The implications of optimum size may be much greater than is realized in most churches and missions.

1. Leadership should be in the hands of a few recognized, gifted leaders. If leadership is not shared, it runs the risk of being dictatorial and occasioning division. If it is shared too widely, it runs the risk of being unwieldy and ineffective.

17. Howard A. Snyder, *The Problem of Wine Skins: Church Structure in a Technological Age* (Downers Grove, Ill.: InterVarsity, 1975), 140.
18. David J. Hesselgrave, "A Propagation Profile of the Soka Gakkai" (Ph.D. diss., University of Minnesota, 1965), 249–64.
19. The lecture was delivered at Trinity Evangelical Divinity School in April 1970.
20. David Barrett, *Schism and Renewal in Africa* (Nairobi: Oxford University Press, 1968), 171.

2. In some cultures it may be extremely difficult for local churches to grow much larger than the upper limits of the size of the small group. Cultures that emphasize the group rather than the individual make it difficult for individuals to follow Christ. When some do believe, the believing family becomes very important to them. But unless an unusual vision and superior strategy for outreach are evident, the need for acceptance and fellowship is met in the small group, and growth may level off at that point.

3. In some situations it will be advantageous to develop cell-group churches from the very beginning. In fact, Ralph Neighbour contends that the cell church is really the church of the future in light of such factors as population explosion, the urbanization of societies, the unavailability of suitable real estate, and the need for belongingness.[21] Church planters would do well to give careful consideration to Neighbour's rationale and his carefully constructed guidelines for establishing cell-group churches.

4. As embryonic churches grow into established churches with ever increasing numbers of believers, it is crucial to maintain small groups. Howard Snyder emphasizes that "theologically, large- and small-group gatherings are the structural implications of the church's being the people of God and the fellowship of the Holy Spirit. . . . Peoplehood implies the necessity of large-group gatherings while community requires small-group structures."[22]

ME-1–3 illustrations: Perhaps the high point of interest in raising up so-called superchurches came in the middle of the 1980s. One expression of that interest was John Vaughan's study of the large church, which he defined as a church with over 5,000 members.[23] A key point in Vaughan's study is that churches grow by division. He notes, for example, that both Donald McGavran and Paul Yonggi Cho advise that when a church reaches a membership of 400 to 500, it should either hive off a new congregation (McGavran) or establish more and more cell groups, each with its own leader and ministry (Cho). Vaughan gives numerous examples of growth through cell groups, including Cho's Yoido Full Gospel Church in Seoul (which at the time of Vaughan's writing had almost 20,000 cell groups) and Charles Stanley's First Baptist Church in Atlanta (which had just appointed a full-time pastor in charge of cell-group development).

---

21. Ralph W. Neighbour Jr., *Where Do We Go from Here? A Guidebook for Cell Group Churches* (Houston: Torch, 1990).

22. Snyder, *Problem of Wine Skins*, 163. Note that Snyder's use of the word "community" does not refer to group size per se.

23. John N. Vaughan, *The Large Church: A Twentieth-Century Expression of the First-Century Church* (Grand Rapids: Baker, 1985).

The Place of Meeting

No doubt about it, the bottleneck in many an effort in church planting is the meeting place. In country after country missionary-evangelists and other church leaders say, "Solve the church-building problem for us, and our program of planting new congregations will go into orbit." It is hard to believe that the church of Christ cannot advance without a generous supply of brick and mortar. At the same time, most of us who have been involved in pioneer efforts over a number of years will confess that an adequate building is usually a big boost to growth.

Biblical Principles and Precedents

It is worthwhile to reflect on the fact that Jehovah's first provision for a special place in which to meet with his people was a tent or tabernacle. At Jehovah's command the people moved. At his command the people camped. Jehovah was present with his people within the tabernacle (Num. 9:17–23). Then came the day when David proposed that a temple be built. He said to Nathan, "See now, I dwell in a house of cedar, but the ark of God dwells within tent curtains" (2 Sam. 7:2). In response Jehovah said:

> Go and tell my servant David, Thus saith the LORD, Shalt thou build me an house for me to dwell in? Whereas I have not dwelt in any house since the time that I brought up the children of Israel out of Egypt, even to this day, but have walked in a tent and in a tabernacle. In all the places wherein I have walked with all the children of Israel spake I a word with any of the tribes of Israel, whom I commanded to feed my people Israel, saying, Why build ye not me an house of cedar? [2 Sam. 7:5–7 KJV]

Howard Snyder concludes, "The truer sign of the presence of God in his earthly church is the tabernacle, and only secondarily the temple. The tabernacle is the truer symbol, for it more accurately shows how God acts in history."[24]

In a sense the New Testament seems to bear out this contention, though it would not be true to say that our Lord neglected the temple. He was taken there as a child. He visited the temple during his ministry, and he cleansed it of merchants and proclaimed that as his Father's house it should be a house of prayer (Matt. 21:13; Luke 19:46). But to the Samaritan woman he said that the time would come when the Father would not be worshiped either on Mount Gerizim or in Jerusalem, but "in spirit and truth" (John 4:23). And he promised that wherever

---

24. Snyder, *Problem of Wine Skins*, 63.

two or three believers would gather in his name, he would meet with them (Matt. 18:20).

After the ascension of their Lord, the early believers met in the temple and in homes (Acts 5:42). As Christianity spread throughout the empire, believers met in the synagogues (Acts 9:20; 13:5; 18:26), in public places (Acts 18:28; 20:20), and in the open air (Acts 16:13). From the very beginning and throughout the New Testament Era, house gatherings were a common feature of Christian corporate life (Acts 2:46; Rom. 16:5; 1 Cor. 16:19; Col. 4:15). In fact, there were no church buildings as we know them for the first 150 years of the church's existence.

We conclude, then, that Christianity has no one sacred spot or shrine and that God will meet with his people wherever they gather to worship and call upon his name. In this, true Christianity is uniquely the universal religion.

Relevant Research

Research on meeting places is certainly not voluminous, but case studies of rapidly growing religious movements in other cultures may be worthy of consideration.[25]

1. One obvious advantage of the house meeting is that it serves to keep the group small. The small-group meetings lend themselves to mutual recognition of participants, dialogue, interaction, and the building of friendships. The others are aware of any member's absence and reestablish contact. Neighbors, friends, and acquaintances find it relatively easy to accept invitations to the house meeting and are quite readily assimilated into the small group. When the group outgrows the limitations of the house (and small-group size), it is quite simple for part of the group to start a new group in the home of another member. In this way the number of meetings, meeting places, groups, and individual members multiplies rapidly.

2. Most religious groups do have central locations where the faithful gather. Some groups of believers do not have such a meeting place in their own community. Nevertheless, they most likely have some accessible building where certain religious activities can be held.

Nichiren Shoshu Soka Gakkai Buddhism claims to have built the largest temple on earth. The Sho-Hondo, as it is called, seats six thousand in such a way that all may view the worship object (*Honzon*) without interference. Standing near the Sho-Hondo are other buildings both ancient and modern that depict Japan's history during the eras of

---

25. David J. Hesselgrave, "What Causes Religious Movements to Grow?" in *Dynamic Religious Movements: Case Studies of Rapidly Growing Religious Movements around the World*, ed. David J. Hesselgrave (Grand Rapids: Baker, 1978), 313–14.

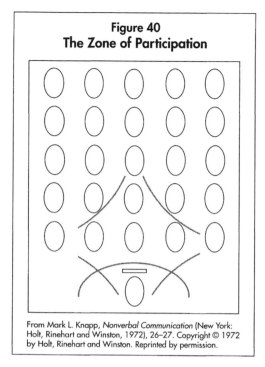

Figure 40
The Zone of Participation

From Mark L. Knapp, *Nonverbal Communication* (New York: Holt, Rinehart and Winston, 1972), 26–27. Copyright © 1972 by Holt, Rinehart and Winston. Reprinted by permission.

growth of Soka Gakkai.[26] The Soka Gakkai claim that this temple area is the earth's center and the location of the coming kingdom.

Some other groups also display architectural grandeur. Consider the Mormons' Temple Square in Salt Lake City. Still others have meeting places characterized by extreme simplicity. Most do have some site or artifacts which are especially meaningful to them.[27]

3. Research shows that the shape of the meeting place and the arrangement of its furniture affect the process of communication. Mark Knapp emphasizes that there is a "zone of participation" which is roughly in the form of a triangle with the base immediately in front of the speaker.[28] People sitting in this area are most likely to respond to what is being said and done in the pulpit area. (See figure 40.) The long, rectangular sanctuaries characteristic of many churches and other places of meeting are not well designed for effective communication. If sanctuaries were better designed for effective communication, much less energy would need to be spent trying to urge people to move to the front pews!

Practical Reflection

As much God-given understanding, creativeness, and patience will be required of church planters at the congregating stage of the Pauline Cycle as at any other. Believers must meet, but where? The answers will be as diverse as the demographics, economics, and cultural preferences that characterize church-planting situations. In most cases it will be de-

26. David J. Hesselgrave, "Nichiren Shoshu Soka Gakkai—The Lotus Blossoms in Japan," in *Dynamic Religious Movements*, 129–30.

27. Hesselgrave, "What Causes Religious Movements to Grow?" 313.

28. Mark L. Knapp, *Nonverbal Communication* (New York: Holt, Rinehart and Winston, 1972), 26–27.

sirable for God's people to have a church building of some kind. Nevertheless, it is well to keep certain fundamentals in mind.

1. The development of new churches ultimately cannot be dependent upon the provision of a church building as such, as desirable as that might be.

2. To broach the matter of a permanent building too soon after beginning a new work may discourage new converts.

3. To saddle any congregation with inordinate debt in order to provide a church building will be counterproductive. It would be helpful for every missionary and church planter to evaluate the situation as an architect might view it. Providentially, a Christian architect, Ray Bowman, has provided us with just such an analysis.[29]

4. Insofar as possible, church buildings should reflect the architectural styles of the indigenous culture. All too often in non-Western cultures, church buildings themselves communicate the idea that Christianity is a foreign religion.

5. When it comes to buildings, more and more emphasis is being placed on the servant nature of the church. The church does not exist to impress people with ostentation, but to minister to them in their need. We should design church buildings with the various ministries in mind, that is, not primarily as a worship shrine but as a ministry center.

The Times of Meetings

Biblical Principles and Precedents

The writer to the Hebrews clearly stated that Christians should not neglect to assemble themselves together (Heb. 10:25). The primitive church followed the practice of meeting often. In fact, in the period after Pentecost they met daily (Acts 2:46).

It cannot be established, however, that there was one certain time when a congregation was required to meet. The Colossians were told not to allow anyone to judge them in regard to feast days or Sabbath days (Col. 2:16). The Romans were told that there was no agreement among Christians in regard to days: "One man regards one day above another, another regards every day alike. Let each man be fully convinced in his own mind" (Rom. 14:5). When entering a city, Paul customarily joined with those meeting in the synagogue on the Sabbath (Acts 17:2). For Christian believers, however, the first day of the week became the customary day to meet. On the first day an offering was to

29. Ray Bowman (with Eddy Hall), *When Not to Build: An Architect's Unconventional Wisdom for the Growing Church* (Grand Rapids: Baker, 1992).

be collected for the poor (1 Cor. 16:2). It was on the first day of the week that the Lord had been resurrected (John 20:1). Therefore, as a testimony to Christ's death and resurrection, it was natural to celebrate the Lord's Supper on the first day of the week (Acts 20:7), which came to be known as the Lord's day (Rev. 1:10). So, although there was no command to meet on a certain day (unless 1 Cor. 16:2 be construed to be such a command), the first day came to be the normal meeting day.

Similarly, it cannot be established from Scripture that the primitive church was required to meet at any specific hour of the day. Some meetings were held at night (Acts 12:6, 12; 20:7). Others were held during the day (Acts 3:1; 19:9). It seems that the churches picked times that were convenient for the worshipers.

Relevant Research

Recent anthropological research has revealed that different cultures have markedly different views of time. In part these differences reflect different philosophies of history. For example, cultures that have a cyclical philosophy of history, according to which history is constantly repeating itself and goes forward at an almost imperceptible rate, can be expected to have a very different approach to time than will a culture with a philosophy where time is always viewed as running out. Local conditions and lifestyles will also have a profound effect.

Time Orientation versus Event Orientation

For better or worse, some audiences will have a good feeling about a meeting only if it begins and ends on time. Other audiences will be relatively unconcerned about punctuality and will entertain a good feeling only if the meeting satisfies their expectations in terms of what should occur. In the former case the "good" meeting starts—or, at least, is dismissed—on schedule. In the latter case, the "good" meeting begins when the people are ready and closes when the objectives have been achieved. The differences between these two cultural (and subcultural) orientations are crucial.

Variation in Schedules

Not nearly so subtle as the previous distinction, but of vital importance to the church planter, are the differences that result from varying local lifestyles. In Nigeria, for example, the week is determined by the market day, which occurs every four or eight days (depending on the tribe). The Igbo tribes mark off the parts of a day by three separate gatherings of liquid from the raffia palm. All appointments are made accordingly.[30] In our culture the differences between urban and rural schedules are frequently of similar significance in the determination of meeting times.

Practical Reflection

Christian leaders need sensitivity to the kind of data we have been considering. They have a tendency to say, "Sunday (A.M.) only," or "no special day," or "meetings begin promptly at 7:00 P.M.," in accordance with their own upbringing and personal preferences. The Bible requires only that believers meet frequently. It also places special emphasis on the first day of the week. Research indicates that some sort of flexibility will be necessary when it comes to setting the schedule for meetings in any given locality. Especially at the beginning of a new work local ideas about time and local lifestyles must be considered if believers are to be congregated and discipled effectively. Only by consulting Scripture and assessing the local situation can it be determined how many meetings are appropriate and when the meetings should be held. Only by a study of Scripture and application of its teachings to the local situation can we be sure that meetings will be pleasing to God and rewarding to his people.

ME-3 illustration: The leaders of one church in Hong Kong took stock of their situation and decided upon two worship services on Sunday—one in the morning and one at night. They correctly reasoned that many business people who were required to work until 5:00 or 6:00 P.M. on Sundays would seldom have the opportunity to meet for regular worship unless a Sunday evening service became a part of the church schedule. Meetings of several thriving youth groups were scheduled for the same time. In addition, evangelistic services were held at times other than Sunday evening; they were well attended, largely because of the location of the church at a busy commercial intersection.

Master Plan Formation

Belongingness

Perhaps what new believers need most immediately following their conversion (whether as individuals or in groups) are clear instruction as to what God expects of his family members and caring Christian friendship. It is the responsibility of the missionary-evangelist to see to it that these two essentials are supplied right away. New believers should receive instruction orally. Culturally appropriate written mate-

---

30. Margaret Green, *Igbo Village Affairs*, 2d ed. (London: Cass, 1964), 22, 24.

Figure 41
Initial-Care Card

Name of new believer(s) _____

Address _____

Phone (if any) _____ Date of profession of faith _____

Name of Christian counselor/friend assigned _____

- -

(Counselor, please note: Those areas where the new believer has already been helped are filled in below. In Christian love please carry out the other assignments, remember the new convert daily in prayer, and fill in the form and return it to the undersigned by _____(date)_____.)

1. Early contacts
     First contact (date) ____   Second contact _____
     Third contact _____   Fourth contact _____
     Fifth contact _____   Sixth contact _____

2. Early instruction. Information and counseling provided concerning:
     Private (home) prayer and Bible reading _____
     Group (church) meetings and activities _____
     Confession of faith _____
     Preparation for baptism _____

3. Material provided:
     Bible or Bible portion _____
     Manual or other printed material _____
     Schedules of meetings, etc. _____
     Other _____

4. Introduction to the believing community (as appropriate):
     New believer introduced to the church or full group (date) _____
     New believer introduced to the following church groups (classes etc.):
     _____ (date) _____
     _____ (date) _____
     _____ (date) _____

                         Assignment made by _____
                         Counselor completing this form _____
                         Date form returned _____

rials such as a Bible (or portions thereof), a brief manual for new believers, and information on meeting places and times should be made available to literates. In most cases identification with the believing group will be aided significantly if some tangible insignia is provided for new converts—a Bible portion with a special imprint, a pin, or a small card.

One of the most important things the Christian worker can do for new converts is to introduce them (as believing individuals, families, or groups) to mature believers who will act as counselors and friends while they are being established in the faith. It is imperative that this be done immediately, since the first forty-eight to seventy-two hours after profession of faith are often absolutely crucial. However this introduction is made, the counselors and friends should receive and later provide specific information regarding the new converts for whom they are responsible. Three simple steps should be followed in this process:

Step One: A list of Christian believers who are mature and willing to take on responsibility for new converts should be compiled.

Step Two: The believer best suited to help the new convert(s) should be prayerfully chosen, and counselor and convert(s) made known to each other.

Step Three: A form like the one in figure 41 should be filled out (as far as possible) and then given to the counselor, with the request that the remaining sections be completed. The form should be returned within a specified time period, in most cases within six weeks.

Groups Projected for the Church

It is just as important to meet the needs of believers and the objectives of the church as it is to add to the total number of believers. This being the case, it is well to plan and (eventually) provide for various groups in the emerging church. Such factors as age, sex, ethnic origins, and educational background must be taken into account in planning for these subgroups. Among other matters that need to be considered:

1. Emerging-leadership groups
2. Small groups for Bible study, discipling, and Christian service
3. The eventual optimum size for the congregation (at what point should consideration be given to starting satellite congregations?)

Place(s) of Meeting

In concert with knowledgeable locals, rate possible places of meeting as good, fair, or poor with respect to each of the factors which will affect

Figure 42
Potential Places of Meeting

	Ease of transportation (distance, parking, etc.)	Availability and economic feasibility	Psychological factors (neighborhood, building, etc.)	Appropriateness for Christian activity (noise, size, atmosphere)
Believers' Homes				
Church Building				
Public Hall				
Theater				
School Building				
Factory				
Office				
Dormitory Lounge				
Other: _____				
Other: _____				
Other: _____				

Figure 43
Potential Meeting Times

Time	Compatibility with working hours, school schedules, traditional meeting times in the community, etc.	Transportation factors (availability of private and public transportation, proximity to believers' residences, etc.)
Sunday: Morning Afternoon Evening		
Weekdays:		
Monday: Morning Afternoon Evening		
Tuesday: Morning Afternoon Evening		
Etc.		

the believers' willingness to participate. Remember to rank potential meeting places for the congregation as a whole and for subgroups separately (see figure 42). Since circumstances change, be prepared to reevaluate these places periodically.

Times of Meeting

In a manner similar to evaluating meeting places, rate possible meeting times as good, fair, or poor in relation to those factors which will affect believers' participation. Remember to rank possible meeting times for the congregation and each subgroup separately (see figure 43).

In this chapter we have been concerned with bringing new believers together in a Christian fellowship. This stage in the Pauline Cycle is exceedingly important, initially in gathering believers together as an embryonic congregation and subsequently in bringing new converts into the fellowship. For every new congregation and for every new believer this stage is temporary. But it is also crucial. Many a congregation has experienced a significant setback because the factors involved were not thoroughly thought and prayed through. Myriads of lost sheep have been found and lost again because undershepherds procrastinated in folding and feeding them.

The Faith Confirmed 13

Confirmation should not be thought of as simply a mental exercise for church youth. Confirmation is for all believers and it is for believers only. Conversion without confirmation and confirmation without conversion are theological contradictions. Conversion is to a new faith and a new life. It anticipates confirmation. Confirmation is in that new faith and life. It presupposes conversion. Let every church planter in whatever culture give serious thought to this indispensable phase of the Christian life.

Objectives

With the foregoing in mind, the following objectives are important in church planting:

1. To establish believers in biblical teachings so they know what they are to believe and how they are to live
2. To encourage and provide opportunities for worship, service, witness, and stewardship that will be pleasing to God and helpful to others, especially fellow Christians

Christian teaching, worship, service, witness, and stewardship—these concepts are so familiar to believers that their meaning and essentiality are usually taken for granted. In our attempt to achieve these objectives, therefore, we will concentrate on various New Testament words and texts specifically related to them.

Faith and Instruction

Biblical Principles and Precedents

The Old Testament is clear that believers were to be confirmed in the faith. God said through Moses:

Hear, O Israel! The LORD is our God, the LORD is one! And you shall love the LORD your God with all your heart and with all your soul and with all your might. And these words, which I am commanding you today, shall

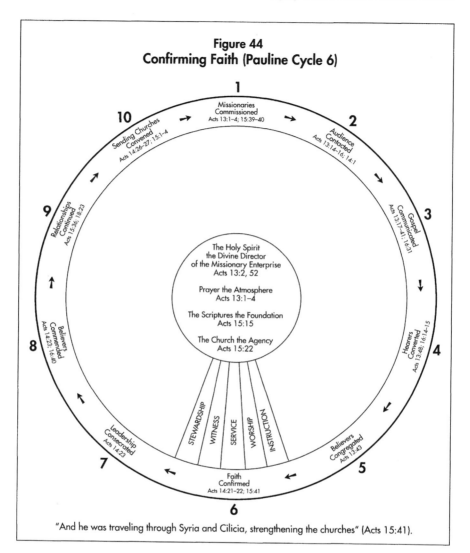

Figure 44
Confirming Faith (Pauline Cycle 6)

1 Missionaries Commissioned Acts 13:1–4; 15:39–40

10 Sending Churches Convened Acts 14:26–27; 15:1–4

2 Audience Contacted Acts 13:14–16; 14:1

9 Relationships Continued Acts 15:36; 18:23

3 Gospel Communicated Acts 13:17–41; 16:31

The Holy Spirit
the Divine Director
of the Missionary Enterprise
Acts 13:2, 52

Prayer the Atmosphere
Acts 13:1–4

The Scriptures the Foundation
Acts 15:15

The Church the Agency
Acts 15:22

STEWARDSHIP WITNESS SERVICE WORSHIP INSTRUCTION

8 Believers Commended Acts 14:23; 16:40

4 Hearers Converted Acts 13:48; 16:14–15

7 Leadership Consecrated Acts 14:23

5 Believers Congregated Acts 13:43

6 Faith Confirmed Acts 14:21–22; 15:41

"And he was traveling through Syria and Cilicia, strengthening the churches" (Acts 15:41).

be on your heart; and you shall teach them diligently to your sons and shall talk of them when you sit in your house and when you walk by the way and when you lie down and when you rise up. And you shall bind them as a sign on your hand and they shall be as frontals on your forehead. And you shall write them on the doorposts of your house and on your gates. [Deut. 6:4–9]

In the New Testament the command of God is equally clear. Jesus told his disciples to teach others to "observe all things whatsoever I have commanded you" (Matt. 28:20 KJV).

Paul possessed both a calling and a passion to reach new peoples with the gospel and plant churches where none had existed previously. But his calling and passion went beyond that. Both in precept and practice he also gave priority to confirming believers and churches in the Christian faith. The word repeatedly used in connection with this part of his ministry is the word *stērizō*, which is variously translated as "confirm," "establish," and "strengthen" (see Acts 14:21–23; 15:36–16:5; 18:22–23; Rom. 16:25; and 2 Thess. 2:17). Paul underscores to Timothy both the necessity and means of accomplishing this task: "All Scripture is inspired by God and profitable for teaching, for reproof, for correction, for training in righteousness; that the man of God may be adequate, equipped for every good work" (2 Tim. 3:16–17). This reminds us of a principle essential in the communicating, converting, and congregating stages of the Pauline Cycle; namely, that the Word of God—all of it and as it is—is vitally important in this business of church planting and development. So that's not new. What might be new is the emphasis on preserving the fruit of previous ministry while at the same time pressing forward to new frontiers.

Elementary Teachings and the Emerging Church

The author of the Epistle to the Hebrews makes a striking statement about the truths to be taught early in the development of the believer. In chapter 6, after expressing his regret that his readers had not become teachers as he had expected, and after noting that some truths are milk and other truths solid food, he urges, "Therefore leaving the elementary teaching about the Christ, let us press on to maturity, not laying again a foundation of repentance from dead works and of faith toward God, of instruction about washings, and laying on of hands, and the resurrection of the dead, and eternal judgment" (Heb. 6:1–2). This statement must be understood in the light of the immediate and larger contexts. It seems that whenever the gospel was communicated to Jews and proselytes in the New Testament, it was done in a way that clearly linked Christ and his work to Old Testament history and prophecy. For examples of this approach review once more Matthew's words in the initial verses of his Gospel (Matt. 1:1–17), the Lord Jesus' approach to the disheartened disciples en route to Emmaus (Luke 24:25–27), Peter's message on Pentecost (Acts 2:14–36), and Paul's message in the synagogue at Pisidian Antioch (Acts 13:16–41).

It follows that the recipients of the Hebrews letter were well acquainted with the big picture. Now Paul—or whoever wrote the letter—selected certain elementary teachings for review in the first five chapters. In his very nature, for example, Christ is superior to the prophets, angels, and Moses. Repentance, faith, baptism, resurrection, eternal judgment—all of these teachings are vital. They are elemental and essential to the growth of a church in any and every culture. This is the nature of biblical theology at its very beginning. Biblical theology underscores the fundamentals. Then it takes us from the elementary teaching about Christ to deeper teachings.

Deeper Teaching and the Emerging Church

The author of the Letter to the Hebrews states that his readers are now ready for deeper teaching (6:1). So he proceeds to discuss the priesthood of Melchizedek and of Christ, and the doctrine of the new covenant. In similar fashion Paul demonstrates that there are deeper teachings which should be given to the more mature believer (1 Cor. 3:1–2). These teachings are best seen in his letters to the older, established churches. The letters to the Philippians, Ephesians, and Colossians should be studied in this regard. What could be more profound than the *kenosis* passage of Philippians 2, the great christological passage in Colossians 1, and the tremendous soteriological passage of Ephesians 1? It is plain that Paul reserved deeper teachings for more mature Christians.

Furthermore, Paul expected more mature practice from these churches. Believers were to seek those things which are above, while mortifying the members of their earthly bodies (Col. 3:1–14). They were to be filled with the Spirit and give evidence of it (Eph. 5:18–6:9). They were to exhibit the unity of the Spirit (Eph. 4:13) and be joyous in all circumstances (Phil. 3:1).

The Church as a Hermeneutical Community

There is yet another aspect of the confirmation stage of the Pauline Cycle that merits careful consideration. It is implicit in Hebrews, but explicit in certain other parts of the New Testament. It has to do with the priesthood of *all* believers. Peter writes to scattered believers and congregations, "But you are a chosen race, a royal priesthood, a holy nation, a people for God's own possession" (1 Peter 2:9). That is part of the new covenant emphasized in the later chapters of Hebrews.

In line with this, Paul Hiebert talks about critical contextualization and emphasizes that the local church constitutes a hermeneutical community.[1] In most cases, the believers of the emerging congregation will be in a better position to exegete the meanings of local religious rituals, linguistic expressions, and cultural practices than will the church

---

1. See David J. Hesselgrave, "Paul Hiebert: Revisiting Contextualization," in *Scripture and Strategy: The Use of the Bible in Postmodern Church and Mission* (Pasadena: William Carey, 1994), 73–84.

planter—especially in ME-2 and ME-3 situations. On the other hand, the church planter will have been trained to exegete the biblical text and determine its meaning. So dialogue is essential. Church planters help laity in the interpretation and understanding of Scripture; laypeople help church planters in the interpretation and understanding of the target culture to which Scripture applies.

Two caveats should be added at this point. William Larkin Jr. notes that Peter Stuhlmacher similarly speaks of the church as a "confessional interpreter."[2] However, Stuhlmacher is thinking of the church in larger dimensions. His point is that the biblical text needs to be read and interpreted in dialogue with the confessional tradition—that is, with the way in which the Scriptures have been understood in the church down through history. No one person is an island. Neither is any church.

For the other caveat we return to the Book of Hebrews. In the final chapter we read an admonition to believers: "Obey your leaders, and submit to them; for they keep watch over your souls, as those who will give an account. Let them do this with joy and not with grief, for this would be unprofitable for you" (Heb. 13:17). The doctrine of the priesthood of all believers does not absolve church planters, other special person-gifts, or other church officers of responsibility for leadership. Emerging congregations need leaders—not autocratic leaders, of course, but servant leaders.

Relevant Research

Growth and Instruction

Studies show that rapidly growing religious movements tend to stress that those who wish instruction should master a basic doctrinal core and, once that has been mastered, go on to the deeper teachings. One could call this process "indoctrination." It is too bad that this term has been linked with brainwashing and therefore has a bad connotation. When coercive methods are employed, indoctrination is to be deplored. Otherwise, it is a good word. But by whatever name the process is a common one. That we disagree with both the methods and the teachings of communism, Scientology, the Unification Church, Jehovah's Witnesses, the Mormons, and Soka Gakkai Buddhists should not blind us to their strengths. Immediately upon believing, Gakkai converts, for example, are introduced to a carefully thought out program of instruction in the basic teachings of the sect. Instruction in small

---

2. William J. Larkin Jr., *Culture and Biblical Hermeneutics: Interpreting and Applying the Authoritative Word in a Relativistic Age* (Grand Rapids: Baker, 1988), 52–54.

groups, special lectures, a believers' manual, a series of voluntary examinations, advancement according to the degree of doctrinal knowledge attained—all of these are parts of the program.[3]

Formal, Informal, and Technical Learning

Anthropologist Edward T. Hall has made the helpful distinction that learning takes place at three levels: the formal level (mistake-correction); the informal level (imitation of models); and the technical level (instruction from a teacher). One of Hall's major contentions is that a far greater proportion of learning than we may suppose takes place at the informal level.[4] One of the implications of this is that much more attention needs to be given to the modeling of biblical truth. Unless truth is exemplified and modeled in terms of changed behavior, its mere recitation probably is not nearly as effective as we ordinarily suppose. This is especially the case in the pioneer situation.

Learning by Listening and Seeing

Studies indicate that, all things being equal, 10 percent of the subject matter is remembered when a lesson is taught by speech alone; twice that amount (20 percent) will be recalled if the lesson is communicated by visual methods alone. But if listening and seeing are combined, 65 percent of the material will be recalled![5]

Learning by Doing

It is a fundamental law of pedagogy that one learns by doing. Learning is not simply a matter of cognition. It is also a matter of action. Learning that is divorced from life, that is only a matter of the accumulation of data, is hardly worthy of the name. The best education, therefore, is that which combines the classroom and the laboratory, that which involves the learner in the employment of information. Using the figure of a split-rail fence to illustrate this approach to learning, Ted Ward stresses that theory and practice go together, and that periodically there should be an opportunity to discuss and analyze what one has learned and experienced (see figure 45). Though Ward's reference to seminars and cognitive input seems especially applicable to colleges and universities, it would be a mistake to think that his point does not apply to the local church and, indeed, to any learning situation.

3. David J. Hesselgrave, "Nichiren Shoshu Soka Gakkai—the Lotus Blossoms in Japan," in *Dynamic Religious Movements: Case Studies of Rapidly Growing Religious Movements around the World*, ed. David J. Hesselgrave (Grand Rapids: Baker, 1978), 129–48.
4. Edward T. Hall, *The Silent Language* (Greenwich, Conn.: Fawcett, 1959), 63–91.
5. Statistics cited in David R. Mains, *Full Circle: The Creative Church for Today's Society* (Waco: Word, 1971), 87.

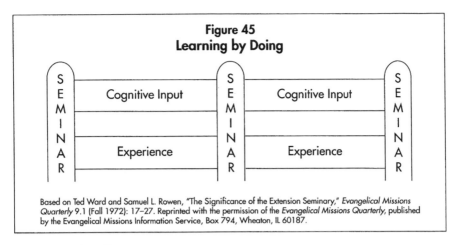

Figure 45
Learning by Doing

Based on Ted Ward and Samuel L. Rowen, "The Significance of the Extension Seminary," *Evangelical Missions Quarterly* 9.1 (Fall 1972): 17–27. Reprinted with the permission of the *Evangelical Missions Quarterly*, published by the Evangelical Missions Information Service, Box 794, Wheaton, IL 60187.

Practical Reflection

We have arrived at a juncture in church-planting strategy where people experienced and knowledgeable in the area of church and mission offer pointed criticisms and proposals. We do well to give careful attention to several of them.

1. One criticism has to do with the role of the missionary church-planter. Jacob Loewen, Paul Hiebert, and various other missionary anthropologists point out that, especially in ME-2 and ME-3 situations, missionaries are often tempted to act as police instead of advocates.[6] Concerned for the purity of the church, they decide upon certain rules, investigate the behavior of believers, and impose punishment upon violators. It should be apparent that this approach is faulty.

The antidote is the practical application of principles inherent in Hiebert's notions of critical contextualization and the church as a hermeneutical community. In the ordinary pattern the missionary or pastor communicates ideas in the form of a monological sermon, and the congregation comes together in business meetings to decide matters of policy and procedure. In Hiebert's pattern, on the other hand, times are scheduled for missionary or pastor to meet with the believers so they in concert can study and apply the Word of God to the local situation. This is the true business of the church!

2. Though the approaches of Roland Allen and Larry Richards are vastly different, they share a similar concern. Early on Roland Allen became concerned lest Christianity be introduced as assent to certain more or less difficult doctrinal statements that have to be maintained

---

6. Paul G. Hiebert, *Anthropological Insights for Missionaries* (Grand Rapids: Baker, 1985), 266–67.

at all costs. Concerning some failed congregations he wrote: "It is vain to say that the doctrine was false or falsely stated, and therefore it failed. It failed not because it was false or falsely stated, but because it was mere doctrine divorced from experience. Experience of the power of Christ to deliver from sin and from fear of the punishment due to sin did then, and does now, induce zeal; and the preaching of that power of Christ is Gospel; but the other by itself is mere doctrine, and like all doctrine, in itself lifeless."[7] Richards expresses himself somewhat differently but with similar intent: "Unfortunately, we evangelicals have been trained to think of and to read Scripture in terms of 'truth to be understood' rather than 'reality to live.'"[8] The solution is to be found in both/and, not either/or. Biblical Christianity consists of truths to be believed *and* a life to be lived.

ME-3 illustration: The work of the Wycliffe Bible Translators among the Tzeltals of Mexico is a scintillating example of the kind of instruction which, according to the data just examined, is most effective. In this particular case the problem of giving Christian instruction to the converts was compounded by a high degree of illiteracy among the Tzeltals. Once the church came into existence, believers gathered for Sunday services that were approximately six hours long! The services were led by Tzeltal leaders on a rotating basis. Comparatively new believers who had qualifications for preaching and teaching assumed those leadership responsibilities soon after being checked out by missionary teachers on the Scripture passages being used. During the Sunday school period the entire congregation was divided up and assigned to classes where the Bible was taught. Each teacher gave the same primary lesson week after week. During the week the members of the class were to share with a neighbor what they had learned. The basic ideas and Scripture passages were memorized. Questions were answered by pointing to relevant Scripture passages, even if the student was illiterate. Believers were allowed to progress to the next class (with its more advanced teaching) only on passing an examination and on the testimony of a neighbor to the effect that they were living according to the truth of the lesson! Within a few years the Tzeltal Church had grown to 8,000 believers, including 120 who could read and possessed the spiritual qualifications of a pastor!

3. A basic target of Donald McGavran's analysis of mission practice was what he called the urge to perfect. Perhaps influenced by Roland

---

7. Roland Allen, *The Spontaneous Expansion of the Church*, 2d ed. (London: World Dominion, 1949), 57–79; the quotation is from p. 68.

8. Lawrence O. Richards, *A New Face for the Church* (Grand Rapids: Zondervan, 1970), 178.

Allen, but certainly informed by mission history and his own experience, McGavran became convinced that one of the pitfalls of the Protestant missionary enterprise has been that once some converts have been won and gathered, missionaries tend to leave off discipling (i.e., making new converts) in order to make good Christians out of the converted. The criticism was, and is, a valid one. At home and abroad the cure is to be found in capitalizing on the newfound joy of converts by encouraging and leading them in witness as part of the confirmation process.

ME-3 illustration: As a follow-up to the *Ee-Taow* video produced by New Tribes Mission (see p. 122), *Ee-Taow Revisited* portrays the fledgling Mouk church as a missionizing church reaching surrounding tribes with the gospel of Christ. It is a thrilling account. The secret to the success of the Mouk believers is that they—at first in the company of the missionary and then on their own—"storied the Bible" in much the same way they themselves had learned it.

This leads us to the basic instructional approach that we referred to previously; namely, that we can do no better than instructing believers in the big story of the Bible. They need to begin what should become a lifelong practice of walking through the Bible over and over again so that the Word of revelation and the world of the Bible become of second nature and primary importance.

ME-2 illustration: On entering a Korean Southern Baptist church just outside of Washington, D.C., one's attention is immediately drawn to a display that covers almost one entire wall in the narthex. The subject of the display is the church-school curriculum. The church is really built around the study of the Scriptures from Genesis to Revelation. Classes are designed and graded for everyone from small children to senior adults; thus every member can study through Scripture at a level commensurate with one's age and background. Upon completing the classes at one level after several years, the student proceeds to another level and goes through the entire Bible again. To make sure that students receive competent instruction, mature and gifted laypersons are assigned to teach specific portions of Scripture on a regular basis. It is their responsibility to keep current and to update their lesson materials. To make sure that the entire membership understands Christian theology and practice, it is expected that all members participate. In addition, all church officers must complete at least one cycle at an appropriate level.

Faith and Worship

Biblical Principles and Precedents

Church planters who are overly influenced by current trends may rather easily mislead the new church in regard to worship. In the first place, worship—and in particular the worship service—may be given too high a priority in relation to other aspects of the confirmation process. In the second place, even though worship may be accorded high priority as an event or exercise, comparatively little attention may be given to the biblical meaning of worship. Strange as it may seem, both of these tendencies are often in evidence at the same time and in the same church. To avoid these problems, let us briefly examine some biblical aspects of worship.

The Biblical Definition of Worship

There are at least six Greek verbs in the New Testament which can be translated "worship." Each one reveals some aspect of biblical worship.

1. *Proskyneō* is the most common word for worship. It is a composite term which literally means "to kiss towards." It can be translated "to pay homage" or "to bow in adoration."

2. *Sebomai* depicts an act of reverential awe and fear. It means "to stand in awe of" or "to venerate." Its noun form was used as a title of the Roman emperors from Caesar Augustus onward. In Acts 25:21 this title is used of the tyrant Nero.

3. The word *eusebeō* is related to *sebomai* and also indicates piety or reverence. The noun form is often translated "godliness."

4. *Therapeuō* literally means "to heal" and "to cure" and, by extension, "to render service or worship."

5–6. *Latreuō* and *leitourgeō* both have reference to a service rendered to God. "*Leitourgeō* is the fulfillment of an office in a representative sense, while *latreuō* is service to the Deity on the part of both priest and laity."[9]

In summary, the New Testament meaning of worship is adoration accompanied by some sort of service rendered to the one who inspires reverence. A good illustration of true worship is seen in the case of the leper who came to Jesus (Matt. 8:1–4). A literal translation of verse 2 would be: "And behold, when a leper had come to him, he worshiped him by saying, 'Lord, if you will it, you are able to make me clean.'" Here the word for worship is *proskyneō*. It involves three elements: a realization of the lordship of Jesus Christ; a recognition of his sovereign will; and recognition

---

9. George Abbott-Smith, *A Manual Greek Lexicon of the New Testament* (Edinburgh: T. and T. Clark, 1964), 266.

of his power. This is true worship. The leper did not worship because he was going to be healed, nor was he healed because he worshiped. He worshiped because he recognized the sovereign power resident in the Lord. If he had not been healed, he still would have worshiped.

The Biblical Pattern of a Worship Service

Strangely, the Pauline Epistles do not use the word *proskyneō* except in 1 Corinthians 14. But this passage is very instructive. It teaches us how true worship is to be encouraged and carried out:

> If therefore the whole church should assemble together and all speak in tongues, and ungifted men or unbelievers enter, will they not say that you are mad? But if all prophesy, and an unbeliever or an ungifted man enters, he is convicted by all, he is called to account by all; the secrets of his heart are disclosed; and so he will fall on his face and worship God, declaring that God is certainly among you. What is the outcome then, brethren? When you assemble, each one has a psalm, has a teaching, has a revelation, has a tongue, has an interpretation. Let all things be done for edification. [1 Cor. 14:23–26]

True worship is prompted by disclosure of the secrets of the heart, detection of the presence of the Lord, and realization of accountability to God. Note that the worship described by Paul is characterized, first of all, by a heavy reliance upon revealed truth. The psalm, the teaching, the prophecy, the revelation, and the tongue all have their origin in God and are revealed to us. Second, there is a total participation by believers. "Each one" is said to have a part. Third, there is clarity of expression. This is the theme of the passage. Prophecy is more useful than tongues because it can be understood. Fourth, there is orderliness. Although each one participates, the participation is by turn (v. 27). Fifth, there is critical reception of the message. While the prophets are speaking, the listeners pass judgment on what is being said (v. 29). This kind of simple service designed to edify the believer prompts genuine worship.

Worship and the Lord's Supper

The Lord's Supper was instituted just before Jesus' betrayal (Matt. 26; Mark 14; Luke 22). It became a regular observance of the early church (Acts 2:42–47; 20:6–7; 1 Cor. 11:20–34). The most complete passages on the Lord's Supper are the Synoptic accounts of its institution and the Pauline direction as to how it should be practiced in the Corinthian church. Though the other apostles had been present when Jesus instituted the Lord's Supper, the apostle Paul claimed to have received his instructions concerning its observance directly from the risen Lord (1 Cor. 11:23), just as he had received his gospel (Gal. 1:11–12). Paul found it necessary to correct certain abuses that had characterized the Corinthian practice of the Supper and did so in 1 Corinthians 11:20–34. Because of its relevance to local church practice, we concentrate here on some important lessons to be gained from this passage.

1. The Lord's Supper had the appearance of a common meal, even though it had a very special significance (v. 21).

2. The observance involved the giving of thanks and praise (v. 24). The word *eucharisteō*, which means "to give thanks," is used here and in Luke 22:19. In Matthew and Mark *eucharisteō* is used with reference to the cup, while *eulogeō*, which means "to speak well of" or "ascribe praise to," is used with reference to the bread.

3. The Supper was in remembrance of the Lord (vv. 24–25). The word *anamnēsis* does not mean simply "memory" of the Lord, however; it connotes a realization of his abiding presence.

4. The frequency with which the Lord's Supper is to be observed is not specified, but the implication of the phrase "as often as" (v. 26) is that it is to be observed regularly and frequently. This interpretation of the phrase is in accordance with what we know of early church practice.

5. Observance of the Lord's Supper is a means of proclaiming *(katangellō)* the Lord's death until he comes again corporeally (v. 26); in the meantime he is spiritually present.

6. The Lord's Supper is for those who are worthy; that is, those who are believers and have examined themselves to make sure that they are in right relationship with the Lord (vv. 27–28).

7. Chastening awaits those who participate in the Lord's Supper unworthily (vv. 29–32).

Erroneous Assumptions

In planting new churches in non-Western cultures, three erroneous assumptions are commonly made. The first assumption is that if people come to faith in God through Christ, they will naturally know how God desires to be worshiped. This is true only in part, if at all. Instruction is needed, particularly on matters like the Lord's Supper.

The second assumption is that the worship that is part of the missionary-evangelist's tradition is biblical worship. The likelihood is that genuine biblical worship would entail much more participation and spontaneity.

The third assumption is that all aspects of indigenous worship are inherently wrong. Not necessarily so. Silent prayer, drums and other native instruments, and certain forms of drama and dance may be used to make worship more biblical and meaningful, though caution must be exercised at this point. In short, neither imported nor indigenous forms of worship should be introduced or discarded uncritically.

The Relation of the Holy Spirit to Worship

No discussion of worship would be complete without some mention of the role of the Holy Spirit. When Jesus spoke to the woman by the well, he said that the hour had come in which true worshipers would worship in Spirit and in truth (John 4:23). In 1 Corinthians 14, which deals with the gifts of the Spirit, a simple worship service is described. From this we may infer that the true worshiper is equipped by the Spirit. When taken together the two passages teach that the Spirit both motivates believers to worship and equips them for worship. Thus no true worship is offered until we are controlled by the Holy Spirit and using the gifts of the Spirit. When this happens, the very life of the believer can be described as a service of worship (Eph. 5:18–20).

Relevant Research

The Nature of Worship

Anthropologists are in general agreement that worship has been a part of human experience from the earliest times.[10] As might be expected, they characterize early worship in accordance with their own biases. Naturalists usually see worship as an effort to placate, cajole, or appease supernatural powers of one sort or another.[11] In his popular book *The Silent Language* Edward T. Hall classifies religious ceremonies under the category of "defense"—along with military defense and health practices![12] As a matter of fact, those who have had any appreciable exposure to non-Christian religions—those who have seen non-Christians at their various shrines, temples, and home altars—will attest that much, if not most, of such worship tends to corroborate the conclusions of social scientists. In fact, the worship of many people degenerates to appeasing the supernatural. But true Christian worship is first and foremost the honoring of God as God, and the ascription of praise and thanksgiving to him for what he is and has done. It does not exclude petition for provision and protection, for God invites his children to approach him for help in time of need. But worship is not wholly, or even primarily, petition. It is a recognition of who God is and that he has already provided life and sustenance and salvation. Thus Christian worship is—or should be—something much different from anything practiced by the unregenerate, and something that will be all but impossible for the unregenerate to understand or interpret.

10. John B. Noss, *Man's Religions*, 3d ed. (New York: Macmillan, 1963), 4–31.
11. Peter B. Hammond, *An Introduction to Cultural and Social Anthropology* (New York: Macmillan, 1971), 258–93.
12. Hall, *Silent Language*, 57–59, 92.

Worship and Environment

Worship is often associated with certain sacred places; while not confined to those places, it is nevertheless rendered more significant and efficacious when practiced in those places. The Samaritan woman entertained just such an idea (John 4:20). Indeed, Judaism with its temple worship reinforced the notion. Biblical Christianity by contrast is a universal faith in that it knows of no spot on earth that is more sacred than any other, or where one ought to worship in preference to any other. At the same time corporate worship does require a place of meeting, and a group of Christians—just as any other religious group—will be affected by environmental factors.

Most such factors will be obvious to all. In many pioneer situations, however, the matter of providing a place for worship will loom so large as to obscure other factors that are important. How else can one explain the lack of provision of simple embellishments (a flower arrangement, for example) which, in even the most simple surroundings, help create an atmosphere for the worship of the God of creation and order? Or how else can one explain the mistakes that are built into numerous houses of worship from the very first? James White, for example, decries both the long, narrow hall and the separated-transept types of church buildings and predicts that, in the future, church architecture will be much more conducive to true Christian worship:

> Probably the present-day experiments which have placed the congregation in transepts or other separate areas will be little imitated. Such arrangements make preaching very difficult. They also foster the illusion of two or more separate congregations instead of one body gathered about the Lord's table.
>
> Most likely the audience-hall type of long naves, sloping floors, and comfortable pews will be rare in the future. It is quite possible that galleries will be little used. With the liturgical centers as close as possible to the congregation, the people will have easier access to them, and the notion of certain places in the church as holy spots, monopolized by the clergy and choir, will be lessened considerably. The impression that God is out beyond the east window will be avoided by centrally planned buildings.[13]

Practical Reflection

Perhaps no aspect of corporate Christian experience has been the object of more criticism recently than has the hour or so of formal wor-

---

13. James F. White, *Protestant Worship and Church Architecture* (New York: Oxford University Press, 1964), 177.

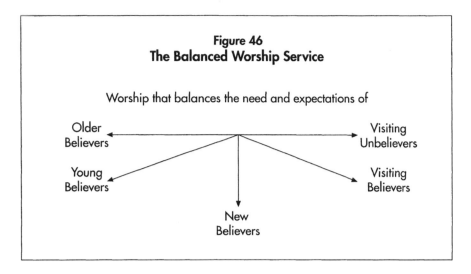

Figure 46
The Balanced Worship Service

Worship that balances the need and expectations of

Older
Believers

Young
Believers

New
Believers

Visiting
Unbelievers

Visiting
Believers

ship on Sunday morning. The criticism is much more evident in the Western world (especially North America) than it is in the non-Western world. Perhaps that is because Westerners tend to be more self-critical. Perhaps non-Westerners simply tolerate the service or, quite possibly, register disappointment by staying away. In any case, reflection is called for.

Eastern peoples often find the usual Christian worship service to be too Western. Western hymns, Western instruments, Western sermons, and Western abruptness—all of these and more give Christian worship a stamp of foreignness that does not necessarily reflect true spirituality.

In the West a major challenge has to do with meeting the expectations and needs of various segments of the average congregation: older believers, younger believers, new believers, visiting believers, and visiting unbelievers. This difficulty can be partially resolved by instructing the congregation in the true nature of worship and by striking a balance as far as the expectations and needs of the various segments are concerned (see figure 46).

Another problem in the West is that many congregations feel that the worship service is uninteresting. David Mains uses the phrase "worship that is pompous and dull" to describe the ordinary Protestant worship service.[14] His basic contention is that leaders err in a number of ways: (1) they mistake the real meaning of worship; (2) they call our hodgepodge of independent and unrelated activities at the 11:00 o'clock hour

14. Mains, *Full Circle*, 52–55.

on Sunday morning a worship service; (3) they see a necessary connection between pews, maroon carpets, elegant chandeliers, and vaulted ceilings on one hand, and worship on the other; and (4) they fail to plan for meaningful worship.

Anne Ortlund agrees—for the most part at least. She insists that we must be scriptural, that we must give creative thought to our worship services, and that neither the repetition of traditional forms nor the supposedly spiritual unstructured service is the answer:

> Where does the idea come from that if you're "in the Spirit" you can eliminate preparations?
>   I'm not sympathetic to the philosophy behind it. . . .
>   But all of our ideas of worship must be rooted firmly in the Scriptures, and I find in them no high praise that was just off-the-cuff. . . .
>   Psalm 34 is a great hymn of praise. Did it just flow out of David like water? Well, we discover it's an acrostic, with the Hebrew alphabet built into the first letter of each line. The Spirit of God inspired it, of course—but maybe it also took David a lot of work to write it.[15]

No doubt it is true that too much originality (as well as too little) can make for a dull church.[16] But if there is anything that we don't need in a new work for Christ, it is simply more of the same thing that we have known previously and elsewhere—especially when it comes to the worship service.

ME-1 illustrations: In recent times numerous churches such as Circle Church and Willow Creek in the Chicago area have revived interest in their worship services by initiating meaningful change. Circle Church was one of the first to attract national attention.[17] Pastor David Mains defined worship in terms of praise and adoration to God. Since emphasis was placed upon the preaching of the Word during the Sunday morning service, he called it the Service of Worship and Instruction. It was usually divided into three sections (though flexibility was the rule):

> The Approach to God in Worship
> God Speaking through His Written Word
> The Response of Obedience

Circle Church has changed greatly and is no longer pointed to as a model church. More recently, the ministry of Pastor Bill Hybels and his

---

15. Anne Ortlund, *Up with Worship: How to Quit Playing Church* (Glendale, Calif.: Regal, 1975), 36.

16. Dan Baumann, *All Originality Makes a Dull Church* (Santa Ana, Calif.: Vision House, 1976).

17. Mains, *Full Circle*, 72–81.

Willow Creek church in the northwestern suburbs of Chicago has attracted national—and, indeed, international—attention. Unlike Circle, Willow Creek attracts large crowds on Sunday mornings by featuring a comparatively brief message that is based on Scripture but does not major on Bible exposition as such. Rather, the message highlights important topics and issues of contemporary concern and is complemented by drama, music, and careful programing. The service is designed to appeal to seekers rather than to mature believers. In-depth and extensive Bible instruction is scheduled for other times.

It is too early to tell what will ultimately become of the Willow Creek approach, though we do know of numerous cases where it has been reproduced with success (as well as cases of failure). It would seem that, if true worship is what we really want, less attention should be given to what pleases us and more attention should be given to what pleases God.

Faith and Service

Biblical Principles and Precedents

The Basis of Service

One of the more extensive themes running throughout Scripture is that of service. It is said that when the Son of God became a man, he became similar to a slave. The implication is that the very nature of humanity is that of a servant (Phil. 2:7). We are commanded to serve (Matt. 4:10). Members of the early church believed that they were converted in order to serve God (1 Thess. 1:9). A solid basis for service is seen, then, in human nature, God's command, and the beliefs and practice of the early church.

The Semantics of Service

The New Testament uses several words in connection with the service of the believer: *doulos, diakonos, leitourgos, latreuō* (a cognate of *latris*), *oiketēs*, and *hypēretēs*.

The *doulos* was a slave. This word in its various forms is the one most commonly used in the New Testament in connection with service. The Lord had much to say about this type of servant. No one can be a slave of two masters (Matt. 6:24). When told to do something, the good slave does it (Matt. 8:9). Those who wish to be great in the kingdom of heaven should first be servants (slaves) (Matt. 20:27). The slave is never greater than his master (Matt. 10:24). An alert slave of God will be rewarded when Christ comes again (Matt. 25:21; Luke 12:37). Christ said this and much more about the *doulos*.

Paul also spoke about the *doulos*. He confessed that he was a slave of Jesus Christ (Rom. 1:1; Gal. 1:10; Titus 1:1). We are slaves of that to which we render obedience (Rom. 6:16). All are slaves to sin (Rom. 6:17, 20). But the believer should be a slave of righteousness (Rom. 6:18). Obedience to one's master is the chief characteristic of a slave (Col. 3:22). Thus attempts to please others may place one's servant (slave) relation to Christ in jeopardy (Gal. 1:10).

Another common word for servant is *diakonos*. While the derivation of this compound word is doubtful, the meaning is clear from its usage. It (including cognates) is often used in connection with the serving of food (Matt. 8:15; 25:44; Mark 1:13; Luke 17:8; Acts 6:2). It is used of bringing relief money to the poor saints of Jerusalem (Rom. 15:25; 2 Cor. 8:4). The idea always seems to be to give to or do for others that which is necessary to their life. In the spiritual realm it is used of bringing to others whatever is necessary for their spiritual life. There are, after all, various ministries—the ministry of the Word of Christ (1 Cor. 3:5), the ministry of reconciliation (2 Cor. 5:18), and the ministry of the Spirit in bringing life (2 Cor. 3:6).

While *doulos* relates the believer to the person of the Lord, *diakonos* relates the believer to the work of the Lord—work to be carried out in the world. Jesus came into the world to be a *diakonos* (Mark 10:45). Greatness requires faithfulness at the level of servanthood (Matt. 23:11). Very soon after the birth of the church, the apostles established the office of deacon (Acts 6:2–6). These men ministered to the physical body (Acts 6:1–3) and to the spiritual (Acts 8:5). Accordingly, those who wished to be deacons had to be highly qualified (Acts 6:3; 1 Tim. 3:8–10).

A third kind of servant was the *leitourgos*. Here was an individual "who discharged a public office at his own expense."[18] The word (and its cognates) is used in connection with the public ministry of the priest in the temple (Luke 1:23; Heb. 10:11), monetary giving (2 Cor. 9:12), the apostle Paul's offering himself in service on behalf of the Philippians (Phil. 2:17), the aid which the Philippian church gave to Paul (Phil. 2:30), government officials ruling for God (Rom. 13:6), the angelic ministry (Heb. 1:7), Christ's high-priestly ministry in the heavenly sanctuary (Heb. 8:2), and the duties of the prophets and teachers in the Antioch church (Acts 13:2). Inasmuch as believers constitute a royal priesthood, the *leitourgos* ministry belongs to all of them (1 Peter 2:5).

The word *latris* also denotes a servant. While the noun form is not found in the New Testament, the verb form, *latreuō*, is used in reference to the service of both priest and people. This type of service was to be rendered exclusively to God (Matt. 4:10). The heathen perverted this service

18. Abbott-Smith, *Greek Lexicon*, 267.

by worshiping the creature rather than the Creator (Rom. 1:25). It is this service which Paul has in mind when he speaks of the offering of the believer's body to God as one's "reasonable service" (Rom. 12:1–2 KJV).

The *oiketēs* was a domestic servant who lived in the house of his master (Acts 10:7; Rom. 14:4; 1 Peter 2:18). Being a house servant, the *oiketēs* had a closer relationship to the family than did most other servants. In Luke's version it is this kind of servant to whom Jesus refers when he says that no servant can serve two masters (Luke 16:13).

Finally, *hypēretēs* is also used for "servant." This compound word literally refers to the "under-rowers" on the ships of the Mediterranean Sea. In the New Testament it is used to denote officers of the Sanhedrin or synagogue (Matt. 26:58; Luke 4:20). It aptly describes the work of John Mark as he accompanied Paul and Barnabas (Acts 13:5), for the word can convey the idea of being a servant to a government minister in an official capacity. John Mark was serving the apostles on an official mission. Therefore he is described as a *hypēretēs*. Paul, in fact, uses the word to characterize himself as an "officer of Christ" (1 Cor. 4:1).

All of these words are used to describe the servant of God. Underlying each is the idea of doing the will of another. This is the gist of being a servant. The servant of God is one who does the will of God.

Relevant Research

In his book *East to Eden?* Charles Corwin points out something that has been almost universally observed by those who have lived and worked in the Orient for a period of time.[19] Despite the popularity of some of the non-Christian Eastern religions in the West, down through history those religions have not produced anything like the outpouring of compassionate service to humanity that has characterized biblical Christianity. Hospitals, leprosaria, literacy campaigns, and many other humanitarian services have accompanied the progress of Christianity across the face of the earth. Christianity's rivals cannot begin to match that record. In fact, research will reveal that works of compassion undertaken by Buddhists or adherents of some other Eastern religion often originated after Christian enterprises of the same stripe were initiated in the general area.

Practical Reflection

It is unfortunate that Christian service and witness often seem to be competing concerns in Christian outreach when, in fact, they are biblical and complementary. Paul said that he was called to be a minister *and*

19. Charles Corwin, *East to Eden?* (Grand Rapids: Eerdmans, 1972).

a witness (Acts 26:16). One reason for tension at this point is that service enterprises such as hospitals and educational institutions have a way of preempting finances and energies so that evangelism and witness tend to get crowded out. Another reason is that some of those in the service enterprises have downgraded verbal witness and insisted that acts of compassion are the only witness that is needed. Still another reason is that some specialist organizations have majored in certain types of Christian service, and others in evangelism—a fact that tends to foster competitiveness within the church. Finally, some missiologists have mistakenly interpreted the church's mission not in terms of the Great Commission, but as everything the church is sent to do in the world.

In any case, the matter of service ministries both within and without a newly planted church is often disregarded or unduly delayed. But as soon as men and women are converted, the matter of their service within and without the church should be considered. As George Peters writes, "Service is not only for the perfect, it is a means of perfecting the saints."[20] That service has often been neglected should not be allowed to set the precedent. Scripture is our guide. The emerging church should constitute itself a caring community. Every believer should have something to do for Christ.

First, special attention should be given to needs within the group of believers. Some way of ascertaining these needs should be determined. Then these needs should become concerns for prayer *and* service. Of course, the needs which arise as a by-product of church life (such as cleaning, ushering, child care, etc.) become opportunities for service as well.

Second, the believing community should make it a matter of high priority to find out the felt and real needs of the target community. Most communities will be so surprised by the presence of a group of believers who really want to serve that they will sit up and take notice of the church—some for the first time.

ME-1 illustration: Several years ago the young people of a church in Lincoln, Nebraska, considered what they could do in order to better serve Christ. They realized that there was not a great deal of poverty in their area, but they knew that there were needs, many of them both felt and real. Which ones could they meet? They decided that they could serve best by offering themselves as tutors of retarded children and slow learners in the community. This they did on a regular basis. For the first time many local citizens looked upon the church as a servant of the community. Unlike the vast majority of their peers whose lifestyle

---

20. George Peters, "Pauline Patterns of Church-Mission Relationships," *Evangelical Missions Quarterly* 9.6 (1973): 116.

made demands upon the community, these young people were giving themselves in meaningful service to others. As a result, the church experienced a renewed growth.

Faith and Witness

Biblical Principles and Precedents

To whom was the Great Commission directed? That question has plagued the church down through the centuries. Most of the sixteenth-century Reformers believed that it was given to—and fulfilled by—the original apostles, and that it does not directly apply to anyone who came after them. However, Adrian Saravia (1531–1613), Justinian von Weltz (1621–68), and William Carey (1761–1834) argued that the Great Commission applies to the church wherever it exists.

There is a sense, of course, in which the various commissionings of the early followers of Christ had special application to them. In the first place, only certain individuals could qualify as witnesses (*martyres*, Acts 1:8) in the sense of having been personally present at our Lord's ministry, death, and resurrection. This was a special qualification of apostleship as such (Acts 1:21–22). In the second place, the risen Lord did give certain persons as special gifts to his church—apostles and evangelists among them. However, it is apparent that witnessing and evangelizing in the early church were not confined to those designated as special apostles. Yielded to and directed by the Holy Spirit, ordinary believers witnessed and evangelized. They went everywhere preaching the Word (i.e., evangelizing—*euangelizō*, Acts 8:4). In fact, as John Nevius asserts, "a great advance had been made before the Apostle Paul was called from his home by Barnabas to assist the disciples already gathered at Antioch."[21] Unquestionably, Nevius is correct when he concludes that it was largely through the efforts of ordinary Christians that Christianity found its way to "Cyprus, Syria, Cilicia, Egypt and as far west as Rome."[22] And it should be remembered that those believers were still young in the faith; they were testifying while still learning. And that, after being formed, churches corporately were witnessing while still growing (1 Thess. 1:8).

While there were distinctions in the early church which were analogous to the distinction we make between the clergy and the laity today, the difference was not that the clergy did the witnessing and evangelizing while the laity simply supported them in such endeavors. Rather,

---

21. John L. Nevius, *The Planting and Development of Missionary Churches* (Philadelphia: Presbyterian and Reformed, 1958), 59.
22. Ibid.

there was a spontaneous witness on the part of the believers that was little short of earthshaking in the Mediterranean world. In the manner of Christ, who instituted the "master plan of evangelism,"[23] the leaders of the early church both served as models and prepared believers for the task of witnessing (1 Cor. 4:16; Eph. 4:11–12). Had the witness of the early church been confined to that of the apostles and evangelists, the growth of that church would have been very different from that pictured in the New Testament.

Relevant Research

The Strachan Theorem

After doing research on communism, Islam, Jehovah's Witnesses, the Latter-day Saints, and other movements, and after a careful study of relevant literature, the late director of the Latin America Mission, R. Kenneth Strachan, articulated a principle which became the cornerstone of the strategy of Evangelism-in-Depth. It is now known as the Strachan theorem: "The successful expansion of any movement is in direct proportion to its success in mobilizing and occupying its total membership in constant propagation of its beliefs."[24] As George Peters points out, it is regrettable that Strachan did not go on to discover other dynamic principles of evangelism and church multiplication, but this theorem is indeed significant.[25] Its validity has been demonstrated in the success of saturation evangelism around the world as well as in the growth of other religious movements.[26]

Life-related Witness

It should be noted that witness seems to be especially effective when it is related to contemporary issues with which people are concerned. One need not completely agree with Gabriel Fackre's indictment of contemporary evangelism in order to appreciate his emphasis on relating Christian faith and witness to contemporary issues such as nuclear war, ecological disaster, abortion, marriage, and biomedical engineering.[27] This is a most natural way of witness, as research into the rapid growth of other religious movements attests.[28]

23. Robert E. Coleman, *The Master Plan of Evangelism* (Westwood, N.J.: Revell, 1963).
24. *Evangelism-in-Depth* (Chicago: Moody, 1961), 25.
25. George W. Peters, *Saturation Evangelism* (Grand Rapids: Zondervan, 1970), 53.
26. David J. Hesselgrave, "What Causes Religious Movements to Grow?" in *Dynamic Religious Movements*, 319–20.
27. Gabriel Fackre, *Do and Tell: Engagement Evangelism in the '70s* (Grand Rapids: Eerdmans, 1973), 56–57.
28. Hesselgrave, "What Causes Religious Movements to Grow?" 306.

The Weakness of Campaign Evangelism

In spite of the potential of lay witness to effect world evangelization and growth in the local church, not all efforts to harness this potential are successful. In fact, such highly organized efforts as Evangelism-in-Depth and Here's Life, America, have sometimes failed to produce the anticipated church growth.[29] The limited success of these and similar campaigns, however, is not due to the employment of lay witness but to the programing of lay witness. If lay witness is to result in church growth, it cannot be imposed upon local churches from the outside or geared only or primarily to one specific period of time. Witness must come from within the churches and be a part of their ongoing outreach. In other words, if believers in the churches are not spiritually alive to their ongoing responsibility in the world, churches will not grow and multiply as they did in the New Testament Era.

Practical Reflection

There can be little doubt that, when it comes to church growth, both the professionals and the nonprofessionals must be involved in witness—the former equipping, modeling, and participating, and the latter learning and doing. When this is the program, God will cause churches to grow. Nevertheless, a variety of breakdowns in this normal pattern of Christian witness have occurred.

Breakdown 1 occurs within the hearts, not the heads, of leaders and laity alike. The apostles had three years of instruction at the feet of the master teacher and example, but they were faltering witnesses at best until they were infused and empowered by the Holy Spirit at Pentecost. By contrast post-Pentecost believers were powerful witnesses even before there was opportunity for them to receive prolonged instruction. The essential ingredient for witness, then, is the inner working of the Holy Spirit. We must wait upon the Spirit to infuse our hearts before we proceed to witness (Acts 1:8).

Breakdown 2 occurs when church leaders fail to encourage the spontaneous witness of new believers. There are risks in such witness, of course. But God takes a risk with every one of us. What is needed is encouragement that engenders confidence. The new believer has a fresh experience to report as well as numerous contacts with the world. Little is to be gained by putting such people on the shelf until they mature,

---

29. See Peters, *Saturation Evangelism*, 72–77, for an analysis of Evangelism-in-Depth's contribution to church growth; and C. Peter Wagner, "Who Found It?" and James F. Engel, "Great Commission or Great Commotion?" *Eternity* 28.9 (Sept. 1977): 13–19, for an analysis of the results of the Here's Life, America, campaign.

except staleness of experience, separation from unbelievers, and sterility of witness.

Breakdown 3 occurs when leaders prescribe witness without preparing witnesses, and when they challenge believers to witness without channeling that witness. This may seem to contradict what we have said earlier, but in reality it is no contradiction at all. All of us have known certain Christians who maintain the spontaneity and simplicity of their initial witness over long periods of time—even throughout a lifetime. But most Christians soon encounter problems and questions from unbelievers, problems and questions that deserve intelligent biblical answers. As a result Christians may experience discouragement and withdraw from the arena of encounter. When this occurs, simply to prescribe witness and challenge the believer to spread the gospel may accomplish little more than to arouse feelings of guilt. Experience teaches us that the wise leader trains people in soul winning and channels their effort into a program of outreach. All may not witness in the same way, or with the same effect, because Christians are people and people differ from one another. But all Christians can be fruitfully engaged in some aspect of a well-rounded program of outreach and witness. Such involvement accomplishes more than a witness to nonbelievers. It also confirms the faith of the Christian!

Breakdown 4 occurs when the outreach programs of emerging churches are patterned after those of the older churches. In new churches a larger proportion of the membership should be actively engaged in outreach than is usually the case in established churches. Donald McGavran emphasizes that if new churches are to grow, a large number of the leaders must head out into the community rather than simply serve within the church.[30]

Breakdown 5 occurs when church leaders place a higher value on imported programs and personnel than they do on the potential inherent within the local church. This is not to denigrate the imports. Personnel and programs periodically imported from without the local church may serve to revive God's people in addition to winning some who are lost. But when such special programs supplant the ongoing outreach of the local believers, or upset that outreach in such a way that it becomes difficult to keep it going, then something is seriously amiss and reevaluation is in order.

ME-1 illustration: One of the best-known programs of lay witness leading to growth in the local church is that of the Coral Ridge Presbyterian Church in Fort Lauderdale, Florida. In 1961 Pastor D. James

---

30. Donald A. McGavran, *How Churches Grow* (New York: Friendship, 1959), 139–40.

Kennedy accepted the invitation of some 45 people who wanted to organize a church. The number dwindled to 17 before the church began to grow. But as a result of a program of visitation evangelism, attendance at worship services increased to over 5,000 in fifteen years.

The basic program of the Coral Ridge church is set forth in the book *Evangelism Explosion.*[31] Its essence has been summarized by Warren Bathke:

> Kennedy's plan is a simple one. Train briefly—then go out immediately. He instructs a small class of ten or twenty people for thirty minutes. Then he sends them out in groups of three into homes in the area. After sixteen weeks, each home visitor becomes a trainer for another person in the program. After nine years of training sessions he had three hundred home visitors going out on visitation.
>
> The emphasis of the training is on learning to tell the Gospel in a positive and gracious manner. Detailed instructions are given from initial contact to total involvement of an individual in a church.
>
> As one might imagine, to put together the elements of many specialists into one harmonious program is a difficult task, yet that seems to be part of the purpose of the church. To have the visitation program stand the test of time is quite another matter.
>
> A church's doctrine does indeed design its mission. For evangelical churches its Gospel mandates outreach and growth. There are many specialists' programs in America that are waiting to be incorporated into one harmonious operation. This is the task of the local church.[32]

The value of Kennedy's approach is attested to not only by the growth of his own congregation, but also by the fact that literally hundreds of other congregations have adopted the plan and profited thereby. Nevertheless, it is only one plan among many. It will not work in every community.

Faith and Stewardship

Biblical Principles and Precedents

Stewardship has to do with all that a Christian possesses—time and talent as well as treasure. Here, however, we are concerned with stewardship of money and material wealth. The essence of biblical teaching on the subject can be reduced to three very simple but crucial statements: (1) all that we have is given by God (1 Cor. 4:7); (2) that which God gives us is ours to do with as we please (Acts 5:4); and (3) since God

---

31. D. James Kennedy, *Evangelism Explosion*, rev. ed. (Wheaton, Ill.: Tyndale, 1977).

32. Warren E. Bathke, "Visitation Evangelism: Do We Need It?" *Evangelical Beacon*, 11 July 1978, p. 19.

has given freely to us, we should also freely give to God and those in need (Matt. 10:8; 1 John 3:17).

It will come as a surprise to many that God has much to say about money and material possessions. It is obvious that God had communicated to Cain and Abel the desirability of sacrifice (Gen. 4). Abraham gave tithes of all that he possessed (Heb. 7:2). The children of Israel were commanded to bring sacrifices and offerings to God (Exod. 30). Jesus reminded us that we should lay up treasure in heaven and that our heart will be where our treasure is (Matt. 6:19–21). We are also told that the "love of money" (not money itself) is the "root of all evil" (1 Tim. 6:10 KJV).

Ralph Martin notes that Paul's teaching on these matters is summed up in seven basic principles emphasized in 2 Corinthians 8 and 9:

1. The basis of stewardship is that God has given bountifully to his people.
2. The most important offering is the commitment of one's own life to God.
3. All Christian giving is prompted by divine grace, yet is voluntary, eager, and cheerful.
4. Stewardship is to be offered in accordance with one's ability and the needs of others.
5. God is no one's debtor.
6. Churches and their people should be fair and open in their financial dealings.
7. Concern for the welfare of others creates a bond of love between giver and recipient and calls forth the praise of God.[33]

Relevant Research

The Protestant Ethic

It was the sociologist Max Weber who developed the concept of the Protestant ethic, though the phenomenon itself has long been a part of Protestantism. Weber simply provided a construct and an analysis of what came to characterize Protestant believers soon after the Reformation: as a by-product of attention to the biblical teaching on stewardship, Protestants tended to be characterized by industriousness and thrift.[34]

Donald McGavran's studies of world missions and churches led him to a very similar (if not identical) conclusion: once people are redeemed

33. Ralph P. Martin, *Worship in the Early Church* (Grand Rapids: Eerdmans, 1975), 84–85.
34. Max Weber, *The Protestant Ethic and the Spirit of Capitalism*, trans. Talcott Parsons (New York: Scribner, 1958).

and enter God's family, they tend to raise their standards of living and productivity. McGavran called this "redemption and lift."[35]

Astute Christians recognize that while this kind of industry is commendable, it is not an unmixed blessing. John Wesley, for example, realized that such industry is likely to result in prosperity and wealth, and wealth is apt to lure the affections of believers away from single-hearted devotion to Christ. He concluded that the only solution to the problem is that as believers earn more, they should give more!

The Sacred and the Secular

Westerners have a deep-seated inclination to make a radical distinction between the sacred and the secular, neatly dividing all concerns and activities into these two airtight compartments. The distinction has now become a commonplace both in scientific analysis and in the popular mind.

Many non-Western and non-Christian societies, on the other hand, do not make this distinction. All of life is intimately related to deities and spirits, worship and ritual. An informative research project was carried out a generation ago at a mission station in the Sepik district of New Guinea.[36] (Perhaps only in a virgin mission field could this kind of study be successfully carried out.) The mission station was a large one with seventy permanent buildings. The closer a village was to the mission station, the more it was involved in the ordinary business concerns of the station. To study the effect upon the spirituality of the churches, certain measurable qualities of spirituality (attendance, stewardship, etc.) were investigated. It was found that the closer the churches were geographically to the mission station, the greater their economic involvement was. Conversely, the farther they were from the station, the greater their spirituality proved to be! It seems clear that the Western tendency to think of the business of living as distinct from stewardship, worship, and spirituality had a negative effect in a society that, in spite of its lack of knowledge of God, nevertheless did not put worship, sacrifice, and ritual in compartments completely separate from the production and marketing of goods!

The Psychology of Value

There seems to be a principle (true in many cases if not all) according to which the perceived value of something is correlated with one's in-

35. Donald A. McGavran, *Understanding Church Growth* (Grand Rapids: Eerdmans, 1970), 270–88.

36. O. E. Fountain, "Religion and Economy in Mission Station Relationships," *Practical Anthropology* 13.2 (1966): 49–58.

vestment in it. To put it another way, intrinsic value is not the only yard-stick by which we evaluate things. If, for example, a person invests energy, money, and time in something, its perceived value goes up accordingly even though the intrinsic value does not change.

This principle is easily testable. Some years ago in our family-owned store we placed identical items in separate displays, one of which was marked at a lower price and the other at a higher price. Though not adjacent, the displays were in the same general location. Our hypothesis was substantiated. Many customers examined the merchandise in both displays and still purchased the higher-priced items; they assumed that whatever cost more had to be superior.

We feel a certain ambivalence about this kind of phenomenon. On the one hand, it is irrational to place a greater value on an item simply because one pays more for it. But there is a principle here that is powerful and pervasive enough to have influenced the policy of many dynamic religious movements. Many of them sell their publications, for example, rather than give them away, or give them only with the understanding that the one who gives them has actually paid for them on the recipient's behalf.

Practical Reflection

It is important that church planters at home and abroad provide the right instruction and follow the right procedures from the very beginning when it comes to this matter of Christian stewardship. Melvin Hodges says, "If we are to attain self-support, it is important that we lay the right foundation from the very beginning of the work, since procedures we establish with the first few converts and in founding the first church will doubtless become the pattern to be followed by the converts and churches which will spring up later in the district."[37] Specifically, church planters need to plan so as to avoid three common and negative tendencies relating to stewardship of money and goods.

1. There is a tendency to postpone instruction concerning the stewardship of money and material goods. This is perhaps more pronounced in the Third World, but it is not confined to the Third World. There are various reasons for this tendency. One reason is that salvation is a free gift of God (though it cost heaven's best), and we want people to understand that they cannot buy it or merit it. Another reason is that religion in the East, and increasingly in the West, is associated with begging and moneymaking; and we want people to understand that we are not charity seekers or charlatans.

37. Melvin L. Hodges, *The Indigenous Church* (Springfield, Mo.: Gospel, 1953), 79.

Of course, we do not err when we do not seek money for God's work from people who do not know God. But we do err when instruction in Christian stewardship is not given to those who do know God, and when we do not encourage them to give proportionately, generously, and gladly.

2. There is a tendency to bring financial aid along with a spiritual ministry, especially into areas and cultures that are depressed or impoverished. This is something that Paul never did. But when outside resources are available, the temptation to tap them is sometimes almost irresistible. In that case we should remember that astute students of mission such as Henry Venn, Rufus Anderson, John Nevius, Roland Allen, Melvin Hodges, and Donald McGavran were basically of one mind in this matter. All discouraged the use of imported funds in church planting, though McGavran did allow for a limited use of funds that primed the pump and did not stifle local responsibility and initiative.

3. Finally, there is the unintended tendency to refashion the spiritual ministry of the emerging church into something approaching an economic enterprise. The church planter can contribute to this process by overemphasizing tithes and offerings, by promoting costly building programs prematurely, or by encouraging the calling of a full-time pastor too soon. When the King's business becomes like any other business and church planters become ministers of finance instead of ministers of the Word, the new church is already in trouble.

ME-3 illustration: For a positive illustration of what can happen when missionaries plan carefully and proceed wisely, we go to a continent and situation where church finances have occasioned numerous problems over the years. By the time Isaac Saoshiro, a missionary from Japan, was ready to begin a church plant in Nakuru, Kenya, it was apparent to him that he faced a serious problem in the area of stewardship. In the first place, the local people looked upon themselves as poor and upon the Saoshiros as wealthy Japanese with access to almost unlimited resources. Second, the indigenes could anticipate crops the year around to meet their basic needs. People lived simply. Planning in general—and financial planning in particular—was quite foreign to their thinking. Third, the denomination of which Isaac Saoshiro was a part did not handle their own finances. All offerings went to a central office where priorities were established for the use of church funds. The church in Nakuru was destined to be different. Indeed, it became instrumental in a denomination-wide policy change. Saoshiro explains how this happened.

1. In starting the work in Nakuru, Saoshiro was faced with the choice of following denominational policies and precedents or adhering to

biblical principles. Providentially, God arranged circumstances so that Saoshiro was free to apply biblical principles without offending denominational leaders.

2. Early on Saoshiro taught biblical principles of stewardship. Just as important, perhaps, was the fact that his personal convictions in this area were somehow communicated to the people. As a result, some of the people voluntarily began to tithe of their wheat, cows, goats, and cash.

3. Uncharacteristically, church finances were disclosed. When believers saw regular reports of church funds, they began to trust their leaders and gave more.

4. With the blessing of the central office, the church in Nakuru became financially autonomous, assuming responsibility for the gathering and dispensing of their own funds. This proved to be an added incentive to sacrificial giving.

5. Saoshiro discouraged dependence on foreign funds. He made it clear that he did not come to help the locals financially, but to work along with them. In fact, he received a salary from them for his work, though he donated it to a development fund.

6. A savings account for the building of a sanctuary was opened in a local bank. Interest rates were relatively high, so when the people saw how the account grew, they were surprised and gave even more generously.

7. It was decided that the people should be encouraged to give in response to the goodness and grace of God, not in response to open pleas and urgings.

Writing of the fruits of his approach both in Nakuru and elsewhere, Saoshiro says: "As a result of the effort mentioned above, most of the building expenses for the sanctuaries, pastors' houses, and polytechnic's classrooms were financed locally, though we accepted some voluntary donations from overseas. Another blessing was that church people volunteered to dig the foundation, poured cement, and built the walls by themselves."[38]

Master Plan Formation

In chapter 12 we were concerned with the initial care of new converts. Here our concern is for their continued welfare and strengthening. We suggest that two types of records be kept for each believer. First, a record should be filled out by the new believer (perhaps over a period

38. Isaac T. Saoshiro, "Missiological Reflections on Church Planting in Kenya" (paper for seminar in church planting, Trinity Evangelical Divinity School, May 1996), 18–19.

Figure 47
Questionnaire for New Believers

Name: _____ Sex: _____

Address: _____

Telephone: _____ Date of profession of faith: _____

Age: Under 20 ___   20 to 30 ___   30 to 40 ___
      40 to 50 ___   over 50 ___

Marital status: Married ___ Single ___ Widowed _____
            Divorced _____

Family members: _____

_____

_____

- -

1. Do you have a Bible? Yes ____ No ____
2. Will you join a Bible instruction class?   Yes ____ No ____
3. Which of the following worship opportunities will you observe?
   a. Public: Sunday A.M. ____ Sunday P.M.____ Other_____
   b. Family _____
   c. Personal _____
4. What abilities and interests do you have which might be used in the service of Christ? _____

5. In accordance with Romans 12 and 1 Corinthians 12, will you look to the Lord for provision of spiritual gifts?

   _____

   And are you willing to receive counseling as to the presence and use of those gifts in Christ's service?

   _____

6. Have you shared your testimony of faith in Christ with your family? ____ friends? ____ fellow believers? _____
7. Are you willing to share your testimony with others as the Lord and church leaders provide opportunity? _____
8. In accordance with Acts 20:35 and 1 Corinthians 16:1, do you recognize the importance of stewardship of material goods? _____

of time) assessing one's talents, interests, and commitments as a Christian (see figure 47). Second, the counselor/friend should record the progress of the new believer until the completion of basic instruction and full integration into the life of the emerging church (see figure 48). The time required to accomplish this objective will vary with the individual and cultural environment, but from six to twelve months might be considered average. (Church leaders will be greatly aided in planning the program of the local church if they will use questionnaires to get a reading on older believers as well as new ones.)

Some will object that the keeping of such records is too laborious and time-consuming. We would argue that secular institutions such as schools keep records and that, above all other institutions, the church of Christ should be interested in individuals. Furthermore, if the counselor and the new believer are given the responsibility of keeping the records up-to-date, the burden on the missionary-evangelist and local leaders is actually reduced. By keeping the records accessible to the leaders (no highly personal information is included) the spiritual welfare and progress of the group can be more readily monitored. When the new believer encounters spiritual difficulties or fails to progress, the counselor can alert the leaders, who will be able to minister accordingly. When individuals come to Christ as a group, it will be helpful to find some way of putting the individual records together so that the progress of the group as well as of its individual members can be monitored. In cases where, by virtue of the number of new converts or other factors, the church planter decides not to use individual records, the progress of the church as a whole must continue to be evaluated carefully.

Faith and Instruction

There should be a record of the progress and commitment of new believers in the areas of instruction, worship, service, witness, and stewardship. The basic principle in regard to instruction is that all believers be trained in the Scriptures with three objectives in mind. First, that they become familiar with the unfolding story of biblical revelation beginning with Genesis and ending with Revelation. Second, that they master the cardinal doctrines of the Christian faith as taught in Scripture and affirmed by the church in historic creeds down through the centuries. Third, that they be equipped in basic rules of biblical interpretation so that individually and in concert they are prepared to search the Scriptures for themselves. Care should be taken that the materials and methods used lend themselves to these ends.

Figure 48
Report on New Believer

A new report form should be completed by the counselor or some other leader at regular intervals until the new believer has been fully integrated into the life of the believing community.

Believer's name _____
Counselor's name _____
Date _____
Date of profession of faith _____ Date of baptism _____
Date of acceptance into informal membership in the group or church _____
Date of acceptance into full membership in the church _____

- -

Bible instruction record:
　　Date of completion of lesson series #1 _____
　　Date of completion of lesson series #2 _____
　　Date of completion of lesson series #3 _____
Etc.

Participation in worship:
　　Public worship:　Regular _____ Irregular _____
　　Family worship:　Regular _____ Irregular _____
　　Personal worship: Regular _____ Irregular _____

Service involvement:
　　Form of service　　　　　　　Supervisor
　　_____　　_____

　　_____　　_____

Witness:
　　Form of witness　　　　　　　Supervisor
　　_____　　_____

　　_____　　_____

Stewardship:
　　Involved _____　　Not involved _____

Faith and Worship

Assuming that the meaning and practice of Christian worship constitute part of the instruction provided for all new believers, our concern
shifts to their actual experience in public worship, group (e.g., family)
worship, and personal worship. Do they participate regularly? Are they
being strengthened spiritually as a result of worship? Do they feel that
God is pleased with their worship? Is the observance of the Lord's Supper an integral part of their worship? The answers to these questions
will be important in planning public worship and counseling concerning private worship.

Faith and Service

It is imperative to find out precisely what talents and spiritual gifts
for Christian service are possessed by believers, and then to provide opportunities for them to develop their talents and spiritual gifts and to
use them in Christ's service. Believers have a responsibility to aid one
another both in the recognition and in the utilization of these talents
and gifts. If this dual responsibility is taken seriously, the chances of
new believers actually serving Christ will be greatly enhanced.

Faith and Witness

We can anticipate that, as a result of the inner working of the Holy
Spirit and proper instruction at the time of turning to Christ, converts
will bear a spontaneous witness to family, friends, and the group of believers. Nothing is quite so refreshing and convincing as the witness of
the newly reborn member of God's family. In most cases, however, it
will be necessary for Christian leaders to provide inspiration, models,
and occasions for a continuing witness. It is precisely at this point that
many cults outdo the church. So let the church planter settle on a program of evangelistic outreach for the local group (simplified, perhaps,
at first). And let all believers have the privilege of participating in it, in
ways great or small.

Faith and Stewardship

Churches have a wide variety of approaches to the stewardship of
money and material goods. Single or multiple freewill offerings, the
pledge system, faith-promise plans, offerings in kind, monies given directly to a church treasurer—these and various other approaches are
used in churches around the world. It is not our intention to evaluate
these various approaches here, but simply to suggest that all believers

be provided with information and materials designed to encourage them to exercise generous stewardship on a regular basis.

The twentieth-century church and its missions have been criticized on two seemingly contradictory counts. On the one hand, we are told that churches in new areas have not grown because of the tendency to concentrate on the first believers until they become what would be considered good Christians. This to the neglect of a continued outreach to the unconverted. On the other hand, we are told that many of our churches are weak because new believers are not instructed and built up in the faith.

Which is right? It would seem that if either criticism is valid, the other must be invalid. But it may be that both are true! Urging believers to become good Christians—and even praying that they do so—is not the same as actually confirming them in the faith! Instruction in the Word, worship of God, service for Christ, witness to the world, stewardship of means—these are the elements of confirmation. It is hard to imagine that churches composed of confirmed believers will not grow. And it is hard to imagine that churches without confirmed believers can be pleasing to the Lord of the church.

The Leaders Consecrated 14

It is common for church planters to desire that groups of new believers organize as soon as possible. The emphasis can be somewhat misguided, however. No organization can be stronger than its leadership. Therefore, to think, pray, plan, and work with a view to raising up spiritual leadership for the organizing church should be of first priority. When spiritual leadership emerges, organization will become practicable and essential.[1]

Objectives

With the above in mind, we will establish three objectives for this stage of the Pauline Cycle:

1. Efforts should be continued to promote the spiritual maturity of all believers in the congregation.
2. The believers should be taught how to recognize and select men and women who are gifted and spiritually qualified for leadership in the local church.
3. The church should be organized in a permanent form that is scriptural, functional, effective, and expandable.

Developing Qualified Leadership for the Local Church

Biblical Principles and Precedents

The Synagogue Background

The churches which Paul founded were not organized in a religious vacuum. Many of the early converts had been members of synagogues.

---

1. For an excellent guide on the subject of leadership and leadership development for Western churches see John J. Westermann, *The Leadership Continuum: A Biblical Model for Effective Leading* (Deer Lodge, Tenn.: Lighthouse, 1997). Church planters would do well to consult this book often, which is based on both Scripture and extensive secular literature.

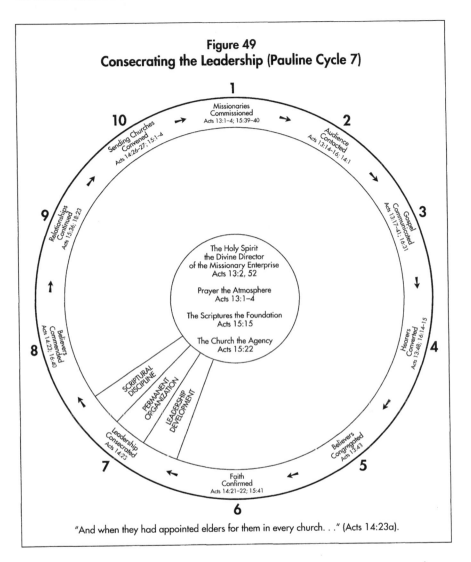

Figure 49
Consecrating the Leadership (Pauline Cycle 7)

1
Missionaries Commissioned
Acts 13:1–4; 15:39–40

2
Audience Contacted
Acts 13:14–16; 14:1

3
Gospel Communicated
Acts 13:17–41; 16:31

4
Hearers Converted
Acts 13:48; 16:14–15

5
Believers Congregated
Acts 13:43

6
Faith Confirmed
Acts 14:21–22; 15:41

7
Leadership Consecrated
Acts 14:23

8
Believers Commended
Acts 14:23; 16:40

9
Relationships Continued
Acts 15:36; 18:23

10
Sending Churches Convened
Acts 14:26–27; 15:1–4

The Holy Spirit
the Divine Director
of the Missionary Enterprise
Acts 13:2, 52

Prayer the Atmosphere
Acts 13:1–4

The Scriptures the Foundation
Acts 15:15

The Church the Agency
Acts 15:22

SCRIPTURAL DISCIPLINE

PERMANENT ORGANIZATION

LEADERSHIP DEVELOPMENT

"And when they had appointed elders for them in every church. . ." (Acts 14:23a).

It was natural for these believers and their leaders to follow the synagogue traditions of worship and patterns of organization.

Briefly look at the synagogue pattern. In order to organize a synagogue or hold meetings it was necessary to have at least ten men. The elders of the congregation selected a ruler (or possibly several of them). The ruler was responsible for synagogue services and properties. He often designated others to lead in the expression of praise, to pray, to read from the Law and the Prophets, and to give exhortations. Several assistants carried out menial duties, inflicted corporal punishment or otherwise disciplined members, and dispensed alms received from the members.

Thus New Testament believers already had a model for church leadership and organization. It is not to be inferred that they followed this synagogue pattern rigidly, however. The point is that the early believers were aware of basic ways and means for conducting corporate spiritual life and business.

The Officers of the Church according to the New Testament

At least five offices of the early churches can be distinguished in the New Testament: the apostle, the prophet, the evangelist, the pastor (elder, overseer), and the deacon. The two latter offices require special consideration here. Local churches need pastors (or elders) and deacons.

1. In the New Testament the terms "pastor," "elder," and "overseer" (or "bishop") seem to be used more or less synonymously. However, the three terms designate separate functions that may have required more than one man to perform. Since the oft-used word "elder" normally occurs in the plural, it seems likely that most early congregations had more than one such person (Acts 14:23; 15:2, 4, 6; 20:17). Passages such as Ephesians 4:11 and 1 Timothy 5:17 seem to differentiate between those elders who primarily governed and those who ministered the Word and shepherded the flock. The common distinction between elder and pastor, therefore, may be one of function as much as one of office.

The specific functions of the elders included responsibility (a) to govern the congregation (1 Tim. 5:17), not by "lording" *(katakyrieuontes)* over it but by example *(typoi)* (1 Peter 5:3); (b) to minister the Word of God; (c) to equip believers in the church so they could minister and build up the body (Eph. 4:11–12); (d) to protect the congregation from false teachers (Acts 20:28–30); and (e) to visit the sick and pray for them (James 5:14).

Polycarp, who was both a disciple of John and an early church leader, summed up the duties of the elder:

And let the presbyters be compassionate and merciful to all, bringing back those that wander, visiting all the sick, and not neglecting the widow, the orphan, or the poor, but always "providing for that which is becoming in the sight of God and man"; abstaining from all wrath, respect of persons, and unjust judgment; keeping far off from all covetousness, not quickly crediting [an evil report] against anyone, not severe in judgment, as knowing we are all under a debt of sin. If then we entreat the Lord to forgive us, we ought also ourselves to forgive; for we are before the eyes of our Lord and God, and "we must all appear at the judgment-seat of Christ, and must every one give an account of himself." Let us then serve Him in fear and with all reverence, even as He Himself has commanded us, and as the apostles who preached the gospel unto us, and the prophets who proclaimed beforehand the coming of the Lord [have alike taught us]. Let us be zealous in the pursuit of that which is good, keeping ourselves from causes of offense, from false brethren, and from those who in hypocrisy bear the name of the Lord, and draw away vain men unto error.[2]

2. Concerning the office of deacon there is little room for question. The deacons in the New Testament churches carried out such duties as waiting on tables and dispensing church funds. By inference we may conclude that they did whatever menial tasks were necessary in order to make it possible for those who preached the Word to give full attention to that ministry (Acts 6:1–6). It should be emphasized that the deacons had a spiritual and essential ministry. Without them corporate activities would have suffered, individual needs might not have been met, and the ministry of the Word would have been hampered. Note also that worthy women participated in this diaconal ministry (Rom. 16:1–2).

The Qualifications of Local Church Leaders

1. The pastors (elders, overseers)
   a. Pastors must be above reproach (1 Tim. 3:2; Titus 1:6–7)
   b. They must be the husband of one wife (1 Tim. 3:2; Titus 1:6)
   c. They must be temperate and self-controlled (1 Tim. 3:2; Titus 1:8)
   d. Pastors are to be prudent, sensible, and just (1 Tim. 3:2; Titus 1:8)
   e. They must be respectable (1 Tim. 3:2)
   f. And hospitable (1 Tim. 3:2)
   g. And be able to teach (1 Tim. 3:2)
   h. No pastor should be addicted to wine (1 Tim. 3:3; Titus 1:7)
   i. Nor pugnacious (1 Tim. 3:3; Titus 1:7)
   j. Nor contentious (1 Tim. 3:3)
   k. Pastors must be gentle (1 Tim. 3:3)
   l. They must be free from the love of money (1 Tim. 3:3; Titus 1:7)
   m. They must manage their household well (1 Tim. 3:4)
   n. Pastors should not be new converts (1 Tim. 3:6)
   o. They must have a good reputation with unbelievers (1 Tim. 3:7)
   p. They must not be self-willed (Titus 1:7)
   q. Nor quick-tempered (Titus 1:7)
   r. Pastors must love what is good (Titus 1:8)
   s. They must be devout and just (Titus 1:8)
   t. They should hold fast to sound thinking (Titus 1:9)
   u. They should exhort others in sound teaching (Titus 1:9)
   v. And refute those holding unsound doctrine (Titus 1:9)

2. Polycarp, "The Epistles of Polycarp to the Philippians," in *Ante-Nicene Christian Library*, vol. 1, *The Writings of the Apostolic Fathers* (Edinburgh: T. and T. Clark, 1867), 72–73.

2. The deacons (and deaconesses as appropriate)
   a. Deacons must have a good reputation (Acts 6:3)
   b. They must be full of the Holy Spirit and wisdom (Acts 6:3)
   c. They must be competent in administration (Acts 6:3)
   d. Deacons should possess dignity, seriousness (1 Tim. 3:8)
   e. They must not be double-tongued (1 Tim. 3:8)
   f. Nor addicted to much wine (1 Tim. 3:8)
   g. Nor fond of sordid gain (1 Tim. 3:8)
   h. Deacons should hold the mystery of the faith with a clear conscience (1 Tim. 3:9)
   i. They must be tested, not new converts (1 Tim. 3:10)
   j. Deacons must be the husband of one wife (1 Tim. 3:12)
   k. They must be good managers of their children and households (1 Tim. 3:12)
   l. Deacons must possess strong personal faith (1 Tim. 3:13)
   m. They should not be given to slanderous gossip (1 Tim. 3:11)
   n. They must be sober (1 Tim. 3:11)
   o. And reliable in all things (1 Tim. 3:11)

Relevant Research

Defining "Leader" and "Leadership"

Leadership has been defined in various ways. Some definitions are most instructive:

1. Field Marshal Bernard Montgomery said, "Leadership is the capacity and will to rally men and women to a common purpose, and the character which inspires confidence."[3]
2. Chinese statesman Li Hung-chang declared, "There are only three kinds of people in the world—those that are movable, those that are immovable, and those that move them."[4]
3. Anthropologist Philip K. Bock writes, "Leaders are specialists in decision-making."[5]
4. Bock gives another definition, which may be the most useful one for our purposes: leaders are those who have a "role involving legitimate exercise of authority over other persons."[6]

The more one thinks about the matter of leadership, the more one is impressed that authority is the key to understanding it. Of course, the kind of authority involved is extremely important.

3. Quoted in J. Oswald Sanders, *Spiritual Leadership* (Chicago: Moody, 1967), 19.
4. Ibid., 19–20.
5. Philip K. Bock, *Modern Cultural Anthropology: An Introduction,* 2d ed. (New York: Knopf, 1974), 118.
6. Ibid., 117.

Various Kinds of Leaders

Bock distinguishes four types of leaders on the basis of the source of their authority:

1. *Hereditary leaders*. The authority of hereditary leaders is based on their position in a kinship group (e.g., the oldest living male in a royal lineage). They are leaders because of who they are by birth rather than what they can do.
2. *Bureaucratic leaders*. The authority of bureaucratic leaders comes by systematically progressing through positions of lesser authority. They have advanced because of both competence and seniority.
3. *Charismatic leaders*. Unique persons may rise to authority in times of great social crisis. By the force of personality they command enthusiastic followers.
4. *Representative leaders*. Representative leaders are chosen by general consensus or election. They are then responsible to their followers. Though many of these leaders possess the distinctive qualities of the other types of leaders, these qualities are not the basis of their authority.[7]

Bock's typology is especially helpful in Western societies. In the tribal societies common in Africa and Oceania it is less so. For example, in these societies a shaman or witch doctor often exercises considerable authority based on heredity, yes, but also on a different kind of charisma—not so much on the force of personality as such, but on the force or power of the medicine at his command. This kind of factor enables us to understand better such phenomena as the prophet movements in Africa and the cargo movements in the South Pacific. It also helps us understand why, when in difficulty, numerous misguided believers in African churches consult their pastor in the light of day but seek out the local witch doctor under the cover of darkness!

The "Peter Principle"

Laurence J. Peter argues that there is a common tendency to promote faithful members of any organization with little regard to their ability to produce at a higher level of responsibility. But success in one position of responsibility in and of itself does not assure success in another position where the demands may be significantly different and greater. An individual elevated to a level above one's capability becomes frustrated and unproductive.[8]

7. Ibid., 118–20.
8. Laurence J. Peter, *The Peter Principle* (New York: Bantam, 1970), 19–27.

Churches must of course recognize faithfulness, competence, and a job well done. Rapidly growing sects are often much more objective and generous in this regard than are the churches. Nevertheless, spiritual gifts and natural abilities must be taken into account in the encouragement and selection of church leaders. Only those who can preach should be requested to preach. Only those with the gift of teaching should be asked to teach. And only those with the ability to administer should be called to administer.

Practical Reflection

Selecting Church Leaders

Leadership in society at large is vastly different from leadership in the churches. Much has been written on making contact with the leaders of a community and winning them to Christ with a view to positively affecting Christian witness and church life. This is well and good provided unconverted, unspiritual leaders of society do not enter the church and become leaders primarily by virtue of their social status and natural leadership ability. We must keep in mind the differentiation that J. Oswald Sanders makes between natural and spiritual leaders:[9]

The Natural Leader	**The Spiritual Leader**
1. Self-confident	1. Confident in God
2. Knows human nature	2. Also knows God
3. Makes one's own decisions	3. Seeks to find God's will
4. Ambitious	4. Self-effacing
5. Originates methods	5. Finds and follows God's methods
6. Enjoys commanding others	6. Delights to obey God
7. Motivated by personal considerations	7. Motivated by love for God and others
8. Independent	8. God-dependent

ME-3 illustration: An unusual experiment in appointing natural societal leaders to positions of leadership in the churches was carried out by the Rhenish Mission in conjunction with its work among the Bataks on Sumatra.[10] Those who were the natural leaders in the society were baptized and appointed as leaders in the churches. The result was that the churches had leaders, but the leaders occasioned numerous and aggravated problems. Those with natural leadership ability and leadership status in society are not thereby qualified to take positions of leadership in the churches. One of the easiest courses to follow in the organization

9. Sanders, *Spiritual Leadership*, 21.
10. Peter Beyerhaus and Henry Lefever, *The Responsible Church and the Foreign Mission* (Grand Rapids: Eerdmans, 1964), 50–53.

of churches is to select those of demonstrated leadership in society for a similar role in the church. In the case of the Rhenish Mission this was by design. In most cases it happens by default. In both instances adverse results can be expected. A spiritual church must have spiritual leaders.

The Church Leader as a Representative Leader

Spiritual leaders are persons both under authority and with authority. They are most like the representative leader in society in that the basis of their authority does not lie in natural qualities of leadership (even though spiritual leaders may well possess them), but in the fact that they are equipped by God and chosen by Holy Spirit–directed churches. As Vergil Gerber writes, "A man cannot normally exercise authority in the church *until that authority has been recognized by the church.*"[11] If this is to occur, it is imperative that believers be instructed concerning the biblical standards for leadership in the local church. These must be held up before believers so that they have a yardstick against which to measure spiritual growth. Not all believers will become leaders, for not all will have the right combination of gifts and abilities. But all should aspire to the highest standards of godliness, and those who attain them should be recognized and invested with special responsibility and authority.

ME-1 illustration: From the beginning the Fellowship Bible Church of Dallas kept the qualifications for church leadership before its members, including new converts. Pastor Gene Getz and his colleagues organized the church into small groups, each of which was led by an elder or undershepherd. When believers thought that they measured up to the standard, and the church leaders agreed, they were given responsibility for one of these groups. Since this was the plan from the beginning of the church, organization and leadership developed simultaneously. Two types of growth—numerical and spiritual—were the result.[12]

Training Leaders in the Churches

It is not enough that certain believers have the potential for leadership. As they give evidence of spiritual growth, they must be given opportunities to utilize their potential and develop as church leaders. This process will make special demands on both missionary-evangelists and the emerging leaders. But the results will justify any sacrifice.

ME-3 illustration: A missionary in Japan, Jim Blocksom, developed a simple and effective program for training potential elders for a newly

11. Vergil Gerber, *Missions in Creative Tension* (South Pasadena, Calif.: William Carey Library, 1971), 284.
12. Gene Getz, *Sharpening the Focus of the Church* (Chicago: Moody, 1974), 105–8.

emerging church in the Kansai area. Each week he met with five mature and able laymen. They reflected on and evaluated Blocksom's expository message of the previous Sunday. Then they studied the Scripture text for the following Sunday's message. After determining the meaning of the text they suggested specific applications for the Japanese context.

When some months had passed, Blocksom arranged to be away for a Sunday and told the laymen that one of them would have to preach. With one accord they all excused themselves on grounds of inability and inexperience. But Blocksom was ready for them with an unanswerable argument: "Since you have helped me so considerably with criticisms and suggestions for all this time, certainly any one of you can be expected to do quite well."

One layman was chosen to preach, and preach he did. Predictably, the missionary found it necessary to minister elsewhere with increasing frequency! By the time the church was organized and a paid pastor was installed, the church had five laymen who could preach, teach, and lead with remarkable ability.

Leaders Heading Out and Leaders Heading In

In his own unique and captivating style, Donald McGavran once made a distinction between church leaders who are "heading out" and those who are "heading in."[13] Once churches become established, the majority of leaders are given responsibilities that have to do with training the children of Christian families, ministering to the needs of the congregation, keeping the organization running smoothly, and maintaining church facilities. Now all of this is good and necessary. But it also hinders growth. The church is constituted to find lost sheep, not just to fold and feed the saved sheep. Sadly, a new church that models itself after the average established church will soon find that the attention and efforts of most leaders will be focused inward, and few will be reaching out to the lost. Stagnation will result. Only by continual and careful study and action will the proper proportion of attention, time, and effort be given to outreach, even in the pioneer situation.

Effecting Permanent Organization in the Local Church

Biblical Principles and Precedents

The Emergence of Church Organization in the New Testament Period

Contrary to the thinking of some, much New Testament church organization was formal. Otherwise the churches would not have been

---

13. Donald A. McGavran, "Principles of Training Leaders for Growing Churches" (lecture given at Trinity Evangelical Divinity School, 16 Oct. 1969).

able to take required actions in a decent and orderly manner. Many early churches undoubtedly were patterned after the synagogue, but the New Testament reveals that there was also a distinct development in church organization and administration.

The germ of church organization existed previous to Pentecost. In the Epistles believers are called saints and brethren and are found in churches. They shared a mutual priesthood (1 Peter 2:9) and a common ministry (Eph. 4:11–15). Only regenerate persons were members of local churches. And all regenerate persons were members of the churches, as far as we know. It does not seem to be the case that any definite number of believers was required in order to organize a local church (as was true of the synagogue). After all, Christ had promised his presence where but two or three gathered in his name (Matt. 18:20).

The early emphasis in the ministry of Paul and the other apostles was upon preaching. With the passing of time, however, more attention was given to matters of church organization. Before any of the Pauline Epistles were written, the Book of James (c. A.D. 48) made reference to the "elders of the church" (James 5:14). And Paul's first epistle requests appreciation of those who are "over you in the Lord" (1 Thess. 5:12).

Organization and leadership go hand in hand. In the case of the Jerusalem church, the leaders were the special apostles themselves. In the case of the Antioch church, some of the first leaders came from Jerusalem (Acts 15:22, 27). In the cases of the missionary churches, leaders were chosen by the missionary-evangelists or the local believers.

Congregationalism and the New Testament Churches

The fact that, as churches developed, they had some leaders who did not come from the local congregation and some who were appointed by missionary-evangelists does not rule out congregationalism. A. H. Strong offers convincing arguments that in the New Testament Era church government was democratic or congregational:[14]

1. It was the duty of the whole church to preserve unity in its action (Rom. 12:16; 1 Cor. 1:10; Eph. 4:3).
2. The whole church had responsibility for maintaining pure doctrine and practice (2 Cor. 11:1–3; 1 Tim. 3:5; Jude 3; Rev. 2 and 3).
3. The ordinances were committed to the whole church to observe and guard (1 Cor. 11:23–24).
4. The whole church elected its officers and delegates (Acts 6:3, 5; 13:2–3; 15:2, 4, 22, 30; 2 Cor. 8:19). (This is a critical point, of

14. A. H. Strong, *Systematic Theology* (Philadelphia: Judson, 1907), 904–8.

course. In making his case Strong understands Acts 13:2–3 as referring to the whole church at Antioch. And regarding passages such as Acts 14:23 and Titus 1:5 he maintains that the appointing by the apostles and Titus does not refer to the mode of appointment and therefore does not rule out the authority of the church community, which is upheld in other passages.)

5. The whole church had the responsibility and authority to exercise discipline (1 Cor. 5:4–5, 13; 2 Thess. 3:6, 14–15).

We must not press these arguments too far. There seems to have been a flexibility in New Testament organization that served the purposes of the churches. The pattern probably differed somewhat from church to church. As Donald Lake says, "Churches can have deacons, elders and pastors or only pastors. . . . The issue of congregationalism is: Where does the authority to elect reside, upon whom does the responsibility fall, and to whom does the power of discipline belong?"[15] Episcopalians will answer, "with the bishops." Presbyterians will answer, "with the elders." Those of us who espouse congregational polity will, of course, answer, "with the congregation."

Relevant Research

Human Government and Authority

Leadership and organization are human necessities. Anarchy is practically impossible. But forms of government do vary radically, and with them the types and authority of leaders, and the methods of their selection. The basic types of human government parallel the alternative forms of church polity:

1. Autocracy—absolute authority exercised by one person
2. Oligarchy—authority exercised by a select and privileged group within the larger society
3. Democracy—authority vested in the members of the society

It should not be overlooked that most human governments can (and perhaps to some degree usually do) exhibit characteristics of more than one of the basic types. A pure form of government is a rarity. Sometimes the form of an autocracy (monarchy) is retained while functionally the government is a democracy. Sometimes the form of a democracy is retained while functionally government is either an autocracy

---

15. Donald Lake, "Congregationalism: Does It Matter?" *Evangelical Beacon*, 16 March 1976, pp. 10–12.

(dictatorship) or an oligarchy. Form and function do not necessarily coincide.

Social Structures and Social Organizations

Elsewhere we drew attention to two distinctions that are particularly relevant here. One has to do with the difference between structures and organizations in human societies.[16] The former has to do with the ways in which members of a society relate to each other with a view to perpetuating traditional values and resisting change. The latter has to do with the ways in which members of a society come together in order to accomplish certain objectives that involve change. Castes, subcastes, and clans are examples of social structure. Fraternities and sororities, farmers' cooperatives, and the thousands of voluntary groups that characterize American culture are examples of social organization.

Church planters and emerging church leaders do well to note this distinction. Social structures in target cultures will likely be resistant to church establishment and growth. Social organizations of various kinds may well provide a new church with helpful insights as to ways in which to accomplish those purposes for which God has placed it in the world. Eventually this tension will necessitate a creative balance. The church is called upon to preserve a tradition of faith and at the same time to be willing to change and stay at the cutting edge. Strong recognized the implications of this dual role of the local church.[17] Only when a church maintains a balance will it become salt and light in a community.

Lineage and Kindred Societies

The second distinction has to do with the difference between lineage and kindred societies.[18] To put it simply, the locus of attention and authority in lineage societies is on ancestors and reaches back to a common ancestor (real or mythological). The locus of attention in kindred societies is upon the ego's changing relationships through life. The differences between these societal orientations will be apparent in almost every aspect of church life, including general perspectives, values, counseling, organizing, and decision making. When moving from a kindred to a lineage culture, for example, church workers should be prepared to deal with a variety of unfamiliar issues—ancestor veneration, different understandings regarding eldership, and decision making by consensus. When an American church-growth analyst asked Hong Kongers why de-

16. See David J. Hesselgrave, *Communicating Christ Cross-Culturally*, 2d ed. (Grand Rapids: Zondervan, 1991), 483–85.
17. Strong, *Systematic Theology*, 892–93.
18. See Hesselgrave, *Communicating Christ*, 477–78.

ceased members were not removed from church rolls, they looked at him incredulously and replied, "Why, you certainly wouldn't revoke their membership just because they moved to heaven, would you?"

Parkinson's Law

There is a pronounced tendency on the part of human governments and most social organizations to grow ever larger and consume an unnecessary and disproportionate part of their total resources upon themselves. This they often do without a commensurate increase in effectiveness in terms of their original and basic goals. Although C. Northcote Parkinson developed this law from his research into business organizations, it has a much wider application.[19]

Decision by Consensus

It may be well to take another look at the method of decision making called decision by consensus. A consensus is a shared conviction that a particular decision is the right one. It is arrived at by a full discussion in which all members of the group are encouraged to share their true feelings. They make known which of the alternatives they can support in view of the goals of the group. The decision to act will represent the best wisdom of the entire deliberative body (though not necessarily the first choice of each individual member). Decisions reached in this way help promote the goals of the organization and assure group harmony in pursuing them. Decision by consensus is as adaptable to democratic institutions at the grassroots level as is the method of decision by discussion and vote.

Practical Reflection

In general, missionary-evangelists who have seen their task as including the planting and developing of local churches have had the best of intentions. Not only so, they have also been relatively successful in establishing churches all around the world. No one who is familiar with pioneer work at home or abroad, however, would be willing to say that what has been accomplished has been done in the most biblical and effective way.

Autonomous or Christonomous Churches?

From the days of Henry Venn and Rufus Anderson, strategists have stressed the indigenous church, which has usually been defined as self-supporting, self-governing, and self-propagating. Overall, when prop-

19. C. Northcote Parkinson, *In-Laws and Outlaws* (Boston: Houghton Mifflin, 1962), 233.

erly conceived and wisely applied, this has been a good emphasis. Recently, however, it has received some healthy reevaluation. The question has been raised, "Is it proper to define churches in terms of *autonomy* (i.e., *self*-governance), etc.? Would it not be more biblical and fruitful to describe them in terms of *Christonomy*, i.e., under the rule of Christ?"[20] Moreover, and in line with this, is it not true that, properly conceived, churches modeled on the New Testament will be indigenous in the sense of "related to the soil"? Is it not the imported cultural expectations of church planters that make new churches something other than indigenous? And for that matter, is it not possible for a church to be indigenous according to the classical definition (self-supporting, self-governing, self-propagating) and still be more or less unrelated to the soil in which it must grow? These questions deserve careful consideration. They point at the heart of church organization.

Should Form Follow Function?

On the subject of form and function Lyle Schaller writes, "In simple language, the primary issue boils down to an either-or type question. Should the structure or organization of the churches determine function? Or should needs and function determine structure?"[21] Schaller gives priority to function. He says that it is a mistake to think that the church leaders of the eighteenth, nineteenth, and early twentieth centuries were great adherents of tradition. Rather, they were innovators who were willing to change, to scrap tradition when appropriate, and to serve Christ effectively rather than simply retain old forms. Schaller could make a similar case vis-à-vis the apostles and leaders of the first century. But were he to do so, he would have to recognize that form and function are so intricately intertwined in New Testament ecclesiology and church polity that to disregard or denigrate one would be to detract from the other. The New Testament churches adopted some common forms associated with Judaism and the advent of Christianity. That having been said, Schaller is no doubt correct in encouraging urban churches especially to give careful consideration to function (in his terminology, "mission" as opposed to "tradition") in the organizing process. Also helpful is his list of criteria for the evaluation of related proposals and plans.

Church Polity as a Reflection of Local Practice

A careful study of representative church polities will reveal that historically they have tended to reflect the social structures of the times and

---

20. Beyerhaus and Lefever, *Responsible Church*, 112–13.
21. Lyle E. Schaller, "Organizing for Mission," in *Toward Creative Urban Strategy*, comp. George A. Torney (Waco: Word, 1970), 220–23.

places of their inception. In spite of what we have said about congregationalism, the early churches did exhibit some episcopal characteristics as a result of the presence of the apostles. Given the social setting of the early centuries, episcopal characteristics continued and even amplified after the death of the apostles themselves; indeed, the doctrine of apostolic succession was later devised in order to reinforce them. The Reformation churches—developed where feudal concepts and clan structures were strong—tended to be presbyterian. Congregational forms as we know them are a more modern development which unfolded along with revolts by minorities against authoritarianism. It should be borne in mind that the congregational form of church government does not necessarily preserve the independence of the local congregation, nor do episcopal or presbyterian forms necessarily abrogate it.

While the form of church polity is important, function is just as important or more so. A form of church government that is foreign to the target culture will tend in one of two directions. Either it will adapt functionally to local ways of governance, or it will greatly impede the growth of the church.

ME-3 illustration: In Zaire some years ago, there was a district business meeting of congregationally organized churches. Three times the meeting had to be recessed when the democratic method of nominating a chairman occasioned pandemonium and worse. The fact is that the participants were working with an unfamiliar form that could not be expected to function well if too closely adhered to! Little wonder that a veteran missionary in attendance remarked, "I wish that we could go back fifty years and undo the mischief we have caused by the organization we imposed."

Just as we err when we disregard New Testament polity or read too much of our own cultural biases into the New Testament, we also err when we push any church polity too far from the form and function of local sociopolitical expressions of government. The emerging church can learn from the local structures (society organized to preserve the traditions) because it too must preserve certain teachings, values, and ways of life. The church can also learn from local organizations (groups formed to effect change) because it too is an agent of change both in the Christian community and in the larger society.

Putting Local Organization "Up for Grabs"

One of the most common errors of church planters who espouse congregational polity is the rather common practice of involving the new church in the construction of its own constitution. The reasons for the practice are obvious. They stem from democratic ideals and notions of congregational responsibility. But the practice is often misguided.

In the first place, a new congregation of believers is usually composed of a number of people who are in the process of adjusting to one another and, in many cases, to biblical teaching. Misunderstandings can easily occur. In the second place, the construction of a biblical and practical instrument of organization is a time-consuming task which diverts attention away from outreach to unbelievers and confirmation of new believers at a time when the fledgling church can least afford it. In the third place, a locally devised constitution (like all other constitutions) will be an imperfect instrument which will soon need revision on the basis of experience. Moreover, it will often prove to be most difficult to revise a constitution in which there are vested local interests.

It is far better to propose a model constitution which has been prepared by the sponsors of the emerging church than to put a constitution up for grabs, so to speak. When the charter members of the congregation realize that they will be able to revise it according to their needs at a later date, they will usually welcome emancipation from this arduous task.

ME-1 and 3 illustrations: The author's personal experience in organizing a local congregation in Urawa, Japan, is a case in point. Devising a new constitution came within a hair's breadth of being rewarded with a church split—a division at the hour of birth! In similar subsequent situations we proposed acceptance of a model constitution under which the congregation could operate for the first several years of its existence. In each case, the results were much happier!

The Tendency to Overorganize

The trouble with many constitutions and the efforts of missionary-evangelists in this regard is that both tend to impose organizational yokes upon fledgling churches that even mature churches have found it difficult to bear. Parkinson's Law is operative in many churches, including new ones!

Churches and their derivative missions and organizations must come to grips with this natural tendency. One church spawned twenty-nine committees! Ultimately a thirtieth committee was appointed to check up on the other twenty-nine! Now, of course, that there are numerous committees in a church is no more than prima facie evidence that Parkinson's Law applies. We must ask what they are doing and how well they are doing it. But the fact remains that Western churches, at least, are often afflicted with too many committees, committees that are too large, and committees that are working too hard and too long on the wrong objectives. To keep the wheels turning does not mean that the church is going anywhere.

Decision by Consensus or by Discussion and Vote?

No church polity (including congregational polity) need be locked in to decision by discussion and vote. That procedure is certainly allowable, but there are at least two aspects of it that may be inimical to Christian purposes. First, the more carefully and passionately the alternatives are presented, the more likely that sides will be taken and feelings hurt. Not all heat produces light! Second, decisions affecting the total life of a congregation that are made by a bare simple majority seem out of keeping with the unity of the body and divine guidance. To introduce decision by consensus in a society that is not acquainted with the process may not be easy, but the change may be like dew from heaven. To introduce any other process in a target area where decision by consensus is traditional may be tragic.

Maintaining Scriptural Discipline

Biblical Principles and Precedents

No good purpose is served by idealizing the early Christian congregations. On the contrary, it is very important that we recognize that they had problems. Only then can we fully understand the importance of discipline in the first century and in the twenty-first.

There were cases of immediate, severe corporal punishment in the early congregations. Ananias and Sapphira (Acts 5:1–11) and those Christians who participated in the Lord's Supper unworthily (1 Cor. 11:28–32) readily come to mind. In those cases God dealt directly with offenders on the basis of his knowledge of their inner motives. God may deal directly with erring believers today as well. But that is up to him. When the churches began to exercise discipline, conditions (but not necessarily the principles) changed radically.

The New Testament teaching on church discipline can be summarized by considering three basic questions: Who? Why? and How?[22]

Who Was Disciplined in the Early Church?

1. *Those guilty of serious doctrinal deviation.* When the purity of the gospel (soteriology) and the truth about the person of Christ (Christology) are at stake, the Bible leaves no room for carelessness or indecisiveness. Such cases are to be dealt with forthrightly and without delay (Gal. 1:6–9; 1 Tim. 1:19–20; 2 John 7–11).

---

22. J. Robertson McQuilkin, "Whatever Happened to Church Discipline?" *Christianity Today* 18.13 (29 March 1974): 8–12.

2. *Those guilty of continued ecclesiastical insubordination.* Diotrephes is a classical example of insubordination (3 John 9–10). Not only did he put himself and his own interests first, he also turned a deaf ear to the apostle and the local believers. He even excluded true Christians from the church. He exhibited those precise characteristics of evil that John had talked about in his first letter—lawlessness and lack of love for other Christians (1 John 2:9–11). There is no room for such behavior in the churches.

3. *Those guilty of flagrant moral indiscretion.* In the First Epistle to the Corinthians we are told of an instance of intrafamily fornication within the church (1 Cor. 5:1–5). The offender of common morality is by no means excused. Paul indicated in no uncertain terms that the one who was guilty in Corinth must be disciplined.

4. *Those guilty of voluntarily being indigent.* Evidently there were some people in the early churches who stopped working but did not stop eating! Paul knew of such persons in Thessalonica. They lived "in idleness, mere busybodies, not doing any work." He commanded that they "do their work in quietness and . . . earn their own living." Otherwise they were to be disciplined (2 Thess. 3:11–14 RSV).

We should not suppose that this is a complete register of those who merited discipline, or that Scripture supplies a complete register. Paul took the occasion of immorality in Corinth to mention idolaters, revilers, drunkards, robbers, and greedy persons, and he prescribed discipline for them also (1 Cor. 5:9–13). It is clear that churches had a divine directive to discipline their members, and they were to do so evenhandedly according to God's standards and not their own.

Why Were People Disciplined in the Early Church?

1. Discipline was exercised in order that offenders might be punished and justice done (1 Thess. 4:6–7). We hasten to add that this was not the chief grounds for cases of New Testament church discipline. Nevertheless, church discipline was to be considered as part of the judgment of God upon wrongdoers.

2. Discipline was to be exercised in order that offenders might be instructed and reclaimed (1 Cor. 5:5; 11:32; 2 Thess. 3:15). This is one of the dominant notes of the biblical teaching on discipline. How could erring believers be brought to their senses, to repentance, to new usefulness, and to all that accrues to salvation? How else, if not by being forced to experience something of the consequences of their evil ways? This biblical teaching needs new emphasis in today's churches. Church discipline is remedial. It is to be undertaken with great sorrow and compassion, and in the hope that the erring brother or sister will be restored to obedience and fruitfulness.

3. Discipline was to be exercised in order that others might be warned and fear God (Acts 5:11). If sin had been overlooked or winked at in the church, sinners might have been encouraged to think that they could continue to sin with impunity. This was not to be.

4. Discipline was to be exercised in order that the church might be purified and protected. This important reason for discipline is underscored by Paul's apt metaphor: "A little leaven leavens the whole lump" (1 Cor. 5:6). That is why those who were in the church and who persisted in sinning could not be allowed to go on without correction. Both unscriptural teaching and ungodly living are infectious among Adam's children.

How Was Church Discipline Carried Out?

The manner of discipline is certainly an important consideration. Church discipline itself becomes an evil when exercised in an unscriptural manner that is hurtful to the body and to the testimony of Christ.

1. Private grievances and public sin were to be differentiated and dealt with accordingly (Matt. 18:15–17; 1 Cor. 5; Gal. 2:11–14; 1 Tim. 5:20). In the passage from Matthew the problem was between private individuals. It was to be dealt with by enlisting the aid of other believers and, if the offender would not listen, by having nothing more to do with him. In the other passages the problems were matters of public record. To deal with them only in private would have been to disregard both the nature of the offenses and the reasons for discipline.

2. Discipline was to be exercised only on the basis of factual knowledge (Matt. 18:15–18; 1 Cor. 5:1; 1 Tim. 5:19). Discipline was serious. Hearsay evidence was insufficient. Our Lord's requirement that there be two or three witnesses fell within the Mosaic pattern, but it had a wider application, as evidenced by Paul's requirement that elders were not to be charged with wrongdoing unless there were two or three witnesses.

3. Discipline was to be carried out with a proper spirit on the part of those who enforced it (Matt. 7:1–5; Rom. 15:1–2; 2 Cor. 2:6–8; Gal. 6:1–4). A spirit of vindictiveness or self-righteousness had no place in church discipline. Rather, responsible believers were to judge themselves, and then to deal with offenders in a spirit of meekness and helpfulness.

4. Discipline was to be carried out by exclusion from *koinōnia* (Matt. 18:15–17; 1 Cor. 5; 2 Thess. 3:14; 2 John 7–11; 3 John 9–11). These passages deal with somewhat different circumstances, but the basic method of discipline was the same in each case. One of the greatest gifts God has bestowed on believers is fellowship with the saints. One of the most severe punishments the churches can inflict is the withholding of it.

Relevant Research

Guilt Cultures and Shame Cultures

In spite of the fact that a great deal of relevant research and writing on the subject has occurred since Ruth Benedict made her well-known differentiation between guilt cultures and shame cultures,[23] the basic distinction is worth noting. Among other differences the people in guilt cultures are more concerned with separate, discrete acts and deplore the transgression of a specific code. Those in shame cultures are more concerned with the overall self and deplore falling short of an ideal. In relation to church discipline, erring believers in guilt cultures tend to suffer inwardly irrespective of whether others in the church fellowship know about their sins. In fact, sin is likely to be thought of as a matter between the individual and God, with little thought given to the consequences of sin for the body of Christ. Erring believers in shame cultures will tend to suffer when they fail to live up to the expectations of others and therefore lose face, bringing shame upon the church.

Of course, the Bible reflects some aspects of both types of cultures. In guilt cultures, like the traditional United States, believers need instruction as to the effect of sin upon the church. And *koinōnia* needs to be developed to the point where the withholding of it would cause real remorse. In shame cultures, such as traditional Japan (or the United States of tomorrow?), believers must be taught that God sees our sin even when our neighbors don't, and that unconfessed sin breaks our relationship with him even though fellow believers may be unaware of the problem.

Belongingness as a Primary Motivation

Numerous studies point to the importance of belongingness in, and acceptance by, a group as a primary motivating force. Abraham Maslow's "motivational pyramid," for example, indicates that when elementary physiological and safety needs are cared for, higher motivations take over.[24] One such higher motivation is the need to belong. No one is an island. When it comes to church discipline, the implications of our need for belongingness are obvious.

Discipline and Group Progress

It is self-evident that groups which have a large proportion of self-disciplined members who are committed to group goals and programs

23. Ruth Benedict, *The Chrysanthemum and the Sword* (Boston: Houghton Mifflin, 1946).
24. Abraham Maslow, *Motivation and Personality*, 2d ed. (New York: Harper and Row, 1970).

will grow faster than those that do not. The validity of this principle stands out in bold relief when we consider the rapid growth of conservative churches in America[25] and the even more rapid growth of such groups as the Church of Jesus Christ of Latter-day Saints and Jehovah's Witnesses.[26] Of course, various factors must be taken into consideration in studying the growth of these movements. But the inescapable fact is that church organizations with great numbers of nominal believers generally are not growing, while those with a high proportion of committed, disciplined members are growing.

Practical Reflection

Whatever Happened to Church Discipline?

J. Robertson McQuilkin has posed the both pertinent and practical question of what has become of church discipline. Discipline, in the churches of the Western world especially, has fallen prey to an easygoing religiosity that bears little resemblance to New Testament Christianity. The reasons are not hard to find.

1. The attitudes and values of Western culture have adversely affected the churches. Therefore, Christians tend to lose sight of the holiness of God and the sinfulness of sin. In addition, the general lack of discipline in Western culture has invaded the churches.

2. The availability of many churches in the same area makes it more difficult to maintain discipline. A member in danger of discipline in one church is apt to look for another church in the same area. Only rarely will the shift of allegiance be questioned when one applies for transfer of membership.

3. Church membership is downgraded in many Christian circles. It is often deemed sufficient to be a member of the universal church. All too often, membership in a local church is considered to be a matter of personal preference.

Little wonder, then, that existing churches do not serve as good models for new churches. Unless missionary-evangelists hold scriptural principles and models before the new congregations, they cannot be expected to become New Testament churches.

Discipline in Relation to the Unity of the Church

It is obvious that discipline has to do with the purity of the church and its testimony. Often overlooked is the fact that discipline is also re-

---

25. Dean M. Kelley, *Why Conservative Churches Are Growing* (New York: Harper and Row, 1972), 20–31.

26. Ibid.; and David J. Hesselgrave, *Dynamic Religious Movements* (Grand Rapids: Baker, 1978), 308–9.

lated to the unity of the church. In fact, as Roland Allen notes, there was a real sense in which Paul put the whole church under discipline when he called for the discipline of one member.[27] Western individualism tends to diminish the pain that the entire body should feel when one member falls, and the shame that the errant believer should feel when disciplined. By contrast, Paul emphasized the unity of the body—not only in theory but also in practice. Therefore, when discipline was exercised in New Testament times, the whole church was intimately involved.

Discipline from the Conscience of the Church

It is important that church discipline be just that—*church* discipline. Pioneers and, later, other church leaders play important roles in investigating accusations of wrongdoing and in dealing with offending members. But discipline is something less than biblical when the conscience of a few leaders is imposed upon the church. Only when the larger body of believers agree that God's standards have been violated, that the purity of the body is jeopardized, and that a certain course of action is in accordance with the revealed will of God—only then can something so distasteful and disagreeable accomplish its divinely intended ends.

Self-Exposure, the Key to Church Discipline

In a singularly helpful article on church discipline, Jacob Loewen emphasizes how important it is for church leaders, including the missionary-evangelist, to expose themselves as being subject to the same temptations and weakness as are other believers.[28] By discreetly but candidly revealing that they too are tempted, sometimes fail, and are always in need of the prayers of God's people, they encourage others to deal honestly and biblically with the problem of sin in themselves and in the church.

Master Plan Formation

Developing Qualified Leadership for the Local Church

Leaders must be both discovered and developed. Essential to both processes is a recognition of the qualities or characteristics of leadership whether natural or spiritual. When both the church planters and the local believers discover these characteristics, they will also dis-

27. Roland Allen, *Missionary Methods: St. Paul's or Ours?* (Grand Rapids: Eerdmans, 1962), 123–25.
28. Jacob Loewen, "Self-Exposure: Bridge to Fellowship," *Practical Anthropology* 12 (1965): 49–62.

cover the leadership that the Lord of the church is providing for the emerging congregation. Then, giving priority to the development of spiritual qualities, these leaders can become a blessing to the entire congregation.

The master plan will involve three steps.

Step One: Plan for some teaching and preaching that clarify the distinction between the characteristics of natural and spiritual leadership, and that hold up the latter as the measure of a spiritual man or woman.

Step Two: Single out those whose ability and testimony occasion the confidence of other believers. In part this will be an automatic process. There is a natural tendency, however, for those who are leaders in secular society to become leaders in the church. Unless spiritual qualities are assigned high priority in the selection process, the emerging congregation may be headed for trouble.

Step Three: Special responsibilities and training should be given to those who are recognized as leaders and potential leaders. If the attention that is involved in praying for and working with this small group is balanced by the delegation of responsibilities, the specter of favoritism will be avoided.

Previously we discussed the notion of optimum size (pp. 204–7) and the relationship between the size of a group and its objectives. In the nature of the case the core leadership group in any church will be relatively small. But in many ways the selection and training of leaders are most important aspects of church planting because these individuals will not only manage church affairs, they will model the faith for good or ill. Whether the leaders number one, three, or twelve, therefore, they are worthy of the concern, time, and effort of missionary-evangelists.

Effecting Permanent Organization in the Local Church

When leaders have developed to the point where other believers will follow them, the time for permanent organization has arrived. Two aspects of the organizational process are all-important and require careful planning: preparation for the organizational meeting and the proposal of an organizing document.

First, the organizational meeting should be preceded by a period of preparation and prayer. To aid in the preparation, a number of questions should be asked:

1. Do the leaders agree that the time is ripe for organizing the church?
2. Is it clear who will be invited to the organizational meeting?
3. Are the agenda and procedure to be followed understood by all?

4. Has the suggested document of organization been made available to everyone?
5. Have the leaders of the organizational meeting been selected and prepared?
6. Has there been an ample period for discussion and prayer on the part of God's people?

If the temporary organization has been functioning effectively, it should not be difficult to plan for the organizational meeting and provide adequate answers to these questions.

Second, special attention should be given to the organizing document or constitution of the church. It should be simple enough to allow for flexibility and initiative in church life, comprehensive enough to provide a common ground for action, and indigenous enough to ensure effective decision-making and smooth functioning in the congregation. A model document will include information concerning various topics:

1. Purpose and goals
2. The duties of leaders
3. The qualities of leaders and methods of electing them
4. The process of decision making
5. Standards of membership
6. Standards of belief
7. Standards of behavior
8. Matters of discipline
9. Matters of finance
10. Ownership of property
11. Items required by the local government

Maintaining Scriptural Discipline

The church that is lax in discipline after its formation will have great difficulty in recovering a biblical level of discipline later. It is imperative that the new congregation apply constitutional and biblical principles of discipline from the very beginning. This is true in relationship to two groups of people: those who are already members and those who will apply for membership. Church planters, therefore, should encourage the new congregation to deal decisively and Christianly with defections from biblical faith and practice. And they should assist where possible in the preparation and examination of new members.

One of the results of the emphasis in Western cultures on the rule of law has been the tendency to see church organization as something separate from the spiritual life of the church. Business meetings of the church are seldom characterized by fervent prayer and warm fellow-ship. Discipline is often lacking because it is regarded as punitive and not as a means of restoring the erring members and of preserving the purity of faith and testimony of the church. Of course, non-Western cultures also have their inbuilt biases and prejudices. Missionary-evangelists can escape these cultural traps by consciously planning for church organization with sensitivity to both Scripture and culture.

The Believers Commended   15

If there is any one area of church-planting evangelism that does not receive adequate attention either in the literature or in the actual planning for a new work, it is the withdrawal of the church planter(s).[1] This is not to imply that the topic needs a voluminous literature. But sound strategy for planting churches must include plans for the withdrawal and redeployment of the pioneer worker(s). In most cases knowing when and how to leave a new work is almost as important as knowing when and where to undertake it in the first place.

Objectives

With the foregoing in mind, our objectives for this stage should be:

1. An amicable withdrawal of the church planter(s) from the established congregation at the most advantageous time (as soon as practicable)
2. An orderly transition of leadership in the congregation
3. A continuation (where possible) of effective ministries that have been undertaken by the pioneer(s)

Preliminary Considerations

The stage of development with which we are presently concerned has posed major problems for both home and overseas missions. Though many of the problems are similar in both cases, some are unique to overseas missions.

Similar Problems in Home and Overseas Missions

1. In both home and foreign missions we have often lacked the wisdom to prepare and deploy (and redeploy) church planters properly.

---

1. A recent helpful contribution in this area is Tom A. Steffen, *Passing the Baton: Church Planting That Empowers*, 2d ed. (La Habra, Calif.: Center for Organizational and Ministry Development, 1997).

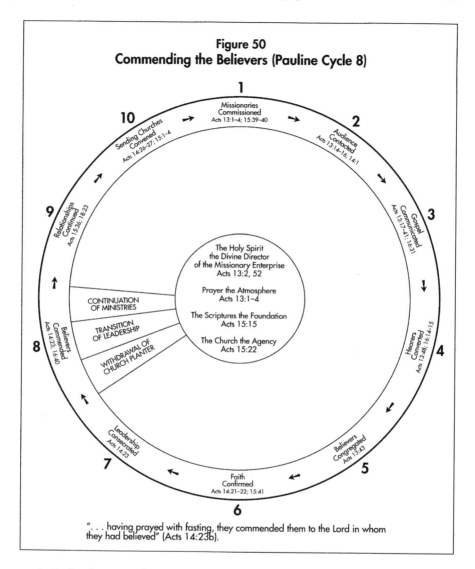

Figure 50
Commending the Believers (Pauline Cycle 8)

1 — Missionaries Commissioned — Acts 13:1-4; 15:39-40
2 — Audience Contacted — Acts 13:14-16; 14:1
3 — Gospel Communicated — Acts 13:17-41; 16:31
4 — Hearers Converted — Acts 13:48; 16:14-15
5 — Believers Congregated — Acts 13:43
6 — Faith Confirmed — Acts 14:21-22; 15:41
7 — Leadership Consecrated — Acts 14:23
8 — Believers Commended — Acts 14:23; 16:40
9 — Relationships Continued — Acts 15:36; 18:23
10 — Sending Churches Convened — Acts 14:26-27; 15:1-4

The Holy Spirit the Divine Director of the Missionary Enterprise — Acts 13:2, 52

Prayer the Atmosphere — Acts 13:1-4

The Scriptures the Foundation — Acts 15:15

The Church the Agency — Acts 15:22

CONTINUATION OF MINISTRIES

TRANSITION OF LEADERSHIP

WITHDRAWAL OF CHURCH PLANTER

". . . having prayed with fasting, they commended them to the Lord in whom they had believed" (Acts 14:23b).

2. In both cases the temptation to build our own little kingdoms instead of Christ's great kingdom must be resisted.

3. In both cases a special bond often develops between the pioneer leaders and pioneer followers. Usually this bond is hard to break. Planning for separation with its tearful farewells is similar psychologically to planning for one's own funeral!

4. In both situations any given church polity has unintended adverse effects unless compensations are made. Churches with a congregational polity, for example, will experience a long and agonizing search

for a new pastor unless a proper procedure is decided on and made clear ahead of time.

The Unique Problems of Overseas Missions

1. Some of the most difficult decisions for ME-2 and ME-3 cross-cultural missions have to do with the transference of authority from mission to national church and from the church-planting missionary to the planted church and its leaders. Theorists have talked about stages of growth leading to independence. Henry Venn coined the phrase "euthanasia of mission" to describe this objective. But the problem persists—and the solving of it presents a challenge to both our theory and our practice!

2. A related problem in which the record of foreign missions is spotty at best is the continuance of missionary-initiated ministries, especially secondary institutional ministries. That the problem has arisen is understandable, but it could be ameliorated, if not erased.

3. Finally there is the problem of the loss of financial support from the home base of the missionary-evangelist—be that in America, Korea, Brazil, or wherever. The newly independent church may have to carry on without whatever finances and material aids the missionary-evangelist supplied. The problem is compounded if an institution such as a clinic or school was closely related to the local church during the church-planting period.

The Withdrawal of the Church Planter(s)

Biblical Principles and Precedents

Leadership Succession in the New Testament

Several elements in the New Testament indicate that there was a succession of leadership in the early days of the church:

1. The preparation of leaders to continue the work
2. The symbolism of the laying on of hands (Acts 13:3)
3. The variety of special gifts the risen Christ gives to his church—some being pioneers, others being consolidators (Eph. 4:11–13)
4. The directions given to those in leadership (e.g., 2 Tim. 2:2)

Those whom Christ has given to the church to preach the Good News where it is still new and plant churches where none has existed should be encouraged to continue in that type of ministry. Those whom Christ has given to the church to preach the Word and shepherd the gathered flock should be encouraged to step in, and to continue and enhance the ministry that others have initiated.

The Temporary Nature of Paul's Ministry

We have already noted that Paul's ministry was a temporary one, as was the ministry of a number of his team members. Theirs was not the kind of temporary ministry that is confined to some simple preaching and a call to commitment, however. It resulted in churches. But once a church was born and established, the pioneer worker(s) usually commended the believers to the grace of God and departed for other fields of service (Acts 14:23; 16:4). Pastor-teachers were then in a position to assume leadership. This was important for the churches; their members were not to become the wards of one leader (1 Cor. 3:4–7). Transfer of leadership was also important for the mission, which was not to be abandoned because a church was born.

Relevant Research

The Change Process

The withdrawal of church planters often constitutes the first major change confronting the new church. If this change has not been part of the thinking of all concerned, it can be especially traumatic. Even when planned for, it can be difficult. In Paul's case it sometimes involved tearful farewells. Of course, the primary source of encouragement and counsel at such times will be the presence and promises of the Lord himself. But a number of helpful studies on change have recently been forthcoming from anthropologists, sociologists, and business experts. Change, in fact, has come to be considered the one constant in this world! Much of contemporary life assumes that change is natural and to be expected, while constancy and continuity are unnatural and in short supply.

Despite limitations church planters can expect to discover in a variety of secular sources helpful insights regarding the nature of change, the characteristics of the process, and coping strategies. At the very least, they will find reinforcement for the kind of planning strategies advocated here. To take one example pertinent to our present discussion, William Bridges deals with our inner resistance to change. He suggests that, rather than always preparing for change, we should start taking the kind of action that culminates in change. If we do not, our natural resistance to change will likely result in making more (and more and more) preparations, unduly delaying the inevitable.[2] Though Bridges's advice is often

---

2. William Bridges, *Transitions: Making Sense of Life's Changes* (Reading, Mass.: Addison-Wesley, 1980), 144–45.

little more than common sense growing out of personal experience, common sense being rather uncommon, such works are worth noting.

Making Way for Other Types of Leadership

We mentioned earlier (p. 98) Eric Hoffer's theory that there is a succession of leadership in growing movements.[3] Now the qualities of the person of words, the fanatic, and the person of action may be found in one and the same individual, but more often than not, the people who begin a movement are not the best qualified to see it through successive stages of development. Study of rapidly growing religious movements reveals that there indeed are various types of leadership and that crises of leadership do occur with the passing of time.[4] Accordingly, Christ has given various types of leaders to his church. Different gifts are needed as the local church is born and as it matures.

Practical Reflection

It has often been said that the job of missionaries is to work themselves out of a job. That is more easily said than done. Nonetheless, church-planting missionaries at home and abroad must ever anticipate the day when they can leave. Accordingly, from the earliest stages the Pauline Cycle points forward to missionary withdrawal—to the passing of the baton as Tom Steffen refers to it. Steffen's ten baton-passing principles (I prefer to call them "requirements") are geared especially to ME-3 church planters, but with slight modifications can be applied to others as well:

1. Build deep relationships
2. Make sure believers share the vision
3. Model ministry before requiring others to take it over
4. Organize to disperse power
5. Call for ministry involvement immediately
6. Expect mistakes
7. Believe in God's people
8. Announce departure plans discreetly
9. Plan programed absences
10. Expect the ministry to increase after departure[5]

3. Eric Hoffer, *The True Believer: Thoughts on the Nature of Mass Movements* (New York: New American Library of World Literature, 1958), 120.
4. David J. Hesselgrave, "Nichiren Shoshu Soka Gakkai," in *Dynamic Religious Movements: Case Studies of Rapidly Growing Religious Movements around the World*, ed. David J. Hesselgrave (Grand Rapids: Baker, 1978), 135–38.
5. Steffen, *Passing the Baton*, 217–18.

The wise church-planter will always have these requirements for withdrawal in mind and take periodic inventory to see if all of them are being met. As Steffen so aptly puts it: "Knowing when to leave a church plant is just as important as knowing when to begin it."[6]

Transition in Christian Leadership

Biblical Principles and Precedents

Christ's Appointment of Peter and Paul

Perhaps both Catholics and Protestants are guilty of neglecting part of the picture in their portrayal of leadership in the apostolic church. Both Peter and Paul were designated as leaders in the transition from Christ to his apostles. In Caesarea Philippi Christ made it clear that Peter would play a leadership role in the building of his church (Matt. 16:18–19). That Peter carried out his responsibility is clear from his acting as the disciples' spokesman on the Day of Pentecost (Acts 2:14–40), his opening the door of faith to the Gentiles (Acts 10), and his speaking out at the Jerusalem conference (Acts 15:7–11).

Christ also made it clear that Paul would take a leading part in the continuation and expansion of the church (Acts 9:1–22, esp. vv. 15–16). That Paul understood and exercised the authority and responsibility that had been given to him is apparent throughout Acts and his letters, especially in such passages as Galatians 1:11–24 and Ephesians 3:1–12.

The supernatural wisdom and power of Christ and the Holy Spirit are, of course, apparent in this transition of authority from Christ to his apostles and then to his church. From a human point of view, two crucial aspects stand out. First, the leadership role of Peter was announced by Christ and accepted by the other apostles and the Jerusalem church. Second, in spite of some minor misunderstandings, Peter and Paul recognized that each of them had been given a place of leadership to be exercised within a specific sphere of responsibility (Gal. 2:7–9).

Paul's Confidence in the Churches, in Their Leaders, and in the Grace of God

Roland Allen has most significant insights into the confidence Paul had in the Holy Spirit to direct the local churches.[7] As an Anglo-Catholic, Allen overplays the importance of the sacraments. He perhaps underplays the importance of sound doctrine. But his emphasis on Paul's con-

---

6. Ibid., 218.
7. Roland Allen, *The Spontaneous Expansion of the Church* (Grand Rapids: Eerdmans, 1962).

fidence in the Spirit-led congregation and its leaders is not misplaced. Paul knew that his fledgling congregations would be tested. But he did not believe that his physical presence was critical to their success in standing for truth and moving forward for Christ. He knew that one measurement of faithful service is abiding fruit (John 15:16). Confident that he had been faithful and that the one who had begun a good work would complete it (Phil. 1:6), Paul could depart from a church after a limited time and begin another. He could speak as though his work was done (Rom. 15:18–24), confident that the members of his churches were evangelizing their environs (1 Thess. 1:6–8). His confidence in the churches was matched by his confidence in coworkers on whose shoulders the mantle of leadership was to fall. He was confident that they understood their task and would carry it out faithfully (Titus 1:5).

Relevant Research

The history of religions provides numerous illustrations of the necessity of an orderly transition of leadership within religious movements. This is especially true in the case of founders (or pioneers) and their disciples.

When we look at the history of Buddhism, for example, we have a classic example of how critical the transition of leadership is. The record of early Buddhism is not entirely clear, but the case of Nichiren Buddhism in Japan is both clear and instructive. When the iconoclastic and nationalistic prophet Nichiren died in the thirteenth century, he did not designate any of his disciples as their leader. Disagreement and division were the predictable results. Not surprisingly, then, when the new Nichirenist lay movement known as Soka Gakkai mushroomed under the leadership of Josei Toda in the twentieth century, observers almost universally agreed that it would languish when he died. They did not reckon on Toda's foresight, however. Toda had groomed a disciple, Daisaku Ikeda, and had him waiting in the wings. Upon Toda's death in 1958, and after a smooth transition of authority to a prepared leader, the movement grew as never before!

Students of religion, however, will be aware that the classic example is provided by Islam. Because Muhammad died suddenly, he had named no successor (caliph). His followers were left to decide who would be their leader and how he would be chosen. The resultant tensions and schisms have plagued Islam for thirteen centuries!

These illustrations may seem far-fetched. After all, they come from outside the Christian tradition and seem far removed from the local Christian church. The more one reflects on them, however, the more one realizes that the principles involved are universal. And the more one will appreciate principles and precedents established by Christ and Peter and Paul and perceptive missionary pioneers at home and abroad!

Practical Reflection

When it comes to transition of leadership in the church, there are two critical concerns:

1. Bible schools and seminaries need to provide training for the kinds of leadership required by growing churches. (This is not to minimize the importance of lay leaders.) Precisely at this point the difference between the West and the Third World is most evident. The Christian training institutions in the West prepare comparatively few pioneers, with the result that few workers are adequately trained for planting new churches. By contrast many Christian training institutions in the Third World prepare evangelists (in the narrow sense of that term) and comparatively few consolidators, with the result that churches languish for want of adequately trained pastor-teachers. These imbalances are easily explained. In the West the educational focus is on hundreds of churches that need pastoring. In the Third World the educational focus is on thousands of unreached areas that need evangelizing. It is easy to lose sight of the fact that there are thousands of churchless communities in the West and thousands of churches in the Third World.

ME-3 illustration: In central Africa missionaries and national leaders in a denomination numbering thirty thousand came to a rather rude awakening some years ago. Hundreds of people were making confession of faith and being baptized. Numerous churches were being planted in villages large and small. Amidst the apparent success, however, one great problem persisted despite efforts to solve it. Members were leaving the churches almost as fast as new ones were joining. Changes in local church programs and leadership personnel had little or no effect. Finally, the primary factor became apparent. The training institution for Christian workers was preparing evangelists, those who could gather crowds, preach the gospel, win the lost, and (in some cases) start churches. But it was not training workers who could manage the church, build up believers in the faith, and minister to families in turmoil. The curriculum and practical assignments were then modified. Institutes were held for those in the ministry. Gradually the local churches began to stabilize.

2. Missionary-evangelists and other leaders in new churches need to prepare themselves and the congregation for a transition in pastoral leadership. In some ways this transition is fraught with the same possibilities for good or ill as is any change in pastoral leadership. This transition is likely to be the most critical, however. After all, successful

church-planting missionary-evangelists must do the work of a pastor, and successful pastors must do the work of an evangelist.

The Continuation of the Ministries

Biblical Principles and Precedents

Paul's confidence was not misplaced. Sometimes members of his team were called upon to continue the ministries in evangelized areas (Titus 1:5). At all times the leaders and laity in local churches were called upon to communicate the gospel and extend the work in their areas (Phil. 2:15–16). But Christians are not perfect. Some leaders fall by the wayside (2 Tim. 4:10), some believers succumb to temptation (1 Cor. 10:12), and some churches are in jeopardy (Gal. 3:1). Paul knew that. Still he expressed confidence in the believers (Gal. 5:10), and he and members of his team pressed forward to win converts and establish new congregations.

Relevant Research

Most of the research and resultant literature relating to the continuation of ministries initiated by pioneer workers has to do with overseas missions. Most of it, moreover, has to do with rather broad geographical areas and a large variety of ministries. Nevertheless, some conclusions are instructive and have implications for churches at home as well as churches abroad.

The Western missionary, so welcome in so many places in post–World War II days, became less welcome in the late 1950s and early 1960s. In fact, in 1964 two books, *The Unpopular Missionary* and *Missionary, Go Home!* served to focus attention on the pleas of some nationals and expatriates to discontinue the role of missionaries and bring them home.[8] Church leaders and conclaves called for a moratorium on missions in certain areas of the world. This reversal of the missionary call undoubtedly had its effect. Revolutions, abortive and successful, had an even greater effect. For whatever reason, missionaries were dissuaded from entering some countries and found it impossible to stay in others.

Whatever legitimacy the plea for withdrawal may have had (when pioneers overstay, it is certainly legitimate to ask them to move on!), the results of a nonstrategic discontinuation of missionary ministries were predictable. In the late 1960s Arden Almquist undertook a study of

---

8. Ralph E. Dodge, *The Unpopular Missionary* (Westwood, N.J.: Revell, 1964); James A. Scherer, *Missionary, Go Home!* (Englewood Cliffs, N.J.: Prentice-Hall, 1964).

needs on several mission fields.[9] Whatever legitimacy the plea for withdrawal may have had in some situations, Almquist concluded that premature withdrawal had had negative effects and also that the attitudes of many national leaders and laypeople had been misrepresented or were changing. In Zaire (the field of Almquist's missionary labors) many ministries had deteriorated or even collapsed in the absence of the missionaries. Almquist noted that pleas for the missionaries to return were not confined to Africa nor to educational and medical missionaries. The churches themselves were still in need of missionaries. For example, with special reference to Indonesia Almquist wrote: "It is recognized by national Christian leadership that unless help is secured from Christians abroad, and soon, much of the harvest may be lost by reversion to the past, or to quasi-Christian sects. Wherever there are sheep without shepherds one hears the cry, 'Missionary, Come Back!' And where there are shepherds whose flocks are too large for adequate pasturing and watering, the cry is also heard."[10]

The truth of Almquist's conclusion has been borne out again and again by subsequent events in Zaire and elsewhere, by a greatly diminished call for moratorium, and by the ever increasing concern for partnerships worldwide. Missions and churches everywhere and always will look back upon the moratorium experiment as a great mistake never again to be repeated. Home missions and local churches as well as overseas missions can learn from it. Partnership is needed at every level—not only between those who minister together at any one time, but also between those who minister at different times and over time.

Practical Reflection

The lessons of the New Testament and of the history of churches and missions are uncomplicated and unequivocal. The ministry of any local church or mission will suffer greatly if the withdrawal of pioneer workers comes either too soon or too late. The baton must be passed to the next runner. When the pioneer leaves the race without passing on the baton, he departs too soon. When he continues to hold the baton until he has exhausted his time and resources, it may be too late.

ME-3 illustration: Two churches were started by church-planting missionaries in the same Asian city. We will call the churches A and B. The missionary who started Church A was especially gifted. Services were crowded, souls were saved, the church flourished. In fact, mission leaders pointed to Church A to show what could be accomplished by a hardworking expatriate in a relatively resistant area. The months and

9. Arden Almquist, *Missionary, Come Back* (New York: World, 1970).
10. Ibid., 58.

years sped by. Just before furlough time a frantic search was made for a national or missionary who could continue the work. Before a replacement was found, the missionary left for the United States. Weeks went by. Attendance at Church A diminished. Finally, a new worker arrived in the church. But with lesser and different gifts he found it impossible to continue the variegated program inaugurated by his predecessor. The church languished. After a few years of struggle it was dissolved.

The history of Church B has been entirely different. With lesser gifts but more foresight, its founding missionary leaned more heavily on his laymen and laywomen. After a relatively short time he encouraged the church to look for a national who might eventually take over the work. By furlough time the ministry of Church B was in the hands of this national worker and qualified laypeople. The transition was smooth. Today, some twenty-five years later, Church B is flourishing with a ministry that reaches well beyond its own community to other parts of the country and even farther.

This tale of two churches has undoubtedly been duplicated in numerous places. There are countless examples of monuments, on the one hand, to the shortsightedness of God's servants and, on the other, to their foresight and wisdom. We repeat, pioneers with a mission come and go. Churches and their ministries spring to life because they come. Churches and their ministries may long outlive them, depending on when and how they go.

Master Plan Formation

The ministry of the missionary-evangelist is a temporary one in any given location. Of course, not all churches are begun under the leadership of specialists. But more could be and probably should be. And even when they are not, the basic problem of the transition of leadership remains, though the process will, of course, differ somewhat from personality to personality, place to place, and culture to culture. To assist in forming a master plan for the withdrawal-transition-continuation process a composite transition schedule will prove helpful (see figure 51).

Withdrawal of the Pioneer Worker

Preparation of the Local Church

The leaders and members of the newly formed local church should not be taken by surprise at the departure of the missionary-evangelist. Theologically, psychologically, and practically they should be prepared for the departure. Otherwise disappointment and even bitterness may result.

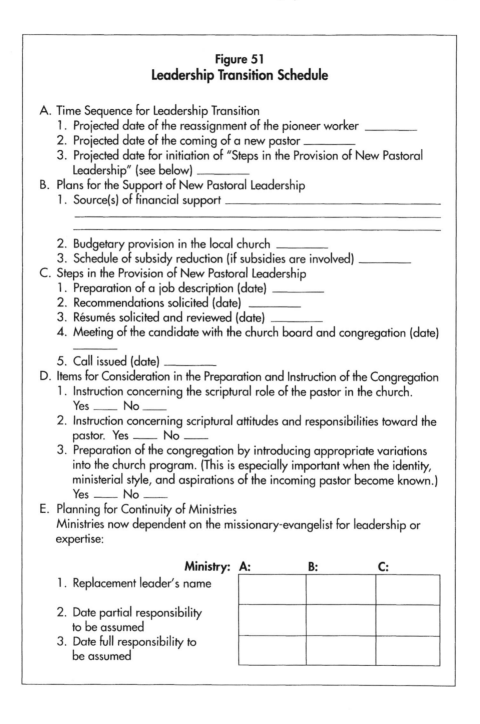

Figure 51
Leadership Transition Schedule

A. Time Sequence for Leadership Transition
  1. Projected date of the reassignment of the pioneer worker _____
  2. Projected date of the coming of a new pastor _____
  3. Projected date for initiation of "Steps in the Provision of New Pastoral Leadership" (see below) _____
B. Plans for the Support of New Pastoral Leadership
  1. Source(s) of financial support _____
     _____
     _____
  2. Budgetary provision in the local church _____
  3. Schedule of subsidy reduction (if subsidies are involved) _____
C. Steps in the Provision of New Pastoral Leadership
  1. Preparation of a job description (date) _____
  2. Recommendations solicited (date) _____
  3. Résumés solicited and reviewed (date) _____
  4. Meeting of the candidate with the church board and congregation (date) _____
  5. Call issued (date) _____
D. Items for Consideration in the Preparation and Instruction of the Congregation
  1. Instruction concerning the scriptural role of the pastor in the church. Yes ____ No ____
  2. Instruction concerning scriptural attitudes and responsibilities toward the pastor. Yes ____ No ____
  3. Preparation of the congregation by introducing appropriate variations into the church program. (This is especially important when the identity, ministerial style, and aspirations of the incoming pastor become known.) Yes ____ No ____
E. Planning for Continuity of Ministries
  Ministries now dependent on the missionary-evangelist for leadership or expertise:

Ministry:	A:	B:	C:
1. Replacement leader's name			
2. Date partial responsibility to be assumed			
3. Date full responsibility to be assumed			

Redeployment of the Church Planter

Reassignment may be no less difficult for the Christian worker's family than it is for the church family. Depending on the length of time spent in the target area, the involvement of family members, and the availability of housing and services, moving may be extremely difficult for modern Pauls! Prior understanding as to when and how decisions relative to withdrawal and relocation are to be reached will go a long way to alleviate the problem. The mobility of the missionary-evangelistic force must be maintained if there is to be a continued outreach.

Leadership Transition

Circumstances differ widely. In ME-1 situations where the church planter does not continue as pastor, the pioneer's ministry will terminate before the ministry of the new pastor begins. In many ME-3 situations a young aspiring pastor will work with the church planter for some time before the latter withdraws. Whatever the circumstance, two primary aspects of leadership transition deserve consideration: the role of lay leaders and preparations for the new pastor.

The Utilization of Lay Leadership

Blessed is the local church whose lay leaders have had actual experience in ministering the Word and in administration of the congregation. That church will be much better prepared to face any eventuality that may attend the transition from missionary to pastoral leadership.

Preparing the Way for the New Pastor

The church planter can do much to assure the acceptance and support of the new leader. By teaching biblical attitudes toward those who minister the Word, by adjusting the church budget in such a way that pastoral support will be available, by introducing flexibility into the program, by personally demonstrating what it means to submit to one another in the fear of the Lord—by these and other such means the way can be prepared for the new pastor.

A word of caution is in order here. These matters are crucial and therefore deserve careful planning. If, for example, the church planter has outside support, perhaps the church budget should take on a corresponding obligation to home missions until the new pastor arrives. Thus the shock of adding this major new item to the budget can be avoided. If the new pastor's support is to be partially subsidized, plans should be made for the subsidy to come to the church (not directly to the pastor) so that responsibility to the congregation is maintained. Even before the new pastor is called, consideration should be given to experientially preparing the congregation for new forms in the worship service. Thus the congregation will be able to adjust to whatever new ideas and ways the new pastor may have.

The Continuation of Ministries

Primary Ministries

If the leaders and lay members of the new church fellowship have been active with the missionary-evangelist in discipling ministries, those ministries will likely continue under the new leadership. Continuation should not be taken for granted, however. Whenever possible, plans should be made to orientate the incoming pastor, either directly or indirectly.

Supporting Ministries

Plans for initiating secondary ministries should include their eventual transference to local leadership. In ME-2 and ME-3 situations secondary ministries are perhaps the most difficult hurdle to keeping missionary-evangelists involved in primary ministries and to keeping a mobile missionary force.

It is no easy task to turn the spiritual results of months (and perhaps years) of self-giving, dedicated ministry over to the care of another. In the face of such a transition, anxiety is to be expected. Will the new leader really care for the flock of God? Will the congregation be accepting? Will the attendant ministries be carried on faithfully? Will the church continue to grow? These and many other questions occur to the missionary-evangelist. They must have occurred to the Lord Jesus. Certainly they occurred to the apostle Paul as time after time he left fledgling congregations just when he had become most aware of their strengths and weaknesses and, in some ways, had become better prepared to lead them to full maturity in Christ.

How can this anxiety be resolved? What will enable the missionary-evangelist to move on in accordance with one's calling? In the final analysis, it will not be the spiritual strength of the congregation, though many of its members may have made great progress in their walk with the Lord. Nor will it be the gifts and dedication of the pastor-elect, encouraging though his reputation might be. In the final analysis, the pioneer worker confidently makes plans and ultimately moves on because of belief in the grace of God and the power of his Spirit. After doing what one can, the church planter commends the congregation to God and departs.

The Relationships Continued 16

"God be with you . . . till we meet at Jesus' feet" is too often interpreted as meaning that we will not meet again until heaven. In actuality most church planters have a number of opportunities to meet their congregations again before they are promoted to their pew in the church triumphant! Paul did. And how he and the congregations cherished the prospect of those meetings!

But human relationships are fraught with all sorts of possibilities for good and ill. It was so then. It is so now. Happy are the church planters, therefore, who have thought through the issues and who lay a solid foundation for future relationships with the new congregation. And happy are those who build continuing and mutually beneficial relationships on that foundation!

Objectives

Sooner or later, with few exceptions, the local congregation will be forced to come to grips with questions of continuing horizontal relationships. These relationships will be of three types: with departing workers (especially the one who established the church); with other churches (especially the fellowship of churches or denomination that sponsored the church); and with the mission (especially the mission of the departing pioneer worker). If wholesome relationships have been initiated before the leave-taking of the pioneer missionary-evangelist, the congregation will be in a much better position to face any difficulties that may attend the departure. If the leaders of the congregation and the pioneer sit down together to pray and discuss what their future relationship ought to be, the congregation will benefit even more. With that in mind we will explore some of the important issues and strive for the following objectives:

1. To establish between the church planter and the church a continuing relationship that will be spiritually stimulating and mutually rewarding
2. To establish between the new church and the fellowship of churches or denomination a continuing relationship that will

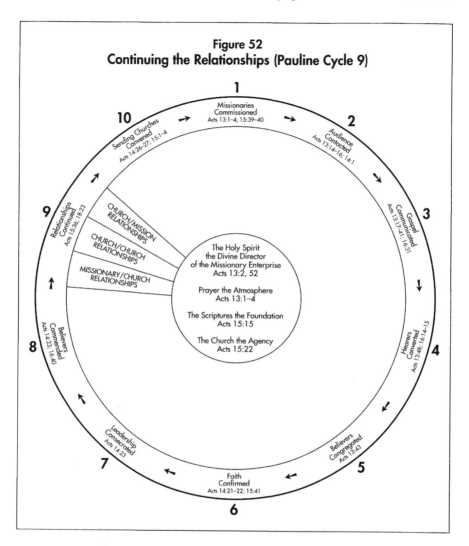

Figure 52
Continuing the Relationships (Pauline Cycle 9)

strengthen their witness to the world and enhance the spiritual
and numerical growth of both

3. To establish between the new church and the founding mission
   a continuing relationship that will further the worldwide mission of the church of Christ

The perplexing and continuing problems that attend these three
types of relationships reflect the fact that the Bible does not speak precisely concerning the details of these relationships. It is probably also
true that we do not carefully heed what the Bible does have to say.

When one adds the widespread reluctance of many Christian workers to deal with these issues until they are forced to do so, that we have problems in these relationships should not come as a surprise.

The Church Planter and the Church

Biblical Principles and Precedents

The relationship that existed between Paul and the churches was manifestly a spiritual one. Even in the case of that great apostle, the relationship could not be characterized as being one of dominion (2 Cor. 1:24). It is best summed up in that important word *koinōnia* (Phil. 1:5). *Koinōnia* is usually translated "fellowship," but it could be justifiably translated "joint participation" or "partnership" (among other possibilities).

The New Testament gives clear indications of what was involved in true *koinōnia*. We can cite, for example, Peter's exhortation to elders (1 Peter 5:1–4) and, especially, Paul's detailed descriptions of his interaction with the churches he founded. From Paul's letters we can deduce the major elements in *koinōnia*:

1. The apostle felt a responsibility for the continued well-being (especially spiritual well-being) of the churches and believers he had fathered in the faith. All of the Pauline letters witness to this. Paul did not wash his hands of the sometimes impure Corinthian Christians once they had said their mutual farewells. He did not write off the churches in Galatia because some of their members had been hoodwinked by the Judaizers. Rather, he had a genuine and abiding burden for these fledgling churches and their members. So much so that he writes of "the daily pressure . . . of concern for all the churches" (2 Cor. 11:28).

2. The churches Paul founded were expected to give special attention to the words spoken, and the example set, by the apostle, precisely because he had fathered them in the faith. Consider Paul's words in 1 Corinthians 4:15–16: "For if you were to have countless tutors in Christ, yet you would not have many fathers; for in Christ Jesus I became your father through the gospel. I exhort you therefore, be imitators of me." (See also Phil. 2:1–2 in this connection.)

3. The churches participated with Paul in his ministry through prayer, gifts, and the sending of helpers (Phil. 2:25; 4:14–16; Col. 4:3). Note, however, that though the apostle greatly appreciated and even solicited some types of partnership, he by no means demanded it nor did he always receive it (Phil. 4:15).

This simple overview does not provide clear answers to many contemporary questions. For Paul's position as a special apostle introduced a unique factor into his relationships. Obviously, Paul (and John and Peter) possessed an authority that church leaders do not possess today. Quite apart from that authority, however, it seems evident that New Testament *koinōnia* involved a reciprocal concern, respect, and obligation between the apostle and the churches he founded, a relationship that went beyond a handshake and a farewell. It entailed an abiding concern, each for the other, and all for the Christian cause.

Relevant Research

Given the individualism, the kinship and value systems, and the mobility of many Western societies, it is understandable that teacher-student, friend-friend, and even parent-child relationships are considerably different from what they are in much of the rest of the world, and also that reciprocal obligations are less demanding. The Chinese still live according to the obligations built into Confucius's system of five relationships. Filipinos consider *utang na loob* (obligations) as extremely important. The Japanese have an intricate network of obligations. It is difficult to describe the attitudes and feelings that attend these obligations. They are deep-rooted, complex, and extend far past the time when they are easy to fulfil. One has to experience them in each society in order to understand them. And yet the basic feeling is something we all know well.

It is true that obligations of various types deter many in non-Western cultures from becoming Christians. That is the dark side of the picture. But it is also true that adherence to the rules governing relationships makes for stability and qualities of trust that the church and its leaders should both emulate and model.

Practical Reflection

Upon parting, the founders of new churches and the churches themselves must walk a tightrope between two extremes. The first is the tendency on the part of some pioneer workers to maintain such close ties with the church (or with friends in the church) that they infringe upon the prerogatives of the new leaders. There is a parallel tendency for some churches to remain emotionally and spiritually dependent upon the pioneer(s) to a degree that discourages the new leaders. The other extreme is the tendency of many church planters and their congregations to part company and practically forget one another. After the first few weeks or months there are negligible communication, little prayer for one another, and minimal mutual concern.

The first extreme (too close ties) is characteristic of churches in the Third World. The latter extreme (broken ties) is characteristic of churches in the West. But both extremes can be seen East and West. How much better that, in every culture, we seek a middle ground between the extremes! Before parting let the pioneer worker and the local leaders briefly discuss their future relationship. Not that it needs to be programed. That would undercut the delight of a spontaneous holiday greeting, an invitation to an anniversary gathering, or a gift for a special ministry. But, avoiding extremes, let there be a continuing *koinōnia* within some basic guidelines.

The New Church and Other Churches

Biblical Principles and Precedents

The matter of the relationship between the New Testament churches presents us with numerous unanswered questions. When the New Testament epistles were written, church relationships were in an early stage of development. When, in the second and third centuries, that development became much more formalized and complete, it was not necessarily more exemplary. Are we, then, left to do as we please? Hardly, for however basic and simple they may appear to be, there are biblical principles and precedents, and they constitute a clear indication that, just as believers are to relate to one another in local churches, so local churches are to relate to one another in a larger fellowship which reflects the church universal.

The Spiritual Basis of Interchurch Fellowship

It is clear that when our Lord said, "I will build My church" (Matt. 16:18), and when he prayed "that they may all be one" (John 17:21), he had one church in mind. It is tragically true that his cobuilders tend to misconstrue and neglect this clear biblical teaching. Take, by way of example, the common interpretation of 1 Corinthians 3:16, "Know ye not that ye are the temple of God, and that the Spirit of God dwelleth in you?" (KJV). Most Christians, without so much as a second thought, interpret this to mean that individual Christians are temples of God. Some interpret the "temple of God" as a reference to the church at Corinth. But note what Henry Alford says about this passage:

> [H. A. W.] Meyer rightly remarks that *"naos Theou* is *the temple* of God, not *a* temple of God: for Paul does not conceive . . . of the various churches as *various temples* of God, which would be inconsistent with a Jew's conception of God's temple, but of each Christian church as, sensu mystico, *the temple of Jehovah.* So there would be not many temples, but many churches, each of which is, ideally, the same temple of God." And,

we may add, if the figure is to be strictly justified in its widest acceptation, that all the churches are built together into one vast temple.[1]

That the biblical emphasis on one church has been used to promote the cause of organizational unity at the expense of other truths does not justify our disregard of this truth and its implications.

Paul and Interchurch Relationships

As far as we know, Paul did not organize the local churches he founded into regional ecclesiastical organizations. Nevertheless, those local churches were not left to themselves. They were bound together in two types of relationships.

1. There was a relationship of authority. By virtue of the presence of the apostles the church at Jerusalem had certain prerogatives. It sent Barnabas to monitor what was happening in the new church at Antioch (Acts 11:22–26). Barnabas stayed on as a teacher in that church (Acts 13:1–2). Paul went to Jerusalem to consult with the apostles as to his message (Gal. 1:18–19). When questions were raised in connection with the conversion of the Gentiles, the missionaries went to the Jerusalem church and submitted the issue to its leaders (Acts 15:1–2).

2. There was a relationship of *koinōnia* in the body of Christ. Mutual obligations were urged upon the churches as the proper expression of their oneness in Christ (Gal. 6:10). The New Testament notes various manifestations of their close fellowship:

   a. The churches founded by the apostles recognized that in Christ they had a common bond with one another—and particularly with the mother church in Jerusalem (Acts 15:1–2; Rom. 15:26–27).
   b. The churches regularly sent Christian greetings to each other (Rom. 16:16; 1 Cor. 16:19–20; Phil. 4:23).
   c. They collaborated on a project to provide money for the poor saints in the Jerusalem church (Rom. 15:26; 1 Cor. 16:1–3).
   d. They sent representatives to one another (Acts 11:22–23, 27; 15:1–2; 1 Cor. 16:3–4).
   e. They supported the apostles' labor in other fields (Phil. 4:15–16).
   f. They shared letters from the apostles (Col. 4:16).
   g. They encouraged one another by modeling the faith (2 Cor. 1:24; 9:2; 1 Thess. 1:7–10; 2:14).
   h. They cooperated in the common cause of evangelism (1 Thess. 1:8).

1. Henry Alford, *The Greek Testament*, vol. 2 (Chicago: Moody, 1958), 495.

It is evident that local churches today are not related to any other church in exactly the same way as those first-century churches were related to the Jerusalem church. Churches today do not have a mother church in that sense. But today's churches are authentic churches only to the extent that they evidence subjection to the same apostolic authority by adhering to the faith and practice of the Holy Scriptures. It is this adherence that marks them as part of the universal church. Moreover, this adherence will lead to *koinōnia* with other churches under the same authority—a *koinōnia* that will find practical expression in cooperation in good works and glad witness.

Relevant Research

There are at least two lines of research that bear out the importance of supralocal authority and participation.

1. Dynamic and growing religious movements of diverse cultures and orientations tend to be decidedly hierarchical in their organization:

> The three branches of Caodai, the "apostle" orientation of the New Apostolic Church and Mormonism, the "prophet" orientation of Zionism and Kimbanguism, the president and board of directors arrangement in Soka Gakkai all exhibit authority patterns which are at once definite and graded. Sometimes the organization extends right down to the local levels with an efficiency and explicitness that is reminiscent of the military (Iglesia ni Cristo, Jehovah's Witnesses). On the other hand, the nomenclature used may seem to be democratic and egalitarian (United Pentecostal). In either case the organizations tend to be authoritarian. Lines of authority are seldom blurred or disregarded. Checks and balances there may be, but these seem to be operative mainly at secondary and tertiary levels of leadership. Believers know where real authority lies, and it is usually at the top![2]

2. The study of distinctly Christian churches in the Third World reveals a similar tendency. In one of the most careful examinations that has been made of the outworking of different approaches to planting churches, Peter Beyerhaus and Henry Lefever conclude:

> It seems to be the universal experience of all Protestant missions that the congregational principle cannot be put into practice by itself in the mission field. Even the independents . . . have found themselves forced to resort, at least temporarily, to a centralized system in order to guarantee

---

2. David J. Hesselgrave, "What Causes Religious Movements to Grow?" in *Dynamic Religious Movements: Case Studies of Rapidly Growing Religious Movements around the World*, ed. David J. Hesselgrave (Grand Rapids: Baker, 1978), 308–9.

the stability of what they had created. Moreover, episcopacy has a strong appeal in nearly all mission fields, even where the actual term is not used, as for example in Sumatra. To the student of missions that throws a new light on the New Testament pronouncements concerning the problem of church order.[3]

We must be careful not to jump to the conclusion that episcopal, hierarchical church order is true church order because it promotes unified belief and action. At the same time, however, we cannot settle for a congregationalism that does no more than mesh with Western democratic and egalitarian ideals. All that we as Christians are allowed to deduce from these studies is that recognizable authority outside of the local group and some measure of subjection to, or at least cooperation with, that authority seem to be related to effective functioning and growth.

Practical Reflection

Westerners (particularly North Americans) have a cultural bias toward promoting overindependency on the part of the churches they establish. Even when their churches actually belong to a larger fellowship of churches, the likelihood of those churches assuming an active role in the larger fellowship is not always great. Certain aspects of interchurch relationships therefore merit special attention by church-planting personnel.

The Necessity of Interchurch Fellowship

There is no substitute for active involvement in an interchurch fellowship. In certain circumstances, individual Christians must survive without the edification provided by fellowship with other Christians. Usually, however, they will be poorer for their isolation. The same is true of congregations. Nothing can replace the deepened faith, enlarged vision, increased sacrifice, and enhanced outreach that participation in a larger fellowship affords.

Churches tied to a specific denomination will thereby have a feeling of unity and fellowship. In the case of churches with congregational polity and in the case of interdenominational missions, however, the local congregation will be largely dependent upon missionary-evangelists and other leaders for guidance. If this guidance is not forthcoming, one of three results is likely to occur eventually. First, the local congregation may become completely cut off from other congregations. Second, the

3. Peter Beyerhaus and Henry Lefever, *The Responsible Church and the Foreign Mission* (Grand Rapids: Eerdmans, 1964), 162.

local group may divide into factions with differing outside loyalties. Third, the congregation may join a suborthodox organization which provides fellowship and unity but at the expense of truth and purity.

ME-1–3 illustration: A well-known missionary organization which is engaged in evangelizing and discipling all around the world has run head-on into the problem of congregational isolation. Because it raises funds on an interdenominational basis, it feels duty-bound not to set up anything resembling a fellowship of churches or a denomination. Consequently, new groups of believers are left to work out interrelationships largely on their own. Some of them join together in what amounts to an area-wide fellowship of independent churches—a denomination of sorts. Many others have fallen into one or another of the three traps mentioned above.

ME-3 illustration: The growing Evangelical Free Church in Japan merits careful study. Urged and guided to form themselves into a viable national organization from the first, the new congregations went considerably beyond their parent body in the United States in effecting cooperation and fellowship. Out of this denomination has come a program for starting new congregations by sending personnel and providing seed money (often hundreds of thousands of dollars) from existing congregations. This is usually done with no thought of repayment but in the anticipation that when the new congregation has grown sufficiently, it will participate in the same type of outreach. This kind of generosity and cooperation has resulted in a high level of stewardship and comparatively rapid growth in a land which many regard as highly resistant to the gospel.

The Uniqueness of the Relationship between Church and Denomination or Fellowship

As the head of the church, Christ rules the churches. He does so primarily through the Holy Spirit–inspired Word which he gave to and through the prophets and apostles. Ultimately, every duly constituted congregation is responsible before God to abide faithful to that Word. It cannot escape that responsibility by simply deferring to a founding denomination or mother church.

On the other hand, it is not too far-fetched to assume that if the individual who fathers believers in the faith has some special prerogatives, the fellowship that mothers a congregation has some special prerogatives also. And the resultant relationship has some very significant benefits. Not only does the new church have a ready-made opportunity to realize a wider fellowship in the gospel. It also enjoys the steadying influence and helpful monitoring that such a relationship can provide. Just as the hazards of the shoreline are left behind a departing ship, so newer churches face difficulties that diminish as progress is made. The local church is far less likely to flounder near the shore if it is able to link up with the universal church through a sponsoring denomination or fellowship. For that reason constitutional and practical reinforcements for this kind of initial and continuing relationship should be provided.

Relationships between Churches and Missions

In recent years one of the most extensively discussed questions in mission circles has been the relationship between the missions and the churches that result from their labors. On the one side are to be found the proponents of fusion or merger. They insist that mission is the responsibility of the church, that missions have no basis for maintaining their separate existence, and that missionary personnel and organizations should be incorporated into the churches they establish.[4] On the other side are to be found the proponents of separation. They insist that the primary purpose for the organizing of missions has been to evangelize the world and plant new churches; that if missions are merged with the churches they establish, this ministry will be impeded or aborted; and that missions must maintain a position of equal partnership with the churches in order to carry out their proper function. In between these polar positions all sorts of compromises have been proposed.

Biblical Principles and Precedents

Even a cursory reading of the Bible reveals that Christ ordained the church (and, therefore, the churches) and gave it a mission. That the apostles and the churches carried out their mission in the first century is equally clear. It is impossible to make the same kind of a case for mission organizations. Paul's team affords the closest New Testament parallel to modern mission agencies. But the differences between Paul's team and the large interdenominational missions of the modern era are probably greater and more numerous than are the similarities.

What, then, can be concluded on the basis of the New Testament? Can we not say that Christ builds the church, that every believer is made a member of that church, that the apostles had a special authority in that church, and that Christ's mission in the world was to be carried out by apostles and believers in the churches as they were led by the Holy Spirit? The Bible, then, does not allow for a missionless church or a churchless mission. It requires that churches be engaged in mission and that they send out missionaries. It allows for organization among

4. See Stephen Neill, *Creative Tension* (London: Edinburgh House, 1959).

those going forth in missionary service. These organized missions are to plant churches, not supplant them.

Relevant Research

Historical and pragmatic cases can be made for elitist fellowships of Christians. It has been pointed out that one reason for the retarded beginnings in Protestant missions after the Reformation was that the Reformers rejected the Catholic orders that had been in the forefront of the missionary enterprise of the Roman Church. Consequently, when the ecclesiastical difficulties and theological questions that discouraged missionary-evangelistic activities had been partially resolved, there were no organizational vehicles for world mission. Protestants had to begin by building their own orders, which, for the most part, cut across ecclesiastical (denominational) lines.

From examples like the Protestant beginnings in the mission enterprise it has been concluded that modalities (vertically structured organizations that include men and women, young and old—such as churches and denominations) need sodalities (horizontally structured organizations that are made up of people with special expertise or interests—such as missions, evangelistic associations, and other parachurch organizations). As Ralph Winter expresses it, "Churches need missions, because modalities need sodalities."[5]

Historically, mission agencies have played a major role in carrying out the mission of the church. The church and missions must work together. Arguments that missionary organizations be separate from (rather than within and under) the organized church are less than convincing.

Practical Reflection

Missionary-evangelists (and the missions) are often caught in the middle between the churches which sent them and the churches which they helped to plant. In some instances, churches as such did not send them at all. In any case the issues are complex because the missions must walk a line which fulfils their responsibility both to those who sent them and to those who subsequently host them. The issues can be resolved only when we keep in view the permanency of the church and the temporary nature of the mission organizations. When this perspective is adopted, mission agencies may remain as partners of the churches while the latter grow and mature. Even so staunch a churchman as Harvie Conn has concluded as much:

5. Ralph Winter and R. Pierce Beaver, *The Warp and the Woof: Organizing for Mission* (South Pasadena, Calif.: William Carey Library, 1971), 62.

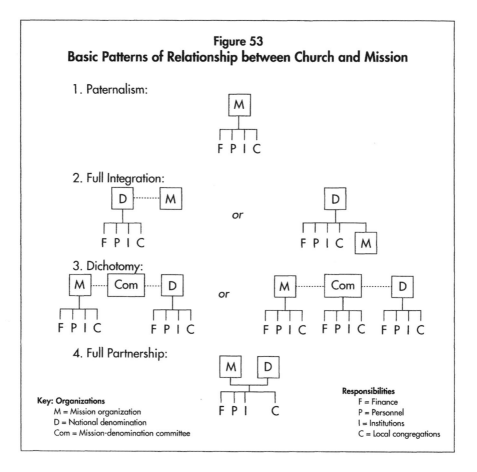

Figure 53
Basic Patterns of Relationship between Church and Mission

1. Paternalism:

2. Full Integration:

3. Dichotomy:

4. Full Partnership:

Key: Organizations
M = Mission organization
D = National denomination
Com = Mission-denomination committee

Responsibilities
F = Finance
P = Personnel
I = Institutions
C = Local congregations

In the awesome complexity of transition between the initiation of evangelistic work in an area, and forming of the structure of the church, the patterns implicit in terminology like "partnership of mutuality" and "cooperation of autonomous equals" are serviceable, as much so as in the transition of a North American home mission work from preaching point to formal organization as a structured body of Christ. But ultimately, the biblical call to unity in the worldwide fellowship Christ has instituted is a call to the consideration of the legitimacy of separate structures.[6]

Conn's call for ultimate integration of church and mission is understandable in the light of the paternalism of many missions in the past and the New Testament emphasis on the church. However, we must not

6. Harvie M. Conn, "Church-Mission Relationships" (paper presented at the Reformed Missions and the Theology of Church Growth Consultation, Westminster Theological Seminary, 24–26 March 1975), p. 18.

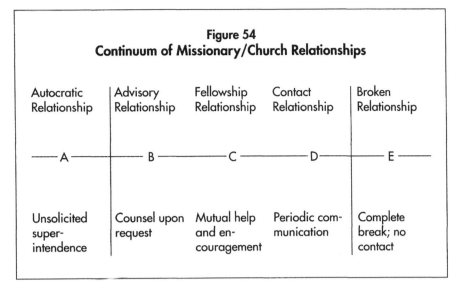

Figure 54
Continuum of Missionary/Church Relationships

Autocratic Relationship	Advisory Relationship	Fellowship Relationship	Contact Relationship	Broken Relationship
——— A ———	——— B ———	——— C ———	——— D ———	——— E ———
Unsolicited super-intendence	Counsel upon request	Mutual help and encouragement	Periodic communication	Complete break; no contact

forget two factors. First, most missions exist under the aegis of sending churches. Second, as long as governments allow missions the freedom to evangelize and extend the frontiers of the church, the responsibility and opportunity to do so should not be forfeited in order to integrate with churches which do not have a vision for that God-given task.

The relationship of field missions and national (and local) churches has been a topic of much debate. We will not add more to the discussion here. However, it does seem that of the basic relationships which have been proposed and practiced (see figure 53), that of full partnership has the most potential for planting new congregations as long as the mission recognizes that it exists to strengthen and add to the national church.

Master Plan Formation

Missionary/Church Relationships

The critical test of the work of a church planter is the ability of the founded church to survive separation and carry on the ministry. Nevertheless, a spiritual bond unites missionary and church, a bond which should find expression in some kind of continued relationship such as is exemplified in the New Testament. Cultural factors and local circumstances should be taken into account. For example, the incoming pastor may be inexperienced. In that case the church may desire that the founder continue in a consultative role (though such a relationship has potential problems).

In a spirit of cooperation and concern, then, let the missionary-evangelist and church leaders discuss future relationships. Avoiding extremes, let them first determine the type of relationship that they want to establish. This can best be done by thinking about the degree of relationship desired (see figure 54).

Second, the church planter(s) and church leaders would do well to project in some detail the form that their relationship will take in the immediate future. For example, if the church decides to support a new effort to be undertaken by the missionary-evangelist, the extent of this support should be clear. Again, if the missionary-evangelist is expected to visit the church periodically, it would be well to spell out the frequency and purpose of such visits. Of course, this kind of planning is not meant to rule out those spontaneous expressions of Christian love which mean so much to the family of God. Rather, such planning is merely to ensure that the continuing relationship, whatever forms it might take, will be built on mutual understanding and respect.

Church/Church Relationships

The master plan should include provision for interchurch relationships of two basic types: those with the sponsoring denomination or fellowship of churches and those with other Christian congregations.

Relationship with the Sponsoring Denomination

The kind of relationship which the local church will have with the sponsoring denomination will be determined by the leadership provided for the new church by the church planter. It is vital, therefore, that the church planter instruct the local leaders as to the nature of that relationship (as reflected in the founding document) and model the relationship in practice.

Fellowship with Other Christian Congregations

If the local church is to avoid an unscriptural isolationism on the one hand and unscriptural forms of ecumenism on the other, both the basis and objectives of cooperation with other churches in the area should be prayerfully considered. A simple statement in the founding document or official records as to the essential items of faith upon which cooperation and fellowship will be based will go far toward averting future dissension or confusion in the local church. To a somewhat lesser extent, the initiation of certain types of cooperation will be important. Consider, for example, cooperation in the following areas:

1. Evangelistic efforts
2. Worship services

3. Special occasions on the church calendar (e.g., Good Friday and Easter)
4. Community projects

Church/Mission Relationships

The relationship between the mission and the national church is generally a matter decided on a nation- or area-wide basis, not at the local level. However, the missionary-evangelist has the responsibility to instruct and guide the local congregation in the fulfilment of its role in the larger scheme of things.

Our Lord said, "I chose you, and appointed you, that you should go and bear fruit, and that your fruit should remain" (John 15:16). Long after the church-planting missionaries have departed, the planted church will live and work within the framework of the relationships dealt with in this chapter. If those relationships are both spiritual and strategic, there is a great likelihood that the fruit of the church-planting labors will remain.

Part Five

The Sending Church and the Christian Mission (Continued)

The Sending Church Convened 17

For the most part, missionary-evangelists who are successful in planting new churches have the backing of sending churches. Why? Because missionary-evangelists sent by Christian churches (as opposed to those who are sent by individual Christians or institutions, or those who go on their own initiative) tend to be church-oriented rather than campaign-oriented and program-oriented. There is another reason. To be successful, church planters—like other servants of God—need encouragement and prayer. And they may need counsel and finances. What better source could one find than the sending church?

In part four we were concerned with the emerging church. We assumed, however, that during the church-planting period missionary-evangelists are in communication with the church(es) that commissioned, sent, and support them. At certain times—perhaps at a missionary conference or school of mission—the members of the sending church should hear a personal report. It is hard to imagine anything more stimulating to a congregation than to hear firsthand how God has used the personnel they have sent, the prayers they have offered, and the other provisions they have made for the establishment of churches in new areas!

Objectives

Definite objectives should be set for the meetings (conference, convention, rally, school of mission, or whatever) where the church planter reports to the sending church. Whatever frills may be thought necessary, nothing should obscure the grand truth that, through his dedicated people and the working of the Holy Spirit, Christ is building his church. Bringing citizens of the kingdom together around the King's business, the local church leaders should have two objectives in mind:

1. To achieve a thorough understanding of what God has accomplished through the missionary-evangelist and how this fits into his purpose for the church

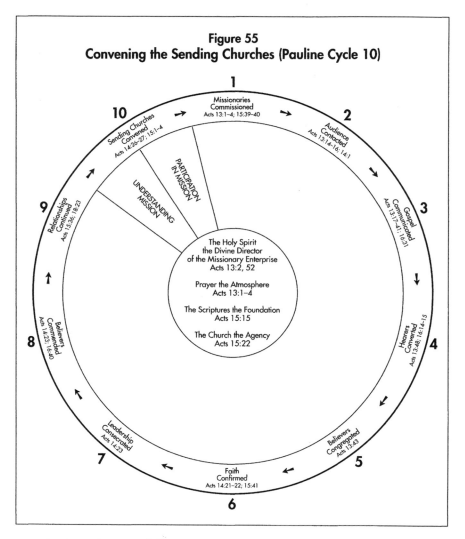

Figure 55
Convening the Sending Churches (Pauline Cycle 10)

2. To achieve a full participation of all Christians in the missionary efforts of the local church

It should be borne in mind that the only way to determine whether these objectives are being reached is to devise some method of testing the understanding of believers and also of monitoring their participation.

Understanding the Church's Mission

There are two essential elements in understanding the church's mission. First, the members of the sending congregation should understand the mission of the church in biblical terms (see part one of this book). Second, believers should understand exactly what has been accomplished through the work of their missionaries, and how it has been accomplished.

Biblical Principles and Precedents

Of course, the biblical prototypes of the kind of reporting which we have in mind are the Antioch and Jerusalem missionary conferences. The Lukan record of the return of Paul and Barnabas to Antioch after the first missionary journey is succinct and stimulating:

> And when they had spoken the word in Perga, they went down to Attalia; and from there they sailed to Antioch, from which they had been commended to the grace of God for the work that they had accomplished. And when they had arrived and gathered the church together, they began to report all things that God had done with them and how He had opened a door of faith to the Gentiles. And they spent a long time with the disciples. [Acts 14:25–28]

The focus of the Jerusalem conference was somewhat different (Acts 15:1–30). At that conference the concern was to understand how the work of the apostles in planting churches among the Gentiles fitted into the larger plan of God.

Paul also returned to Antioch after his second missionary journey (Acts 18:22) and to Jerusalem after his third journey (Acts 21:17–19). He sent Epaphroditus back to the Philippians with instructions that they should "receive him in the Lord with all joy, and hold men like him in high regard" (Phil. 2:29). He sent Tychicus and Onesimus to Colossae so that the Colossians might be informed and encouraged (Col. 4:7–9). A prominent note in all of these meetings was encouragement, joy, and praise to God for what he had done.

Relevant Research

American Opinion about Organized Religion

A 1977 study revealed a considerable degree of skepticism as to organized religion's "honesty, dependability, and integrity," and "ability to get things done."[1] The ratings achieved by organized religion and some (not all) of the other groups included in the questionnaire are given in figure 56 so that a comparison can be made. If we can assume that "organized religion" is more or less synonymous with the Chris-

---

1. *The Study of American Opinion, 1977,* Marketing Concepts, Inc., 1235 N. Avenue, Nevada, Iowa.

Figure 56
American Opinion about Various Key Groups

	Honesty, Dependability, Integrity			Ability to Get Things Done		
	Poor	Average	Good	Poor	Average	Good
The White House	23%	55%	17%	29%	54%	9%
The Supreme Court	19%	41%	33%	19%	45%	25%
U.S. Military	19%	53%	21%	16%	51%	22%
Educators	14%	56%	23%	19%	57%	14%
Organized Religion	14%	48%	30%	16%	53%	19%
Medical Profession	14%	53%	28%	9%	52%	29%
Science and Technology	4%	46%	41%	5%	45%	38%
Large Business	25%	60%	9%	10%	54%	25%
Broadcast News Media (TV news, radio news)	15%	51%	26%	8%	45%	35%
Print News Media (news magazines, newspapers)	15%	58%	21%	9%	51%	29%

tian church, it becomes apparent that churches have to prove themselves in these areas. At least, this is so as far as the general public is concerned.

The Opinions of Christian Youth regarding Christian Mission

The opinions gathered in a survey of some five thousand youthful delegates to the 1967 Urbana Missionary Convention are still pertinent.[2] Of the scores of questions and responses in the survey, several speak clearly to the need for the kind of instruction and reporting we are advocating here. (It should be noted that 85 percent of the respondents were church members, and 93 percent attended church regularly.)

First, when the delegates were polled as to what they regarded as the primary missionary occupation, "personal evangelists" rather than "church planters and developers" was the number one choice. In fact, many delegates selected "technicians and engineers" as most important. (For the full results see figure 57.)

Second, in answer to the question, "If you were going to be a missionary, in which field would you most like to serve?" about five times as many delegates chose to be in education as chose to be in church planting and development. (Figure 58 gives the complete results.)

Some thirty years have passed since the Urbana survey was taken. No comparable survey of such a wide spectrum of Christian youth has been taken in the interim. But it has become clear that the broad interpretation of mission implicit in the 1967 responses is still the general understanding. And that should be a matter of concern and study. We are not saying that the various occupations mentioned in the questionnaire and now evident in contemporary mission enterprises are not worthy. Of course not. It is Christian to do good to all people, and especially to other Christians (Gal. 6:2). But Great Commission mission is more focused than that. The 1967 responses revealed a need for instruction as to what the basic mission of the church is. They also pointed up the importance of communicating the excitement of what is actually happening around the world as missionary-evangelists develop churches made up of people who have been reconciled to God in Christ and, as a result, enter into a new relationship to one another and the world around them. Subsequent history indicates that we still have a long way to go when it comes to helping God's people to understand biblical mission and to support the building of Christ's church worldwide.

2. Paul F. Barkman, Edward R. Dayton, and Edward L. Gruman, *Christian Collegians and Foreign Missions: An Analysis of Relationships* (Monrovia, Calif.: Missions Advanced Research and Communications Center, 1969).

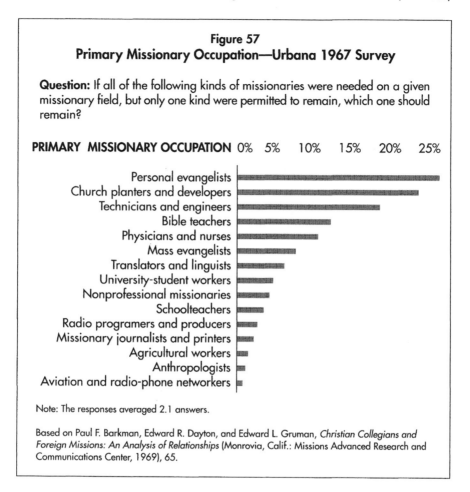

Figure 57
Primary Missionary Occupation—Urbana 1967 Survey

Question: If all of the following kinds of missionaries were needed on a given missionary field, but only one kind were permitted to remain, which one should remain?

PRIMARY MISSIONARY OCCUPATION 0%   5%   10%   15%   20%   25%

Personal evangelists
Church planters and developers
Technicians and engineers
Bible teachers
Physicians and nurses
Mass evangelists
Translators and linguists
University-student workers
Nonprofessional missionaries
Schoolteachers
Radio programers and producers
Missionary journalists and printers
Agricultural workers
Anthropologists
Aviation and radio-phone networkers

Note: The responses averaged 2.1 answers.

Based on Paul F. Barkman, Edward R. Dayton, and Edward L. Gruman, *Christian Collegians and Foreign Missions: An Analysis of Relationships* (Monrovia, Calif.: Missions Advanced Research and Communications Center, 1969), 65.

Practical Reflection

The annual missionary conference held by many churches is certainly not the only way to teach and promote mission. Many other missionary meetings and emphases are needed throughout the church year. But attendance at, as well as interest in, the missionary conference is a fairly accurate measurement of the mission pulse in most churches. It will be instructive, therefore, to focus on its state of health and suggest a way of revitalizing it. The following paragraphs penned after a conversation with a nationally known mission-conference speaker may be helpful:

Is the mission conference still a relevant part of the local church program? Missionaries frequently stop by my office while "on the circuit,"

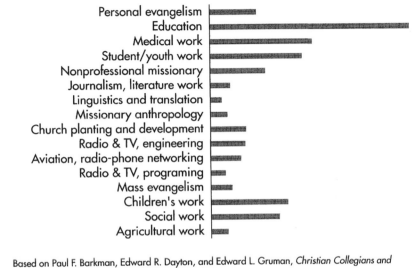

Figure 58
Desired Missionary Occupation—Urbana 1967 Survey

Question: If you were going to be a missionary, in which field would you most like to serve?

DESIRED MISSIONARY OCCUPATION 0% 5% 10% 15% 20% 25% 30% 35%

Personal evangelism
Education
Medical work
Student/youth work
Nonprofessional missionary
Journalism, literature work
Linguistics and translation
Missionary anthropology
Church planting and development
Radio & TV, engineering
Aviation, radio-phone networking
Radio & TV, programing
Mass evangelism
Children's work
Social work
Agricultural work

Based on Paul F. Barkman, Edward R. Dayton, and Edward L. Gruman, *Christian Collegians and Foreign Missions: An Analysis of Relationships*, 79.

and give vent to various frustrations related to conferences. One evangelical mission leader said to me, "Dave, I've almost given up on missionary conferences in the churches. They're like treadmills, always covering the same ground and seemingly going nowhere."

These critics are not professional crepehangers who would be happy with the sudden demise of mission conferences. Quite the contrary. They want an infusion of new vitality, wider participation, more "get up and go." They would be among the first to appreciate the appraisal of the pastor who said, "Without the annual missionary conference down through the years, our program of outreach would have died on the vine!"

The fact remains that many fear the mission conference may be suffering from a malady similar to that which incapacitated the evangelistic services and Bible conferences in many churches a decade or two ago. . . .

What can be done about these problems? Let us assume that we have a concerned pastor, a mission committee which is ready to go to work, and a congregation with allegiance to our Lord Christ who started this vast enterprise and wills its continuance and consummation!

First, Scripture and strategy must be in clearer focus. I am convinced that Bible emphasis is a necessary condition for a successful conference. The whole mission enterprise needs to be grounded in the revealed purpose of God. Sympathy for men in their poverty and diseases is noble, but not enough. There are too many heathen who are wealthy and well! Nothing less than the will of God is sufficient basis for a world-encompassing self-sacrificing mission. Mission is in the Bible from Genesis to Malachi, and from Matthew to Revelation. God the Father is the Sender, and the Son is the Sent One, and the Spirit is the Missionary Spirit. The successful mission conference must be set in the context of a continuing preaching and teaching emphasis on what God says about mission.

And then we come to strategy. We are in the twentieth century. "Reports from the field" are important, but to be up-to-date they must be more than a report of "the work." . . . Christians have been urged to pray and give if they cannot go as missionaries. An increasing number of contemporary Christians remain unchallenged by this approach. They find little compulsion to support that which they do not understand or that of which they do not feel themselves to be a real part. A credibility gap has emerged—not because the average Christian does not trust the missionary, but because he is unable to enter into mission problems and possibilities with real understanding.

The credibility gap can be closed. Real issues and realistic plans must be discussed. Reports must be factual with maps, charts, and graphs that show clearly where, how, why, and to what extent the church of Christ is growing. When people "see" they will interact.[3]

Participation in the Church's Mission

Biblical Principles and Precedents

The fundamental biblical principle related to the sending church's participation in mission is found in 2 Corinthians 8:1–5:

> Now, brethren, we wish to make known to you the grace of God which has been given in the churches of Macedonia, that in a great ordeal of affliction their abundance of joy and their deep poverty overflowed in the wealth of their liberality. For I testify that according to their ability, and beyond their ability they gave of their own accord, begging us with much entreaty for the favor of participation in the support of the saints, and this, not as we had expected, but they first gave themselves to the Lord and to us by the will of God.

The reference, of course, is to the provision made for the poverty-stricken saints in Jerusalem. The Macedonians had given far above the

---

3. David J. Hesselgrave, "The Mission Conference Treadmill: How to Get Off," *World Vision*, Sept. 1972, pp. 12–13.

expectation of the apostle. Why? What was their motivation? The obvious answer is love—not just love for the Jerusalem saints, but love for the Lord. *They gave of their means to others because they had given themselves to the Lord!* The Macedonian Christians had acted upon the truth that Paul had tried to drive home in his first letter to the Corinthian Christians: "Do you not know that . . . you are not your own? For you have been bought with a price" (1 Cor. 6:19–20).

Here, then, we have the mainspring of actual participation in God's great program for his church on earth. Giving oneself in love to the Lord and consequently to others accounts for the fact that when the church members in Jerusalem were subjected to suffering at the hands of Saul the persecutor and were scattered, they "went about preaching the word" (Acts 8:4). It accounts for the fact that, after his missionary campaigns throughout Asia Minor, Macedonia, and Greece, Paul the persecuted insisted upon returning to Jerusalem despite warnings of impending suffering, the believers in Caesarea said, "The will of the Lord be done," and started down the road with him (Acts 21:14–16). And it accounts for the fact that, in spite of lapses and failures, great numbers of ordinary believers were involved in one way or another in the great mission spearheaded by the apostle Paul.

Relevant Research

There is much evidence in the field of comparative religions that indicates the essentiality of lay involvement at the cutting edge of religious movements. It is noteworthy that some of the really successful religious movements of our time are lay movements entirely. Out of the numerous examples that could be cited, we choose but one.

Since 1960 the Bahai movement has grown rapidly (though not rapidly enough to justify its claim of being the fastest growing religion in the world). In slightly more than ten years (from 1960 to 1971), Bahai membership in the United States increased from just under 10,000 to over 100,000, and the number of assemblies from about 200 to 837. One of the factors in the growth of that period was the encouragement of small groups of believers to band together and emigrate to new communities where they functioned as embryonic groups and started new assemblies.[4]

Practical Reflection

We live in an unusual day. Consider how easy it is to travel throughout the Mediterranean lands where our Lord and his apostles carried

---

4. William J. Petersen, *Those Curious New Cults* (New Canaan, Conn.: Keats, 1973), 182.

out their mission. In a matter of hours we can motor from Dan to Beersheba—a distance that once took days of exhausting travel on animal or by foot. In two or three hours we can fly over seas and lands which required weeks and months of treacherous travel on the part of the apostle Paul. The technology of modern transportation and communication makes it possible for ordinary Christians to participate in the worldwide mission of the church with a facility never dreamed of in the first century. Yet to many Christians mission is little more than responding to pleas for money to support missionary-evangelists and sustain the needy. If the field is the world, let believers in new churches as well as older ones be encouraged to actively participate in claiming additional territory for Christ, whether it be near at home or far away.

The possibilities for active participation in the mission of the church today are almost unlimited. Consider a few:

1. Established churches can set up relationships with emerging churches at home or abroad on the pattern of sister cities. Communication can flow back and forth. Visits can be exchanged.
2. Young Christians can establish pen-pal or e-mail relationships with young people in pioneer areas.
3. Foreign nationals can be invited into the homes of local Christians. Many of them can be won to Christ and will become witnesses in their home areas.
4. Teams of local Christians gathered from one or several churches can be sent out to aid in pioneer work at home and abroad.
5. Groups of local Christians can relocate and become the vanguard of a church in a new area.
6. Retirees and specialists can go to a pioneer area at their own expense in order to aid the work of Christ.

ME-1–3 illustration: One of the secrets of the success of the Southern Baptist Convention in establishing churches has been their program of "evangelizing and congregationalizing."[5] And one of the secrets of that program has been the preparation and involvement of teams of laypersons in reaching a target area. Laypeople of sponsoring churches are deployed in home visitation, special meetings, and Bible-study groups. In fact, teams of laypersons have often been utilized in carrying out a special witness in sections of our country far from their home, and even in mission fields abroad. This kind of commitment and in-

5. *Evangelizing and Congregationalizing: Guide for Establishing New Churches and Missions* and *Associational New Work Campaign* (N.p.: Home Missions Board, Southern Baptist Convention, n.d.).

volvement goes a long way to explain why the Southern Baptists evidenced continued growth during a time when many other large denominations experienced a decline in membership.

Prayer for guidance ascended to the Lord of the church. Potential areas for a new work were surveyed and evaluated. Pioneer workers were selected and sent. Plans were carefully laid. Then contacts were made, the gospel was communicated, converts were won, believers were congregated, faith was confirmed, leadership was consecrated, the church was commended to the grace of God, and the missionary-evangelists were relocated. From the beginning it was in their hearts that, once established, the new churches would become the bases for the prayers, plans, and participation essential to enter still other territories for Christ both at home and abroad. And so the Pauline Cycle has been and will be repeated, on and on, over and over, until Christ comes again and the church militant becomes the church triumphant. Maranatha!

Bibliography

Allen, Roland. *Educational Principles and Missionary Methods*. London: Robert Scott, 1919.

———. *Missionary Methods: St. Paul's or Ours?* Grand Rapids: Eerdmans, 1962.

———. *The Spontaneous Expansion of the Church*. London: World Dominion, 1927; 2d ed., 1949.

———, and David M. Paton. *The Ministry of the Spirit*. Grand Rapids: Eerdmans, 1962.

Almquist, Arden. *Missionary, Come Back*. New York: World, 1970.

Anderson, Andy. *The Growth Spiral: The Proven Step-by-Step Method for Calculating and Predicting Growth Potential in Your Church*. Nashville: Broadman and Holman, 1993.

Anderson, Efraim. *Churches at the Grass-Roots*. London: Lutterworth, 1968.

Anderson, Rufus. *To Advance the Gospel*. Edited by R. Pierce Beaver. Grand Rapids: Eerdmans, 1967.

Ayres, Francis O. *The Ministry of the Laity*. Philadelphia: Westminster, 1962.

Bannerman, D. Douglas. *The Scripture Doctrine of the Church*. Grand Rapids: Eerdmans, 1955.

Barkman, Paul F., Edward R. Dayton, and Edward L. Gruman. *Christian Collegians and Foreign Missions: An Analysis of Relationships*. Monrovia, Calif.: Missions Advanced Research and Communications Center, 1969.

Barrett, David. *Schism and Renewal in Africa*. Nairobi: Oxford University Press, 1968.

Baumann, Dan. *All Originality Makes a Dull Church*. Santa Ana, Calif.: Vision House, 1976.

Bavinck, J. H. *An Introduction to the Science of Missions*. Translated by David H. Freeman. Grand Rapids: Baker, 1960.

Bayly, Joe. *The Gospel Blimp*. Grand Rapids: Zondervan, 1960.

Benedict, Ruth. *The Chrysanthemum and the Sword*. Boston: Houghton Mifflin, 1946.

Benjamin, Paul. *Analyzing the Community*. Cincinnati: Standard, 1973.

———. *The Growing Congregation*. Cincinnati: Standard, 1972.

Bennett, Charles. *Tinder in Tabasco*. Grand Rapids: Eerdmans, 1968.

Benson, Donald. *How to Start a Daughter Church*. Quezon City, Philippines: Filkoba, 1972.

Beyerhaus, Peter, and Henry Lefever. *The Responsible Church and the Foreign Mission*. Grand Rapids: Eerdmans, 1964.

Blauw, Johannes. *The Missionary Nature of the Church*. New York: McGraw-Hill, 1962.

Bock, Philip K. *Modern Cultural Anthropology: An Introduction.* 2d ed. New York: Knopf, 1974.

Boer, Harry R. *Pentecost and Missions.* Grand Rapids: Eerdmans, 1961.

Bowman, Ray (with Eddy Hall). *When Not to Build: An Architect's Unconventional Wisdom for the Growing Church.* Grand Rapids: Baker, 1992.

Bradshaw, Malcolm R. *Church Growth through Evangelism-in-Depth.* South Pasadena, Calif.: William Carey Library, 1969.

Braun, Neil, P. W. Boschman, and T. Yamada, eds. *Experiments in Church Growth: Japan.* Kobayashi City, Japan: Church Growth Association, 1968.

Bridges, William. *Transitions: Making Sense of Life's Changes.* Reading, Mass.: Addison-Wesley, 1980.

Brow, Robert. *The Church: An Organic Picture of Its Life and Mission.* Grand Rapids: Eerdmans, 1968.

Brown, Arthur Judson. *The Why and How of Foreign Missions.* New York: Eaton and Mains, 1908.

Brown, Stanley C. *Evangelism in the Early Church.* Grand Rapids: Eerdmans, 1963.

Busia, K. A. *Urban Churches in Britain.* London: Lutterworth, 1966.

Carson, D. A. *The Gagging of God.* Grand Rapids: Zondervan, 1996.

Church Expansion Handbook. New York: American Baptist Home Mission Societies, 1958.

Clark, Charles Allen. *The Korean Church and the Nevius Methods.* Ph.D. diss., University of Chicago, 1929.

Clark, Sidney J. W. *The Indigenous Church.* London: World Dominion, 1923.

Coleman, Robert E. *The Master Plan of Evangelism.* Westwood, N.J.: Revell, 1963.

Collins, Gary. *How to Be a People Helper.* Santa Ana, Calif.: Vision House, 1976.

Cook, Harold R. *Historic Patterns of Church Growth.* Chicago: Moody, 1971.

———. *Missionary Life and Work.* Chicago: Moody, 1959.

———. *Strategy of Missions.* Chicago: Moody, 1963.

Corwin, Charles. *East to Eden?* Grand Rapids: Eerdmans, 1972.

Dana, H. E., and L. M. Sipes. *A Manual of Ecclesiology.* Kansas City, Kans.: Central Seminary Press, 1944.

Davies, J. G. *Worship and Mission.* New York: Association, 1967.

Davies, W. D. *A Normative Pattern of Church Life in the New Testament: Fact or Fancy?* London: James Clarke, n.d.

Davis, John Merle. *New Buildings on Old Foundations.* New York: International Missionary Council, 1945.

Dobbins, Gaines S. *The Churchbook.* Nashville: Broadman, 1951.

Dodge, Ralph E. *The Unpopular Missionary.* Westwood, N.J.: Revell, 1964.

Durkheim, Emile. *Suicide: A Study in Sociology.* New York: Free, 1951.

Engel, James F. *How Can I Get Them to Listen? A Handbook on Communication Strategy and Research.* Grand Rapids: Zondervan, 1977.

———, and H. Wilbert Norton. *What's Gone Wrong with the Harvest? A Communication Strategy for the Church and World Evangelism.* Grand Rapids: Zondervan, 1975.

Evangelism-in-Depth. Chicago: Moody, 1961.

Evangelizing and Congregationalizing: Guide for Establishing New Churches and Missions and *Associational New Work Campaign*. N.p.: Home Missions Board, Southern Baptist Convention, n.d.

Fackre, Gabriel. *Do and Tell: Engagement Evangelism in the '70s*. Grand Rapids: Eerdmans, 1973.

Festinger, Leon. *A Theory of Cognitive Dissonance*. Stanford: Stanford University Press, 1957.

Fiers, Alan Dale. *This Is Missions*. St. Louis: Bethany, 1953.

Firth, Raymond. *Elements of Social Organization*. Boston: Beacon, 1963.

Foster, George M. *Traditional Cultures and the Impact of Technological Change*. New York: Harper and Row, 1962.

Gerber, Vergil. *God's Way to Keep a Church Going and Growing*. Glendale, Calif.: Gospel Light, 1973.

———. *A Manual for Evangelism/Church Growth*. South Pasadena, Calif.: William Carey Library, 1973.

———, ed. *Missions in Creative Tension*. South Pasadena, Calif.: William Carey Library, 1971.

Getz, Gene. *The Measure of a Man*. Glendale, Calif.: Regal, 1974.

———. *Sharpening the Focus of the Church*. Chicago: Moody, 1974.

Green, Margaret. *Igbo Village Affairs*. 2d ed. London: Cass, 1964.

Green, Michael. *Evangelism in the Early Church*. Grand Rapids: Eerdmans, 1970.

Greenway, Roger S. *Guidelines for Urban Church Planting*. Grand Rapids: Baker, 1976.

———. *An Urban Strategy for Latin America*. Grand Rapids: Baker, 1973.

Griffiths, Michael C. *You and God's Work Overseas*. Chicago: InterVarsity, 1967.

Grimley, John B., and Gordon E. Robinson. *Church Growth in Central and Southern Nigeria*. Grand Rapids: Eerdmans, 1966.

Hall, Edward T. *Beyond Culture*. Garden City, N.Y.: Doubleday, 1977.

———. *The Silent Language*. Greenwich, Conn.: Fawcett, 1959.

Hamilton, Keith. *Church Growth in the High Andes*. Lucknow, India: Lucknow, 1962.

Hammond, Peter B. *An Introduction to Cultural and Social Anthropology*. New York: Macmillan, 1971.

Harre, Alan F. *Close the Back Door: Ways to Create a Caring Congregational Fellowship*. St. Louis: Concordia, 1984.

Hawkins, O. S. *Drawing the Net: 30 Practical Principles for Leading Others to Christ Publicly and Personally*. Nashville: Broadman, 1993.

Hay, A. R. *New Testament Order for Church and Missionary*. Audubon, N.J.: New Testament Missionary Union, 1947.

Hesselgrave, David J. *Communicating Christ Cross-Culturally*. 2d ed. Grand Rapids: Zondervan, 1991.

———. *Scripture and Strategy: The Use of the Bible in Postmodern Church and Mission*. Pasadena: William Carey Library, 1994.

———, ed. *Dynamic Religious Movements: Case Studies of Rapidly Growing Religious Movements around the World*. Grand Rapids: Baker, 1978.

————. *Theology and Mission*. Grand Rapids: Baker, 1978.

Hesselgrave, David J., and Edward Rommen. *Contextualization: Meanings, Methods, and Models*. Grand Rapids: Baker, 1989.

Hiebert, Paul G. *Anthropological Insights for Missionaries*. Grand Rapids: Baker, 1985.

Hiscox, Edward T. *The Hiscox Guide for Baptist Churches*. Valley Forge, Pa.: Judson, 1964.

Hodges, Melvin L. *Build My Church*. Springfield, Mo.: Assemblies of God, 1957.

————. *A Guide to Church Planting*. Chicago: Moody, 1973.

————. *The Indigenous Church*. Springfield, Mo.: Gospel, 1953.

Hoffer, Eric. *The True Believer: Thoughts on the Nature of Mass Movements*. New York: New American Library of World Literature, 1958.

Hoffman, Ronan. *Pioneer Theories of Missiology*. Washington, D.C.: Catholic University of America Press, 1960.

Hollis, Michael. *Paternalism and the Church*. New York: Oxford University Press, 1962.

Hsu, Francis L. K. *Clan, Caste, and Club*. Princeton, N.J.: Van Nostrand, 1963.

Idowu, Bolaji. *Towards an Indigenous Church*. New York: Oxford University Press, 1965.

Jackson, Paul R. *The Doctrine and Administration of the Church*. Des Plaines, Ill.: Regular Baptist, 1968.

Jenkins, Daniel. *The Protestant Ministry*. Garden City, N.Y.: Doubleday, 1958.

Kane, J. Herbert. *Christian Missions in Biblical Perspective*. Grand Rapids: Baker, 1976.

————. *A Global View of Christian Missions*. Grand Rapids: Baker, 1971.

————. *Twofold Growth*. Philadelphia: China Inland Mission, 1947.

Keesing, Felix. *Cultural Anthropology: The Science of Custom*. New York: Holt, Rinehart and Winston, 1966.

Kelley, Dean M. *Why Conservative Churches Are Growing*. New York: Harper and Row, 1972.

Kennedy, D. James. *Evangelism Explosion*. Rev. ed. Wheaton, Ill.: Tyndale, 1977.

Klapper, Joseph T. *The Effects of Mass Communication*. Glencoe, Ill.: Free, 1960.

Knapp, Mark L. *Nonverbal Communication*. New York: Holt, Rinehart and Winston, 1972.

Knight, William Henry. *Missions in Principle and Practice*. Nashville: Sunday School Board of the Southern Baptist Convention, 1929.

Köstenberger, Andreas J. *The Missions of Jesus and the Disciples according to the Fourth Gospel*. Grand Rapids: Eerdmans, 1997.

Kraemer, Hendrik. *From Missionfield to Independent Church*. London: SCM, 1955.

Kuiper, R. B. *The Glorious Body of Christ*. London: Banner of Truth Trust, 1966.

Küng, Hans. *Structures of the Church*. New York: Nelson, 1964.

Lapham, Henry A. *The Bible as a Missions Handbook*. Cambridge: W. Heffer, 1925.

Larkin, William J., Jr. *Culture and Biblical Hermeneutics: Interpreting and Applying the Authoritative Word in a Relativistic Age*. Grand Rapids: Baker, 1988.

Laubach, Frank C. *How to Teach One and Win One for Christ*. Grand Rapids: Zondervan, 1964.

Lawson, E. LeRoy, and Tetsunao Yamamori. *Church Growth: Everybody's Business*. Cincinnati: Standard, 1971.

Leeming, Bernard. *The Churches and the Church: A Study of Ecumenism with a New Postscript*. 2d ed. Westminster, Md.: Newman, 1963.

Lees, Harrington C. *St. Paul and His Converts*. London: Robert Scott, 1910.

Lindsay, Thomas M. *The Church and the Ministry in the Early Centuries*. 2d ed. London: Hodder and Stoughton, 1903.

Lindsell, Harold. *Barriers to Church Growth*. Grand Rapids: Eerdmans, n.d.

————. *Missionary Principles and Practice*. Westwood, N.J.: Revell, 1955.

Longenecker, Harold L. *Building Town and Country Churches*. Chicago: Moody, 1973.

Longenecker, Richard. *The Ministry and Message of Paul*. Grand Rapids: Zondervan, 1971.

McCall, Duke K., ed. *What Is the Church? A Symposium of Baptist Thought*. Nashville: Broadman, 1958.

McGavran, Donald A. *The Bridges of God*. New York: Friendship, 1955.

————. *Church Growth in Jamaica*. Lucknow, India: Lucknow, 1962.

————. *Church Growth in Mexico*. Grand Rapids: Eerdmans, 1963.

————. *How Churches Grow*. New York: Friendship, 1959.

————. *Understanding Church Growth*. Grand Rapids: Eerdmans, 1970.

————, ed. *Church Growth and Christian Mission*. New York: Harper and Row, 1965.

————. *Eye of the Storm: The Great Debate in Mission*. Waco: Word, 1972.

MacLeish, Alexander. *Jesus Christ and the World: Christian Missionary Principles*. London: Lutterworth, 1934.

MacNair, Donald J. *The Growing Local Church*. Grand Rapids: Baker, 1973.

McQuilkin, J. Robertson. *How Biblical Is the Church Growth Movement?* Chicago: Moody, 1973.

Mains, David R. *Full Circle: The Creative Church for Today's Society*. Waco: Word, 1971.

Malphurs, Aubrèy. *Planting Growing Churches for the Twenty-first Century: A Comprehensive Guide for New Churches and Those Desiring Renewal*. Grand Rapids: Baker, 1992.

Manson, T. W. *Ministry and Priesthood: Christ's and Ours*. Richmond: John Knox, 1958.

Marshall, Thomas William M. *Christian Missions: Their Agents and Their Results*. 2d ed. 2 vols. New York: Sadlier, 1864.

Martin, Ralph P. *Worship in the Early Church*. Grand Rapids: Eerdmans, 1975.

Mathews, Basil. *Forward through the Ages*. New York: Friendship, 1960.

Mavis, W. C. *Advancing the Smaller Church*. Grand Rapids: Baker, 1968.

Merton, Robert K. *Social Theory and Social Structure*. Rev. ed. New York: Free, 1957.

Miller, Paul. *Group Dynamics in Evangelism*. Scottdale, Pa.: Herald, 1958.

Missionary Methods—Candidate Seminar Manual No. 2. Cleveland: Baptist Mid-Mission, July 1964 revision. See the articles by Gordon D. Mellish ("Pioneering") and Denzel L. Osburn ("The Indigenous Church").

Montgomery, H. H. *Principles and Problems of Foreign Missions*. Westminster, Eng.: Society for the Propagation of the Gospel, 1904.

Montgomery, James H. *Dawn Two Thousand: Seven Million Churches to Go*. Pasadena: William Carey Library, 1989.

———. *Then the End Will Come: Great News about the Great Commission*. Pasadena: William Carey Library, 1997.

———, and Donald A. McGavran. *The Discipling of a Nation*. Colorado Springs: Overseas Crusade, 1980.

Munro, Harry C. *Fellowship Evangelism through Church Groups*. St. Louis: Bethany, 1951.

Nederhood, Joel H. *The Church's Mission to the Educated American*. Grand Rapids: Eerdmans, 1960.

Nee, Watchman. *The Normal Christian Life*. Washington, D.C.: International Students, 1962.

Neighbour, Ralph W., Jr. *Where Do We Go from Here? A Guidebook for Cell Group Churches*. Houston: Torch, 1990.

Neill, Stephen. *Creative Tension*. London: Edinburgh House, 1959.

Nevius, John. *The Planting and Development of Missionary Churches*. Philadelphia: Presbyterian and Reformed, 1958.

Nida, Eugene A. *Message and Mission: The Communication of the Christian Faith*. New York: Harper and Row, 1960.

Norbie, Donald L. *New Testament Church Organization*. Chicago: Christian Libraries, 1955.

Noss, John B. *Man's Religions*. 3d ed. New York: Macmillan, 1963.

Olson, Gilbert. *Church Growth in Sierra Leone*. Grand Rapids: Eerdmans, 1969.

Ortlund, Anne. *Up with Worship: How to Quit Playing Church*. Glendale, Calif.: Regal, 1975.

Packer, J. I. *Evangelism and the Sovereignty of God*. Chicago: InterVarsity, 1965.

Palmer, Donald C. *Explosion of People Evangelism*. Chicago: Moody, 1974.

Peill, S. G., and W. F. Rowlands. *Church Planting*. London: World Dominion, n.d.

Pentecost, Edward. *Reaching the Unreached*. South Pasadena, Calif.: William Carey Library, 1974.

Perry, Lloyd Merle, and Edward John Lias. *A Manual of Pastoral Problems and Procedures*. Grand Rapids: Baker, 1964.

Peters, George W. *Saturation Evangelism*. Grand Rapids: Zondervan, 1970.

Petersen, William J. *Those Curious New Cults*. New Canaan, Conn.: Keats, 1973.

Pickett, J. Waskom. *Christian Mass Movements in India*. New York: Abingdon, 1933.

———. *Christ's Way to India's Heart*. Lucknow, India: Lucknow, 1960.

———. *Church Growth and Group Conversion*. Lucknow, India: Lucknow, 1962.

———. *The Dynamics of Church Growth*. New York: Abingdon, 1963.

Planning and PERT (Program Evaluation and Review Technique). Monrovia, Calif.: Missions Advanced Research and Communication Center, 1966.

Porter, H. Boone, Jr. *Growth and Life in the Local Church*. South Pasadena, Calif.: William Carey Library, 1974 reprint.

Prior, Kenneth F. W. *The Gospel in a Pagan Society*. Downers Grove, Ill.: Inter-Varsity, 1975.

Randall, Max W. *Profile for Victory: New Proposals for Missions in Zambia*. South Pasadena, Calif.: William Carey Library, 1970.

Read, William R. *New Patterns of Church Growth in Brazil*. Grand Rapids: Eerdmans, 1966.

———, Victor M. Monterroso, and Harmon A. Johnson. *Latin American Church Growth*. Grand Rapids: Eerdmans, 1969.

Reese, J. Irving. *A Guide for Organizing and Conducting a Baptist Church*. Elyria, Ohio: J. Irving Reese, 1962.

Richards, Lawrence O. *A New Face for the Church*. Grand Rapids: Zondervan, 1970.

———. *A Theology of Christian Education*. Grand Rapids: Zondervan, 1975.

Richardson, Don. *Peace Child*. Glendale, Calif.: Regal, 1974.

Richardson, William J., ed. *The Modern Missionary Apostolate*. Maryknoll, N.Y.: Maryknoll, 1965.

Ritchie, John. *Indigenous Church Principles in Theory and Practice*. New York: Revell, 1946.

The Role of the "Diakonia" of the Church in Contemporary Society. New York: World Council of Churches, 1966.

Ross, Byron W. *Training Lay Workers*. New York: Christian and Missionary Alliance, n.d.

Rowland, Henry. *Native Churches in Foreign Fields*. New York: Methodist Book Concern, 1925.

Rowlands, W. R. *Indigenous Ideals in Practice*. London: World Dominion, n.d.

Roxburgh, Alan J. *Reaching a New Generation: Strategies for Tomorrow's Church*. Downers Grove, Ill.: InterVarsity, 1993.

Sanders, J. Oswald. *Spiritual Leadership*. Chicago: Moody, 1967.

Saunders, J. Roscoe. *Men and Methods That Win in the Foreign Fields*. New York: Revell, 1921.

Schaeffer, Francis. *The Church at the End of the Twentieth Century*. Downers Grove, Ill.: InterVarsity, 1970.

Schaller, Lyle E. *Assimilating New Members*. Nashville: Abingdon, 1978.

———. *44 Questions for Church Planters*. Nashville: Abingdon, 1991.

———. *Hey, That's Our Church!* New York: Abingdon, 1975.

Scherer, James A. *Justinian Welz: Essays by an Early Prophet of Mission*. Grand Rapids: Eerdmans, 1969.

———. *Missionary, Go Home!* Englewood Cliffs, N.J.: Prentice-Hall, 1964.

Schmidt, Otto Henry. *St. Paul Shows Us How.* St. Louis: Concordia, 1950.

Schramm, Wilbur. *Mass Media in National Development.* Stanford, Calif.: Stanford University Press, 1969.

Schuller, Robert H. *Your Church Has Real Possibilities.* Glendale, Calif.: Regal, 1974.

Schweizer, Edward. *Church Order in the New Testament.* Naperville, Ill.: Alec R. Allenson, 1961.

Scopes, Wilfred, ed. *The Christian Ministry in Latin America and the Caribbean.* New York: Commission on World Mission and Evangelism, World Council of Churches, 1962.

Shearer, Roy. *Wildfire: Church Growth in Korea.* Grand Rapids: Eerdmans, 1966.

Smith, Ebbie C. *God's Miracles: Indonesian Church Growth.* South Pasadena, Calif.: William Carey Library, 1970.

Snyder, Howard A. *The Problem of Wine Skins: Church Structure in a Technological Age.* Downers Grove, Ill.: InterVarsity, 1975.

Sogaard, Viggo. *Media in Church and Mission.* Pasadena: William Carey Library, 1993.

Speer, Robert G. *Missionary Principles and Practice.* New York: Revell, 1902.

Stedman, Ray. *Body Life.* Glendale, Calif.: Regal, 1972.

Steffen, Tom A. *Passing the Baton: Church Planting That Empowers.* 2d ed. La Habra, Calif.: Center for Organizational and Ministry Development, 1997.

Street, T. Watson. *On the Growing Edge of the Church.* Richmond: John Knox, 1965.

Subbamma, B. V. *New Patterns for Discipling Hindus.* South Pasadena, Calif.: William Carey Library, 1970.

Sunda, James. *Church Growth in the Central Highlands of West Guinea.* Lucknow, India: Lucknow, 1963.

Swanson, Allen J. *Taiwan: Mainline versus Independent Church Growth.* South Pasadena, Calif.: William Carey Library, 1973.

Taylor, John V. *The Growth of the Church in Buganda.* London: SCM, 1958.

Tippett, A. R. *Church Growth and the Word of God.* Grand Rapids: Eerdmans, 1970.

———. *Verdict Theology in Missionary Theory.* Lincoln, Ill.: Lincoln Christian College Press, 1969.

———, ed. *God, Man and Church Growth.* Grand Rapids: Eerdmans, 1973.

Tonnies, Ferdinand. *Community and Society.* Translated and edited by Charles P. Loomis. East Lansing: Michigan State University Press, 1957.

Toward Creative Urban Strategy. Compiled by George A. Torney. Waco: Word, 1970.

Trueblood, Elton. *The Company of the Committed.* New York: Harper and Row, 1961.

Vaughan, John N. *The Large Church: A Twentieth-Century Expression of the First-Century Church.* Grand Rapids: Baker, 1985.

Vicedom, Gary F. *Church and People in New Guinea.* New York: Association, 1961.

———. *The Mission of God*. St. Louis: Concordia, 1965.

Wagner, C. Peter. *Church Planting for a Greater Harvest*. Ventura, Calif.: Regal, 1990.

———. *Frontiers in Missionary Strategy*. Chicago: Moody, 1971.

———. *Your Church Can Grow*. Glendale, Calif.: Gospel Light, 1976.

———, ed. *Church/Mission Tensions Today*. Chicago: Moody, 1972.

Warren, Rick. *The Purpose-Driven Church*. Grand Rapids: Zondervan, 1995.

Wasson, Alfred. *Church Growth in Korea*. New York: International Missionary Council, 1934.

Waymire, Bob, and C. Peter Wagner. *The Church Growth Survey Handbook*. Santa Clara, Calif.: O.C. Ministries, 1980.

Weber, Hans-Ruedi. *Salty Christians*. New York: Seabury, 1963.

Weld, Wayne. *An Ecuadorian Impasse*. Chicago: Department of World Missions, Evangelical Covenant Church of America, 1968.

Wells, David F. *Turning to God: Biblical Conversion in the Modern World*. Grand Rapids: Baker, 1989.

Wendt, Harry N. *The Divine Drama: A Study of the Christian Faith in Word and Diagram*. Minneapolis: Crossways International, 1983.

Westermann, John J. *The Leadership Continuum: A Biblical Model for Effective Leading*. Deer Lodge, Tenn.: Lighthouse, 1997.

White, James F. *Protestant Worship and Church Architecture*. New York: Oxford University Press, 1964.

Winter, Gibson. *The Suburban Captivity of the Churches*. New York: Macmillan, 1962.

Winter, Ralph, and R. Pierce Beaver. *The Warp and the Woof: Organizing for Mission*. South Pasadena, Calif.: William Carey Library, 1971.

Wold, Joseph Conrad. *God's Impatience in Liberia*. Grand Rapids: Eerdmans, 1968.

Woodson, Leslie. *Evangelism for Today's Church*. Grand Rapids: Zondervan, 1973.

Worley, Robert C. *Change in the Church: A Source of Hope*. Philadelphia: Westminster, 1971.

Yamamori, Tetsunao. *Church Growth in Japan*. South Pasadena, Calif.: William Carey Library, 1974.

———, and E. Leroy Lawson. *Introducing Church Growth*. Cincinnati: Standard, 1975.

Yoder, J. H. *As You Go: The Old Mission in a New Day*. Scottdale, Pa.: Herald, 1961.

Zook, Mark. *Church Planting Step by Step*. Sanford, Fla.: New Tribes Mission, 1989.

Scripture Index

Subject Index